Not a Lot of Work
or
Life Before D'Oyly Carte

A memoir of the years 1943-1975

David Mackie

Grosvenor House
Publishing Limited

This book is published by
Grosvenor House Publishing Ltd
Link House
140 The Broadway, Tolworth, Surrey, KT6 7HT.
www.grosvenorhousepublishing.co.uk

A CIP record for this book
is available from the British Library

ISBN 978-1-83615-197-5

In memory of my parents

David Stanley Mackie
(1906-1980)
and
Margaret Reeves Laughlan
(1913-2006)

without whom none of this would have happened.

Acknowledgements

It is seldom that any book is finished without some assistance from other people, and I would like to express my thanks to the following who have helped in many different ways to make this one possible. In alphabetical order they are Norman Adam, Ros and John Bagshaw, Arthur Black, Charles Crawford, Shona Dickinson, Carol Downes, Cathie Frenilla, Gordon and Dorothy Gunnee, Bob Harvey, Sandy Leiper, Sandra Lewis, John MacLeod, Patricia MacMahon, Fergus and Marion Malcolm, Tom Malone, Ken McAllister, Jim and Helen McCulloch, Allan McEwan, Nina McKechnie, Kate and Stewart McMillan, Peter Morrison, Matt Neilson, Sandy Oliver, Kareth Paterson, Wilma Poland, Clare Shirtcliff, Christine and David Sinclair, Andrew Smith, John Smith, Harry and Jean Stevenson, Fiona Stone and John Whenham.

I have not been able to ascertain the name of the artist of the Royal Scottish Academy of Music drawing, but should this come to light due acknowledgement will be made in any future edition.

Finally, I would like to thank Julie Scott, Jasmine Damaris and staff at Grosvenor House Publishing Ltd for their help with this third volume of memoirs.

I offer my apologies to anyone I have omitted to thank. Any mistakes and inaccuracies are entirely my own, and any shortcomings must be laid at my own door.

Introduction

My first book, *Nothing Like Work or Right in the D'Oyly Carte* (2018), was not just about my own experience of being part of the world-famous D'Oyly Carte Opera Company, but about what the Company did in its final years following its centenary in 1975. It was not an 'official' history: I simply wanted to give a first-hand account of our tours throughout Great Britain and of the two foreign tours that I took part in – the United States and Canada in 1978, and Australia and New Zealand in 1979. (There was a tour of the United States and Canada in 1976 which didn't include me although I was retained by the Company and worked for five months in the office which at that time was in the Savoy Hotel.) I also wanted to mention events of particular interest such as the Royal Command Performance at Windsor Castle in 1977 (Jubilee year) and the Company's involvement in the making of the film *Chariots of Fire* in 1980.

I joined D'Oyly Carte in its centenary year during which there were numerous toasts to the next hundred years. I thought I had landed a job for life, but, sadly, the Company only lasted for another seven seasons (not quite a full seven years). While much had been written about D'Oyly Carte, up to and including its centenary season at the Savoy Theatre, little had yet been written about those final years, and as those coincided with my time there it seemed a good idea to get it all down on paper – from the inside, as it were. I had no thought of writing anything else after this, but several people suggested that I should write about what I did after D'Oyly Carte closed on February 27, 1982. I resisted this for some time, but eventually I wrote a second book called *A Bit More Like Work or Life After D'Oyly Carte* (2021). This covered the years from 1982 to 2020, during which time I became a free-lance accompanist, repetiteur and conductor.

The lockdown in 2020, following the onset of Covid-19, seemed a convenient place to end this account of my working life: writing the book also helped to pass many long weary hours. When lockdown was eventually lifted, work slowly started up again, but as it was very much a continuation of the same (albeit at a greatly reduced level) it was hardly worth putting pen to paper to record what little there was, and I assumed that I wouldn't write any more. But having now covered my working life from 1975, I gradually began to think about a prequel, and so I have now completed a trilogy by writing about my early life up to the time I joined D'Oyly Carte. Memory can play tricks, and there will inevitably be mistakes and inaccuracies, but it is an honest attempt to recall my earlier years.

The title *Not a Lot of Work* refers to the fact that during this period I only worked full-time for just four years, having been a student for no less than nine years.

Chapter 1: Beginnings and early recollections – 1943–1948

I was born at no. 12 Ardgowan Street, Greenock on November 25, 1943. Greenock was then in Renfrewshire: it is now part of the council area of Inverclyde. The Second World War was still ongoing, and even at that stage it wasn't entirely clear who would win. I weighed 8½ lbs at birth, and I took my first steps at 10½ months. I don't remember this, of course, but these details were duly entered into a little book, *Year by Year/Story of Our Baby,* by my mother. Home births were much more common in those days; in attendance were Dr D.L. Baxter and Nurse McLeod. My parents were members of Martyrs Congregational Church in Roxburgh Street, and I presume that I was baptised there as I still have a Cradle Roll Certificate that states that I was enrolled as a member of the Cradle Roll Department of Martyrs Congregational Sunday School on January 16, 1944. During her pregnancy, my mother regularly saw a midwife who later became a good family friend.

Ardgowan Street is in the West End of Greenock. This is a roughly rectangular area of broad streets bounded by the Firth of Clyde to the north and hills, including a golf course, to the south. It is still considered the best part of the town in which to live. The West End traditionally starts at Nelson Street. This runs roughly north/south, and separates the West End from the East End which was at one time much more industrial with numerous shipyards and associated businesses (sugar refining was another major industry), and, as so often in industrial towns, with some very poor housing. My father often talked about some of the poorer areas that he remembered from the

1

1930s, particularly a street called the Vennel. Dr Baxter, who helped usher me into the world, told my parents that he once attended a confinement in the town where the woman was lying on an earthen floor: this was Greenock in the twentieth century.

The properties starting at Nelson Street are mainly tenement blocks. Larger detached and semi-detached houses come later: the further west you go, the larger the houses. At one time, there were some very substantial mansions, but most of those that have survived have become care homes or have been divided into smaller units. Our house was a flat in a tenement block between Nelson Street and Kelly Street. It was on the first floor, and it consisted of a lounge (always called 'the front room') that looked on to Ardgowan Street, and a kitchen and bedroom that looked on to the back green. We had an inside toilet with a window that looked on to the landing: no bathroom, but it was at least better than some tenement houses in Greenock at that time which still only had access to a shared toilet on each landing. No. 12 and its identical neighbour, no. 14, are still standing, and I often wonder what has been done to upgrade the flats as they are very small, with little room to incorporate a bathroom. There was a large walk-in cupboard in the hall (we called it a 'press'), and this may have become a shower room in each flat.

There were very few shops in the West End proper, but there were quite a few in the area just immediately west of Nelson Street (although there were none in Ardgowan Street) which was very convenient for us. There were several in Kelly Street, the nearest one being a Co-op (which was then the GCCS – Greenock Central Co-operative Society). It was not, of course, a supermarket as they are today, but as we had no fridge we got fresh milk and meat there almost daily. When I was sent to the Co-op for 'the messages' (a Scottish term for shopping) I had to give our dividend number which, constantly drummed into me, I can still remember – 20490. Just up from the Co-op was a very run-down shop. It was presided over by

l-r - nos. 14, 12 and 10 Ardgowan Street, Greenock in 1978.

John B. Nimmo, who seemed to have few customers and who was always reading a paper when you went in. In earlier Greenock Directories he was described as a 'fruiterer and grocer', but now he seemed to sell nothing but bleach, bundles of sticks for firewood and the Sunday papers: every so often he would also have toffee apples, and these were very popular. My mother said that when certain goods became available again after the Second World War, and word got around that Mr Nimmo had, say, some bananas, a queue would form outside the shop. He would then come out and shout at people "Don't bother standing there if you're not one of my regular customers!" This clearly didn't endear him to the shoppers, and it doubtless caused his trade to fall away. The kenspeckle proprietor and his dingy shop were a constant source of fascination to us youngsters: there are few such characters and establishments nowadays.

Several doors up from Mr Nimmo was a 'proper' grocer, proprietor Mr McGregor, where we got items such as ham, cheese, butter (cut from large rounds as you waited), and biscuits which were loose in a glass cabinet and put into a bag or 'poke' (few things pre-wrapped as today). Children would sometimes be given a free bag of broken biscuits, the inevitable bits and pieces that always accumulated in these cabinets. Next door to Mr McGregor was a butcher, Mr Martin, and round the corner in Brisbane Street were the bakery and main shop of Thomas Auld & Sons (still in existence), McGavin's general store, a newsagent/post office and Purdie's dairy. The newsagent/post office was run by Mr McInnes. His son, Hamish (who preferred to spell his surname MacInnes) became a well-known mountaineer, explorer, author and leader of the Glencoe Mountain Rescue Team. Between the post office and the dairy there was an entrance leading to a yard where Hamish MacInnes managed to build a little car from scratch at the age of seventeen: you could watch him at work from the street. The dairy, which was run by Mr Purdie and his daughters Olive and Iris, wasn't like a normal shop: it was more like a kitchen or scullery, and it had an open drain in the floor. They got their milk from a farm at Kilmaurs in Ayrshire, and this came in large churns on the back of a lorry. Watching these churns being unloaded was another fascinating childhood pastime.

There were also shops at the opposite (north) end of Kelly Street, among them Robert 'Bertie' Paterson's hairdressing shop where we boys were regularly given a 'short back and sides'. Later, we became aware that hairdressing shops were a place where contraceptives could be had (an almost under-the-counter transaction at that time), but in our young days we knew nothing of this: we were much more innocent than today's children. There was also a fish shop that was run at one time by my Aunt Betty, a sweet shop, and, on the corner with Union Street, John Scott the chemist. Above this shop lived the afore-mentioned John B. Nimmo. His house was accessed from Kelly Street via a 'close' (entrance passage way: 'close' with a soft 's' as in 'close encounter') and a flight of stairs. The close also led to a small bakery at the back of the shops. This was run by William Strawbridge, who delivered locally in a very ramshackle van that later got him into trouble with the police. His daughter, Ann, was in my class at school. Further down Kelly Street there were a few more shops, among them another sweet shop that was run by two rather intriguing sisters, the Misses MacArthur. There were other shops in Union Street, next to the chemist, although my parents didn't use those very much. But we still had most of our immediate needs within walking distance of no. 12 Ardgowan Street. (The name Ardgowan comes from the Ardgowan Estate: Ardgowan House, the seat of the Shaw-Stewart family (the local landowners), is at the nearby village of Inverkip.)

For some time after I was born, the street lighting and the lighting on the tenement landings was still by gas; someone from the Corporation came round each evening to light the lamps with a long brass implement. I believe that our house had gas lighting when my parents moved in, and I can clearly remember that we kept gas mantles. The heating, presumably in all of the houses (certainly in ours), was primarily by coal fires. The coal came in sacks on a lorry, and it was stored in cellars in the basement – one cellar for each house. (Once electricity had been installed you could then have electric fires.) There was no lighting 'down the dunny' (as we used to say), and you needed a torch or a candle to see what you were doing. I would sometimes go down with my father to fill our coal scuttle, but the darkness was quite frightening to a young child. The cellars were in passageways either side of the main passage out to the back green where there was a communal wash-house. When people moved into a flat, they would be told which day was their wash day. It was invariably the women who did the washing which was then hung on washing lines in the green to dry – not an easy thing to accomplish in Greenock as the town had, and still has, a notorious reputation for rain.

5

My mother, one of six children (four girls and two boys), was born in Greenock in 1913, the second child of my grandparents Peter Laughlan and Margaret Ireland. My grandfather was an electrician, and he worked in the famous Scotts' [sic] shipyard in the town. Even in the early years of the twentieth century, he sometimes worked in submarines, but these were much smaller than they are today, and my mother said that he would often come home with severe backache, complaining that he had to crawl into small and very awkward places to check circuits or effect repairs. 'Home' for the Laughlans was in a tenement in Belville Street in the East End of Greenock. Despite the size of the family (my grandparents, my mother, her sisters Esther, Betty and Catherine (who died as a baby) and her brothers Jim and Billy), it was just a two-room attic flat with a shared toilet on the landing: on visits to my grandparents I thought how lucky we were to have an inside toilet all to ourselves. Some years later, my Uncle Billy moved into an even smaller house opposite (a one-roomed flat known as a single-end), and although there was one other family on that landing it meant that the outside toilet was used mainly by the members of one family: comparative privacy.

My grandfather died in 1956, and I can still see his body lying in an open coffin in the little flat in Belville Street. Members of the family and friends turned up to pay their last respects before the coffin was sealed, a common practice at one time although something of an ordeal for everyone, particularly for a young person. I had never seen a dead body before, and the experience made a big impression on me.

My great-grandparents, William and Esther Ireland, and their two eldest children, went out to Australia in the 1880s – a very long journey by sea in those days. According to my mother, they were effectively pioneers in the outback, and the experience seemed to be too much for them, particularly with the 'creepy crawlies', so much so that after only six months they returned to Scotland – yet another very long journey. As a child, my mother would often say "Tell me about Australia,

Granny", but the reply was always "Be quiet now: nothing to do with you". Children then were to be 'seen and not heard'. My mother often said that she wished that she had pestered her grandmother in the hope that she might have learned something interesting. Granny Ireland spent her last days in Greenock's Medical Aid Home, and she lived just long enough to be aware of my entry into the world, dying not long afterwards in 1944 in her eighty-ninth year.

My father, the youngest of five children, was not a native of Greenock. He was born in Dundee in 1906, but the family moved to Aberdeen when he was about three, and so he always thought of himself as an Aberdonian. His eldest brother, my much-admired Uncle John, had been born in 1887, and a second child, George, was born in 1889. Aged just sixteen, George went to sea on a sailing ship in 1905. One day, a crew member who dealt with the rigging fell ill, and Uncle George volunteered to go up the mast. Unfortunately, he lost his footing, fell onto the deck, and was killed. The crew, who thought that the captain should not have allowed him to volunteer, then took over the ship and sailed it all round the South Atlantic until they had to call in at a port when provisions ran out. It was months before word of Uncle George's death got back to Dundee. My father was born the following year. Another brother, Walter, fought in the First World War but luckily survived: my father remembered the family going down to the station in Aberdeen to welcome him home. My Aunt Alice, who was apparently a good singer and was able to accompany herself on the piano, married a dental mechanic called Barnard (known as Barney) Porter, and they came to live in Greenock. When my grandparents died in the late 1920s (within six months of each other) my father, who was still unmarried, spent much time with his siblings (all married by this time), and it was during an extended stay with Aunt Alice and Uncle Barney that he met my mother. They were married on March 29, 1939, not in a church but in Mackay's restaurant in West Blackhall Street in Greenock.

Above the restaurant was a dance hall with a wonderful sprung floor.

I took some time to make my entrance, but with the uncertainty of those days, culminating in the declaration of war in September of that year, my parents may have decided to wait before starting a family. However, I have a feeling that my mother rather dreaded the idea of childbirth, and the fact that I am an only child perhaps confirms this view. After their marriage, my parents moved into no. 12 Ardgowan Street: living (if only just) in the exclusive West End, my mother definitely felt that she had moved up in the world. My parents didn't own the house: few owned property in those days. Like the other residents, they paid rent to a factor. I believe the man who owned the property lived in Glasgow.

I can still picture the little flat clearly. The front room was the best room, and we always used it when visitors came, but we spent most of the time in the kitchen. In my early days, the kitchen still had an old-fashioned coal-fired black range where a kettle could be kept on the boil if required (we had no running hot water – there was just a black sink with a brass swan-necked cold water tap), but this range was later replaced by a modern tiled fireplace. These were very popular at the time: a contemporary advertisement showing one appeared in my school magazine for 1951. We had no fridge or telephone. The bedroom, where my parents slept, was quite small, but I slept there too when I was younger. With very little space, my bed was right beside the fireplace. I had a stone hot water bottle (known for some reason as a 'pig'), and one night I accidentally pushed it out of the bed. It landed on the solid hearth and broke: I was not very popular. The kitchen and the front room each had a large walk-in space that could be used for storage or as a bed recess (the one in the front room had a door on it). To make a bed, a soft mattress was placed on a frame with springs which itself rested on wooden supports. These beds were certainly comfortable and snug, particularly if there had been a coal fire in the room. This was usually the

Studio portrait by Lockhart Auld, Greenock, 1940s.

case in the kitchen. When I was older, I slept in one or other of these recesses in turn.

One early memory of no. 12 Ardgowan Street is of a birthday party, the room being in darkness apart from the candles on the cake. Later, I convinced myself that the darkness was part of the wartime blackout, but as this was lifted when the war ended in 1945 I would not have been old enough to remember it: the light had probably been switched off while I attempted to blow out the candles. But this may still have been one of my earliest memories. Another memory, from a slightly later time, is of being sent into the East End to acquire the services of a chimney sweep who lived in an old property just off East Shaw Street, near the former Royal Infirmary in Duncan Street.

Sometime during my early days at school, although I can't remember exactly when, I was very ill with what was called 'congestion of the lungs', and I was off school for several weeks. I spent much of the time in the bed recess in the kitchen (the kitchen being the warmest part of the house), with kaolin poultices being slapped on my chest: they had to be as hot as you could bear them. Despite having survived this ordeal, I still suffer from a weakness in the chest.

Greenock was badly bombed over the nights of May 6 and 7, 1941. When the air raid sirens sounded you were supposed to take shelter in the cellars, but my father refused to do this and just went out into the street. A neighbour of ours, who worked at Walker's Sugarhouse, was blown down a flight of stairs in the refinery by the blast from a hit although luckily he was not too badly injured. Several tenements in Belville Street were hit, but no. 51, where the Laughlans lived, was spared. However, other members of the family were not so lucky: several cousins of my mother lost their lives during the second night's raid. Many years later, there were still gaps in the town where buildings had once stood; yet another early memory is of being taken by my mother to the East End on some errand, and passing a number of these bomb sites.

Just opposite no. 12 Ardgowan Street was St Mark's Church (Church of Scotland), now demolished: a block of flats currently occupies the site. There was an open grassy area between the church and Kelly Street, but the church hall, at the far end, was at right angles to the church itself, with its end wall flush with Kelly Street. My parents had now become members of St Mark's, but they seldom attended services except perhaps at Easter and Christmas. The first minister that I remember was the Rev. James Murray. Like my parents, I have never had strong religious feelings, and I complained that I had to go to Sunday School every week while they rarely went to church. The reply was that it was just something that you had to do – like going to school. I empathised with my childhood storybook hero 'William' (Richmal Crompton's engaging creation), who was equally vehement about being sent to Sunday School. Later, I did become a member of the church, but again only because I thought it was something that you had to do. But I did it without any strong conviction.

I remember a Christmas party in the church hall, where there was a large tree glittering with fairy lights; I also remember one Sunday School picnic, and particularly how we got there. Our Sunday School teacher, Gordon Tennant, whose father ran a radio business in the town, had a large 1940s Wolseley of a type used by a number of police forces, and he packed quite a number of us into the back of this seemingly cavernous vehicle to take us to the picnic site. Not having a car ourselves, this was a great treat. At that time, I can only recall one person in our section of Ardgowan Street who owned a car: it was a 1930s Morris, and it belonged to a lady, Mrs Fisher. With so little traffic, you could play in the street quite safely. If a car came along you would see and hear it in plenty of time to get on to the pavement before continuing whatever game you were playing – back in the middle of the road. This may have been potentially dangerous, but at least we were outside: you seldom see children playing outside nowadays. When we went out to play there was always the warning "Don't talk to strange men…" invariably coupled with "…and make sure you're back for your tea".

If we tired of playing in the street, there was another diversion that we occasionally indulged in. Most of the tenements had two flats on each level, the doors being on opposite sides of the landing. But in some tenements the two doors were side by side on each landing, and this suggested a prank, namely to tie the two door knobs together, ring both door bells and then make a run for it. There was usually someone, invariably a woman, at home during the day, but we never dared to stay behind to see what might happen. It seems harmless enough now, if doubtless somewhat tiresome for whoever did answer the doors, but we thought we were very daring, and we always had a good giggle when we were far enough away from the scene of the crime.

Although I remember that particular Christmas party in St Mark's church hall, I don't have very clear memories of Christmas itself at home. That may be because we didn't have large family gatherings (almost impossible in a small flat), and even with just three of us I don't recall special Christmas dinners – certainly not turkey and all the trimmings. Nobody had much money at that time (I usually only got a few pence for pocket money although you could get a gobstopper for a halfpenny: another treat, a 'Merry Mac's Lucky Bag', might have cost threepence or more) and my mother's main interest was in dressmaking, not cooking (or baking). But there was still rationing for several years after the War, and so nothing much was available anyway. For regular meals, we existed on a diet of mince and potatoes, fish and chips, sausages, macaroni cheese, or perhaps cold meat (often corned beef) with a salad that would consist of little more than lettuce, cucumber and a tomato. On Sundays, we might have some silverside: chicken was considered something of a luxury. For desserts, I can only recall basic dishes such as semolina and prunes and custard, but a regular treat at week-ends was to have ice cream. As we had no fridge, this had to be bought on the day, and I would be sent down to one of the Italian cafés with a jug to get enough for three people – "and don't forget the raspberry sauce". There were numerous cafés in the town, most of them run by Italian families (there was even a family called Rossini who had a café in Grey Place), but my father thought that Spella's café in West Blackhall Street had the best ice cream, and so I had to go there.

When I was young, there were no lavish Christmas presents, but I do remember hanging up a pillow case rather than just a stocking – ever hopeful. There might be fruit, one or two books (invariably including a *Rupert* annual) and a couple of Dinky Toys. One present I do remember was a garage for my Dinky Toys that my Uncle Billy, my mother's youngest brother, had made for me. It was quite large, painted green, and had a sliding door; it even had a little ramp up to the door. I was thrilled with this, and it remained a favourite toy for many years. But one really exciting thing was getting food parcels, usually including tinned meat, chocolate and chewing gum, from Canada. These were sent in the years after the Second World War through a connection with some young Canadian service personnel who had been stationed in Greenock during the War in what had been the old Smithston Poorhouse and Asylum (it had been renamed Niobe). My parents apparently met them one night in one of Greenock's cinemas when one of them, sitting next to my father, turned to him and said "Got a light, chum?" (Just about everyone smoked in those days.) My parents then invited them up to our little flat, and they became good friends. After the War, the parents of two of the boys were so grateful for the hospitality that my parents had shown them that they sent these food parcels from time to time. They also sent toys for me, one of which was a 'Log Cabin Building Set' which was probably quite unlike anything available in Britain at the time. I was very proud that I had a toy that none of my classmates had. Many years later, I was able to meet one of the 'boys', Clare (Clarence) Townson, and one of the 'girls', Ferne Stonham, when I visited Canada in 2009: they were both almost ninety then, but they still retained fond memories of Greenock.

While Mrs Fisher's Morris was the only permanent car in the immediate neighbourhood, we did see other ones from time to time. One was a large taxi owned by a local firm, P. B. Wright (next door to Spella's café), and it was driven by Mr Stewart who lived on the ground floor of no. 12. It was an American Packard, number plate DAH 333, and sometimes it sat outside no. 12 if Mr Stewart came home for his dinner (as we would have called lunch in those days). An occasional treat, if you were going to some function in the town, was to hire the Packard: it was even bigger than Gordon Tennant's Wolseley. It may have come over from the United States during the preparations for D-Day, but I believe that some American cars had been available in Britain before that. I often wonder what happened to it. Mr Stewart later became a bus driver for the Western SMT.

I enjoy watching the television adaptations of Agatha Christie's Hercule Poirot novels with Sir David Suchet as the fastidious little Belgian detective. In each of them there is meticulous attention to period detail, and at least two – *The Murder of Roger Ackroyd* and *Hercule Poirot's Christmas* – have featured an old Rolls-Royce, its number plate clearly visible – VS 2172. This was an original Greenock registration, and the car had presumably belonged to a well-to-do family, possibly one with shipping or sugar interests, residing in one of the mansions in the West End. Whoever now owned the car was obviously renting it out to film or television companies when a vehicle of that vintage was required. But I have yet to see DAH 333 in any similar programme.

As to D-Day itself, there seemed to be an unusual amount of activity in the river in 1944, and most people sensed that something big was about to happen. My father took me down to Greenock's Esplanade (at the tender age of not quite a year old) so that I could say with some truth that I 'saw' something of the preparations for this historic event. Later that year I had my first birthday, and my mother entered the following in the appropriate page in the *Baby's Story* book: "Really slept through it all! With the aid of a little whisky before hand!!" (So that's when I got the taste for it.) My mother then seemed to lose interest in marking my progress in such things as 'Baby's First Hair Cut' and when 'Baby's First Tooth Appeared' as, despite the book having pages for notes up to 'Seventh Birthday', there are no further entries.

Another car that made an occasional appearance at our 'close mouth' (communal entry into the tenement) was an old Hillman owned by my Uncle John, my father's eldest brother. He was the one member of that family who had done well for himself. Around the time that I first became aware of him, he had acquired the nickname 'Mappy'. This, I gathered later, came from an attempt by one of his grandchildren to pronounce the name Mackie. He worked in the jute industry in Dundee, and was sent out to India at an early age, certainly before the First World War (I have his own copy of the once popular balled *Love, could I only tell thee* (by Clifton Bingham and J.M. Capel) on which he had written 'John Mackie,

Calcutta, Septr. 1913'). He also travelled widely, and he regularly sent postcards home from literally all over the world: my father had kept the ones that he had been sent (one was of San Francisco's Golden Gate *without* the Bridge: it opened in 1937) and this gave me the impetus to start collecting postcards (cartology) myself. Uncle John later became a stockbroker. He eventually lived in Edinburgh, but he continued to travel. Having said that he had already had a very full life, he decided to sail to Australia in 1961 on one of Alfred Holt's 'Blue Funnel' ships: these were essentially cargo vessels with accommodation for a small number of passengers.

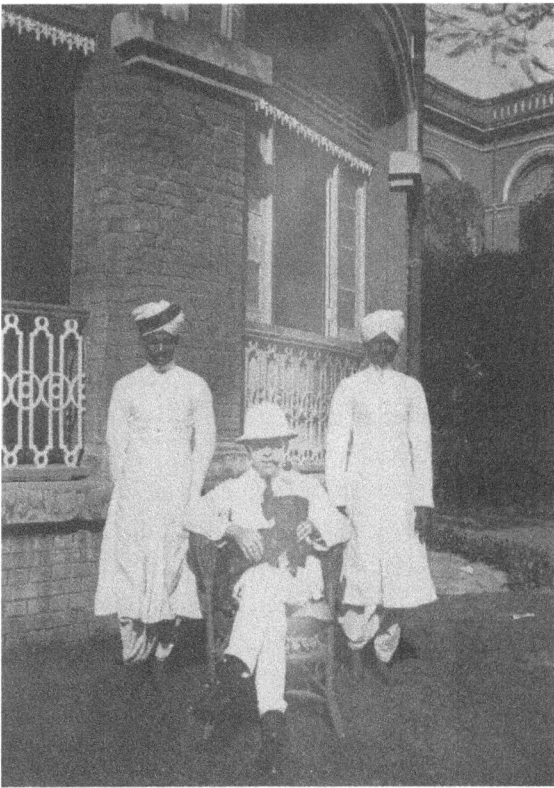

Uncle John in India, pre-1914.

If 'Mappy' had business dealings in Largs, some fourteen miles from Greenock, he always took the opportunity to visit us. He was very dapper, and invariably wore a bow tie. My father always looked forward to his visits, and I thought the world of him. He was able to talk endlessly about anything and everything, and as he owned a car and was always smartly dressed I thought he must be a millionaire (it was the only word I knew that fitted such an unusual personality), and I proudly told my friends so. When the car arrived at no. 12, children would gather round to look at it – a measure of how different things were then and how the world has changed. We didn't have room to put him up, and so he stayed at the nearby Tontine Hotel in Ardgowan Square. His visits were always greatly appreciated.

When I was very young, my grandfather often read to me, and as he was doing so I would look at the page to try to make sense of the letters that I saw and match them to what I was hearing. I was obviously successful in this as I could read before I went to school, and have remained an avid reader and bibliophile ever since. Soon, too, I was reading comics such as *The Dandy*, with 'Korky the Cat', *The Beano*, with 'Biffo the Bear', and, later, and from the same stable (the Dundee based D.C. Thomson), *The Topper*. There was, too, *The Eagle*, with 'Dan Dare' and 'the Mekon', 'Harris Tweed – extra special agent' (pompous but inefficient) and his young assistant (much the cleverer of the two), who was always addressed as 'Boy', and the wonderful cutaway sections in the middle that showed the inside of a plane, a ship, a steam engine or whatever. We didn't have many books in the house, but my father enjoyed the novels of Edgar Wallace (once enormously popular), and he had a number of these as well as reference books and books on various aspects of Scotland and its history. When I was about five we acquired *The Children's Encyclopedia* [sic] (again, once enormously popular), all ten volumes of it. My parents must have sent away for it as I clearly recall the day the books arrived in three cardboard boxes. It was a big thrill opening them.

One childhood incident that I cannot actually recall, but which my mother often mentioned, occurred when I apparently overheard my parents saying that I needed a haircut. My mother, a dressmaker by training, also worked for some time in a large hairdressing establishment (for both men and women) run by Freddy Holms and his wife. It was next door to the Regal cinema in West Blackhall Street. I knew where the shop was as I had been there with my mother, and so, hearing that I needed a haircut, I set off alone one day when I was supposed to be playing in the street. I found my way there, and announced that I needed a haircut (this was clearly before I started to patronise Bertie Paterson who was just around the corner from us in Kelly Street). Mrs Holms recognised me, and told another assistant to take me home again. I don't know if I did get my hair cut that day, but even at that tender age I seemed confident enough to find my way into town: clearly I was exhibiting an early touch of the wanderlust.

At an early age, too, I joined the Watt Library, a private library with origins dating back to 1783: the present building in Union Street dates from 1837. It is very near where we lived in Ardgowan Street: I could almost get there without having to step off the pavement, the one exception being the brief crossing of Watt Street. The library, which later became part of Greenock Public Library (which I also joined eventually: at that time it had an excellent music section), had a good selection of children's books, and I devoured these. As well as Richmal Crompton's 'William' books I enjoyed many of Enid Blyton's stories (including the 'Five', 'Mystery' and 'Adventure' series); also the 'Biggles' books and the 'Billy Bunter' books: they all told of a world that was quite new to me, and different to anything I had experienced so far. The library also had *The Children's Newspaper* that was once very popular. You

could read it there but not borrow it. It ceased publication in
1965. The librarian at the time was Herbert Henderson, a
well-known figure in the town.

As well as visits to my grandparents in Belville Street, I
sometimes saw my mother's siblings. My Aunt Esther was
twice married, but she had no children. Aunt Betty and her
husband Jimmy eventually lived further west of us in a housing
estate built in the grounds of one of the town's larger mansions,
Stoneleigh. They had three boys – Jim, Peter and John. Uncle
Billy, also twice married, had four girls – Edith, Audrey,
Shirley and Sandra. Edith was a talented dancer; she and my
mother got on well together. The other brother, Uncle Jim, had
moved to Grimsby. We seldom saw him although I remember
his two little girls, a few years younger than me, visiting us
once in Ardgowan Street.

My mother was also very fond of her Aunt Margaret, my
grandfather's sister, who lived in an old house in Union Street,
near Greenock Cricket Club, and we often visited her. Her
husband, Donald, whom I never met, had been in the Navy,
and his sword hung in the hallway. From an early age I was
obsessed with swords: I would even draw them on photographs
of people in books or magazines, something l later regretted.
Uncle Donald's sword was an endless source of fascination for
me, and was one reason why I was always happy to visit Aunt
Margaret (my great-aunt) with my mother.

On my father's side, we also visited my Aunt Alice and
Uncle Barney. They lived at 177 Dunlop Street, a semi-
detached two-storey Corporation house next to the Rankin
Park and the main road to Inverkip. With 'upstairs', a
bathroom and both a front and back garden, it seemed untold
luxury to me. The family had previously lived in nearby
Bannockburn Street, but that was before my time although my
father remembered the house. The Porters had seven children
– Winifred, Alison, Cyril, Mina, Stanley, Henry and Ian. Cyril
eventually had no less than thirteen of a family: it would have
been fourteen, but there was a set of twins, one of which died.

My father, who hadn't seen Cyril for some time, met him in the town one day and asked him how he was getting on. "I'm driving a milk float now, Uncle" said Cyril. "I think you'll need most of that for yourself" said my father.

As well as my real aunts and uncles, my parents had close friends that I could call Aunt or Uncle rather than Mr or Mrs. My father was a clerk in the RNTF (Royal Naval Torpedo Factory), and he had a good friend there whose name was Stanley Foster. Stanley and his wife, Chrissie, lived near us in Kelly Street (above Mr Martin, the butcher), and we saw them regularly; so they became Uncle Stan and Aunt (usually Auntie) Chrissie. They had a daughter, Pat, who was roughly my age. The midwife whom my mother had seen regularly, Mrs Lawrence, also became a good friend, but for some reason she was always known by her surname as Auntie Lawrence rather than by her Christian name as Auntie Martha. She and her husband, Alec, also lived near us, in Nelson Street, and we saw them regularly too. Auntie Lawrence, who was probably in her fifties when I was born, was one of a large family from the island of Coll in the Inner Hebrides, and she often spoke of life there when she was growing up in the 1890s. Supplies could only come in by sea, but with no pier the ships would either have to be beached (if they were small, like puffers) or anchored offshore, with goods being brought in by smaller boats. Apparently, this often took place overnight by the light of the moon.

One of Auntie Lawrence's sisters, Mary, had married a shepherd, Charlie Crawford, and they worked on a farm at Arrochar at the head of Loch Long. I don't think my mother had been very well after my birth, and Auntie Lawrence said that the Crawfords would be happy for us to have a holiday there. This was very successful, and the Crawfords joined a growing rank of surrogate relatives as Auntie Mary and Uncle Charlie. They had a son, also Charlie, who was a few years older than me. Although I was just a young child at the time, I clearly remember the farm and the Crawfords' cottage. The farm buildings included a barn in which a swing had been set up. It consisted of a rope hanging from the roof, with a very large knot tied at the bottom. You took the rope, got yourself up on to a ledge, sat on the knot, held on tightly to the rope, and then took off and had a good old swing. There are photographs of me at the farm (although not on the swing) taken in 1947.

Another of Auntie Lawrence's sisters was Bella, who lived at Benderloch, just north of Oban, and we also had holidays there. I don't recall Bella's husband, but one of her nieces, Peggy, worked in the local 'big house': her husband, Jimmy, was the head gardener. The house was just west of the village, and it overlooked a lovely beach. Once, when the owners were away, Peggy took us down to see the property. This was a big thrill as we were not supposed to be there, but I have always been fascinated by these large mansions.

The beginnings of my friendships with local children are difficult to pinpoint with accuracy. Perhaps my first friend was Donald Stewart, son of taxi-driving Mr Stewart, as we lived in the same building. Donald had other siblings, including an older brother, Francis, but Donald and I were, I think, the same age. Directly below us lived Mr and Mrs Wylie. They had a family of two boys, Jim and Freddie, and a girl, Ella. But they were all older than me, and so they were not my 'playmates'. There was another boy, Craig Speirs, who lived in the next tenement, no. 10 (a more up-market one as the flats were bigger and had bathrooms), but he too was older, and so again he didn't play with us. Craig eventually became a doctor. Also in no. 10 was the McTavish family, two of whom, Duncan and Catherine, were well-known in the sporting world. But, once again, they were older than me. Another boy, roughly my age, was Jim Beaton who lived in the biggest house in our stretch of Ardgowan Street between Nelson Street and Kelly Street. It was set back from the road, and although a somewhat plain building, it impressed me greatly. Later demolished, a modern church now stands on the site. Previous generations of the Beaton family had been involved in a contracting business in the town.

But my longest-lasting friendship has been with Allan McEwan, who lived round the corner in Kelly Street, although again I can't say for sure when we first became friends. Allan and I went to the same school, but he was a year older, and we were in different classes: another boy, William (Bill) Harkness, who lived next door to Allan, was the same age as me, and we were in the same class. But although I didn't see Allan very much in school, we played together regularly. We had an interest in Dinky Toys, and we purchased these (when money was available) from Thomas Templeton's shop at 32 Inverkip Street near Brachleston Square. It seemed to sell nothing but Dinky Toys, and there only ever seemed to be a lady serving in the shop – possibly Mrs Templeton. (While the building is still standing, the shop, like so many 'corner shops', has now been converted into a house.) We were also interested in vehicles, generally, and would often spend time collecting car numbers, a favourite pastime. In those days, most of the vehicles that we saw would have been local, and they would have had a Greenock VS registration. Anything else was unusual, e.g. an XS registration: that was from Paisley, less than twenty miles away, but still quite rare. Uncle John's Hillman had an EYV registration; that was *very* rare! Simple pleasures. The McEwans later moved to another part of the town but I still managed to keep in touch with Allan.

I don't recall many friendships at that time with local girls. One, Sheila Robertson, lived with her mother in Kelly Street in a tiny ground-floor single-end at the rear of the tenement whose entrance was between the Co-op (GCCS) and John B. Nimmo's shop. I hardly knew Sheila, but I remember Mrs Robertson: she only had one arm, presumably the result of an accident. Next door to us, in no. 14 Ardgowan Street, lived Anne McDougall, who was, I think, two years older than me. I liked Anne, but she didn't play with us: perhaps she thought we were too young. She had an older sister, Agnes, who seemed very grown up although at that time she too was still at school. Another two were sisters Grace and Caroline Cameron: they lived in one of the tenements between Kelly Street and Patrick Street. But it was only when I went to school myself that I had my first romance – with a very pretty little girl in my year called Dorothy Somerville, who also lived in Kelly Street. Another girl, younger than me, was Kareth Paterson. Kareth lived further west in Ardgowan Street, but I only saw her occasionally. Years later, through a mutual friend, and when we both lived south of the border, we met up again; by chance, and quite independently, we both came back to live in the West of Scotland (although neither of us in Greenock) at almost the same time.

The girls, of course, had their own street games, one of which was peever (another word for hop-scotch). This consisted of a long frame of squares, possibly with a semicircle at one end, and with a number in each square, drawn out in chalk on the street. The game seemed to consist of hopping from one square to another, presumably trying to avoid landing on the lines (I never quite grasped the rules of play!) I believe our local girls also called this 'beds'. The boys usually played football. I may have joined in with them, but I was never good at games, or even particularly enthusiastic: I lacked, and still lack, that essential ingredient – competitiveness. I was happier playing with my Dinky Toys. But I was quite adventurous, and I enjoyed climbing trees. This usually resulted in various scratches, torn garments and small splinters of wood in my hands. My mother had to extract these with a pair of tweezers. We called a little splinter like this a 'skelf'.

Another early interest was the cinema, and Greenock had seven of them: the Pavilion, the Regal, the B.B. cinema, the Central, the King's (formerly a theatre and later renamed the Odeon), the Palace (later the Gaumont) and the La Scala. Port Glasgow had the Plaza, and Gourock, the Picture House, but visits to these two were rare. The Pavilion was considered something of a flea-pit, and the Central, which was unusual in having an open fire in the entrance hallway, was known as the Ranch as it always seemed to be showing cowboy films although I remember seeing one of the longer Laurel and Hardy films there. This was *Fra Diavolo* (a burlesque of Auber's famous light opera), and I came out humming the well-known aria "On yonder rock reclining". Another film at the Ranch contained the popular song *Deep in the Heart of Texas*, and as it was very catchy I came out of the cinema humming that too. On Saturday mornings there were children's programmes at the Regal.

There were continuous performances during the day, and it was quite normal to go in halfway through a film, either the main or the second feature; consequently, you stayed in when the next showing began so that you could catch up with the bit you had missed. People would say "Oh, this is where we came in", and would then get up to leave. This usually caused some disruption, often at a pivotal moment in the film when you could easily miss a vital part of the plot. I often went to the 'flicks' on my own; sometimes I stayed on to see a film twice (very naughty) if it really held my attention. One I recall was *The Story of Robin Hood and his Merrie Men*, with Richard Todd, which I saw at the B.B. cinema; another was *The Great Locomotive Chase*, with Fess Parker, which I saw at the La Scala. Having seen a film twice, I would come out in fear and trembling in case the doorman realised that I had been there too long, but luckily I was never caught. The Robin Hood film also had a musical interest for me as the character Alan-a-Dale was played by the guitar-playing entertainer Elton Hayes. The film contained some attractive numbers such as "Whistle, my love" and "Oh I sing a song, a rollicky song". Again, I came out of the cinema singing these (well, I had heard them more than once). Elton Hayes was often on the radio programme *Children's Favourites* (with 'Uncle Mac' – Derek McCulloch), singing another song that I found very attractive – *The Whistling Gypsy*.

The seeds of my future career in music were clearly planted early. I can recall my mother playing the piano before I started to have lessons; also my father playing the violin. Sometimes, he would play along with radio programmes, a particular favourite being *Grand Hotel*: I can never hear its signature tune, Johann Strauss II's *Roses from the South*, without thinking of those childhood days. My father also played in the Buckeridge Light Concert Orchestra, a small group conducted by Frank Buckeridge. It rehearsed in the E.U. (Evangelical Union) Church in Nelson Street. The church itself was at street level, but the hall was underneath the church as the ground fell away sharply to the back: access to it was via a stairway from the street. My father used to take me to the rehearsals, and eventually they made me the honorary librarian. The orchestra's Light Music repertoire was very much the norm of similar groups, with items such as the overture to Suppé's operetta *Pique Dame*, Frederic Curzon's *The Boulevardier,* Kéler Béla's *Lustspiel-Ouverture* [sic] and selections from shows such as *Lilac Time* (1922) which used the music of Schubert arranged by G.H. Clutsam. At the time, I didn't know where all these individual numbers came from in Schubert's output, but the selection gave me a love of the composer's music that has never left me. Sometimes there were less familiar items. One was a selection from *The King Steps Out*, a 1936 film with music by the famous violinist Fritz Kreisler. There was one number in this selection that I really liked; I eventually found out that it was one of his short pieces, *Marche miniature viennoise*. Despite much serious musical study in later years, this early introduction to the lighter side was almost prophetic as most of my professional life has been with the lighter side of music in all its forms. The orchestra sometimes performed at Cragburn Pavilion in Gourock. This building was later demolished, and flats now stand on the site.

As there was no television in my early days (apart from a few sets in the London area), most people only had radio, or 'the wireless' as it was usually called. Listening, as opposed to watching, gives your imagination greater scope, and people used to sit at wireless sets, conjuring up their own ideas as to what was going on (women would often be knitting as well). Indeed, you needed a bit of imagination for shows like *The Goon Show* and *Journey into Space* which were all the better for not having a visual element.

There was much music played throughout the day on the radio in programmes like *Bright and Early* and *Morning Melody* (most of this coming into the category of Light Music), and there were many comedy programmes such as *Ray's a Laugh* (with comedian Ted Ray) and *Life with the Lyons* (with the real-life Lyon family – Ben Lyon, whom I would meet in Los Angeles many years later, his wife Bebe Daniels and their children Barbara and Richard). This programme also featured the well-known Scottish character actress Molly Weir as Aggie, the family cook. Another popular programme was the lunchtime *Workers' Playtime*, a variety show that was broadcast from different factory canteens throughout the country and had live audiences. On one programme, I remember hearing the off-beat Scottish comedian Chic Murray (another Greenock man) telling one of his long, rambling shaggy-dog stories which was greeted at the end with an embarrassing stony silence. It took some time for Chic's droll humour to be fully appreciated, particularly in England.

The regions had their own programmes, one of the Scottish ones being *Clan Clash* (a great favourite of my father) with the well-known Glasgow broadcaster Jack House. My own favourite was *The McFlannels*, written by Helen W. Pryde, which was about a family who lived in a typical Glasgow tenement. The family consisted of Willie and Sarah, and their children Matt, Peter, Polly and Maisie; there were also occasional visits from the amusing and adenoidal Uncle Mattha. Other characters were given surnames based on different fabrics, cleverly associated with their own characteristics with a 'Mc' attached – McVelvet, McTweed,

M'Corduroy and M'Cotton. The radio stories were later issued in book form.

There were also radio Aunties and Uncles for *Children's Hour* (from 5.00 pm to 6.00 pm), and in Scotland we had Auntie Kathleen (Kathleen Garscadden) – I can still hear her saying "Hello children" in her warm and very distinctive voice. Many of the programmes were set in Scotland; they included serials written by the well-known Scottish writer Angus MacVicar. Sometimes we had programmes from London, among them *Norman and Henry Bones, the Boy Detectives* (one of whom was played by the actress Patricia Hayes) and *Tiger and Snort Investigate* (which had a naval setting), the signature tune of which was *Plymouth Hoe (a Nautical Overture)* by John Ansell. This soon became another favourite piece of music.

It was always exciting when the fairs came to town. I particularly remember one being set up in what had been part of the Lady Alice Park, between Inverkip Road and Brachelston Street. The entrance to this area was in Brachelston Street, just across the road from the west end of Dempster Street, and there was a slope down to the level of the current Lady Alice Bowling Club. Later, on this site, came the Hector McNeil Memorial Baths, but this building was demolished when the Greenock Waterfront Leisure Centre opened. (Hector McNeil was a politician and Member of Parliament for Greenock, during which time he was, briefly, Secretary of State for Scotland.) I also have an idea that there was a fair, or at least some temporary entertainment, in or around Arthur Street at Charing Cross (not far from my grandparents' home in Belville Street), but that may just be my imagination.

When it snowed, there was the fun of sledging. Greenock has a number of hilly streets, but even then, despite the lack of traffic, it was not safe to sledge on the streets. A favourite spot for this activity was in what was known as Macaulay's field, an equally hilly area between Lyle Road and the golf course, running west from the south end of Madeira Street. We didn't have a sledge at home, but I used to borrow a tin tray that served the purpose. There was a culvert in the field that ran from the foot of the hill to an exit further north nearer the river. It was quite a large tunnel, and those of us of an adventurous disposition would often venture inside. Macaulay's field has long since been built over.

Some of these recollections are from my earliest years, but others are from my schooldays which can be dated more precisely.

Chapter 2: Schooldays – 1948–1961

1. Primary – 1948-1955

I was educated at Greenock Academy, a grammar school that was just two streets away from where we lived. The main (and original) building faced east on to Nelson Street, and the school covered an area bounded by Nelson Street, Finnart Street to the north, Newton Street to the south and, to the west, a narrow pedestrian lane that ran between upper and lower Kelly Street. This lane, which had no official name in any older town Directory that I have seen, was always known as the Dardanelles – the famous narrow stretch of water now in Turkey but once part of the old Ottoman Empire. On the other side of the Dardanelles was the Territorial Army Drill Hall. An Ordnance Survey map of 1896 shows that the lane did not exist at that time, the Drill Hall area being contiguous with the Academy grounds. Also, the original building was on a different site to the one I remember, approximately on what is now the north-east corner of Finnart Street and Kelly Street. The lane presumably dates from the time when the larger building was constructed further west.

The school sometimes used the Drill Hall as an extra gymnasium, and there were tales of men enjoying the sight of the girls in their school knickers! When the First World War started in 1914, the Drill Hall was the headquarters of the 5th Argyll and Sutherland Highlanders (Territorials), who fought at Achi Baba in the disastrous Gallipoli campaign in 1915.

If the lane was in place then, it is perhaps through this connection that it got its unofficial name, its narrowness presumably suggesting to the soldiers the narrowness of the real Dardanelles. The original Greenock Academy and the later Drill Hall were both demolished to make way for the present James Watt College, and the lane was moved some way to the west. But it does finally appear to have been granted official status, being dignified with nameplates at each end that read 'Dardanelles/To Kelly Street'.

At one time, during my schooldays, the Drill Hall played host to Hermann Goering's staff car, an interesting survivor from the Second World War: presumably it was being exhibited all around the country. Allan McEwan and I made a point of seeing it; with no-one seemingly in attendance we even managed to get into it. Today's security would not allow that to happen.

Greenock Academy (Latin motto *hinc vera virtus*) was founded in 1855, and it lasted on its original site until 1964 when the school moved to a new building further west, the old one being demolished the following year. Although not a private school (it came under the Renfrewshire Education Authority), there were modest fees. The original block had been added to over the years; it housed the main Secondary classrooms, the gymnasium and a room that was once used to serve meals: these were brought in as there was no kitchen. A separate block, built in 1909-10, housed most of the Primary classrooms and, on the upper floor, the art, music and geography rooms. Primary 1 and Primary 2 were housed in a wooden annexe built in 1931 at the western end of the playground. At the back of the annexe was the school's boundary wall, then the Dardanelles and the Drill Hall. The janitor's house was in the south-west corner of the playground, and between that and the annexe there was space for two or three cars. In 1950, a domestic science unit and a dining hall and kitchen were built in front of the main block, the old dining area in the main building becoming the library.

The Academy had both Primary and Secondary departments, and it was the only school that I, and most of my classmates, ever attended, but the Secondary department did have intakes from other Primary schools. To start at Primary 1 at the Academy you had to be interviewed, even at that tender age; this would have been sometime during 1948 when I was about four and a half. I was given a rectangular box with seven cubes in it, four of one colour on one side and three of another colour on the other side, and I was asked to move them around (without taking them out of the box) so that the colours finished up on the opposite sides. I managed to do this, demonstrating a modicum of intelligence, and, with the answers to several questions, I must have made the right impression as I gained entrance to the school, starting at the annexe in the autumn of 1948. I was not yet five years old, but many of my classmates had already reached that age.

The annexe consisted of a corridor running the full length of the building, with four classrooms (two each for Primary 1 and Primary 2) on the east side looking on to the playground. There were obviously too many of us for one classroom, but I'm not sure how we were divided: it may have been alphabetically, or possibly by age (some had birthdays much earlier in the year). I can't remember, and I was too young to think about it at the time. There were several smaller rooms on the west side of the corridor, one of them being a medical room, another possibly a staff room. On the walls of the corridor were murals that seemed to owe something to Great Britain's colonial past.

I don't recall very much of my two years in the annexe, but I remember my first day at school. One of my new classmates was crying for his mother, and I treated this with scorn; then my mother came to collect me, and I treated this with indignation, telling her that I was quite old enough to look after myself. She never came again. Later, I apparently told my parents that when I grew up they wouldn't see very much of me as I had a lot to do! Something of an independent free spirit was clearly manifesting itself at an early age. I also remember having our daily milk ration in the annexe. This was, I think, just a third of a pint; it came in a little bottle with a cardboard top.

The subjects covered in those two Primary classes were English, arithmetic, writing, drawing and hand work, and there were even two written reports each year, in December and June, on the standard reached in each subject. The assessment varied from 'fair' through 'fairly good' and 'good' to 'very good', and I was in each category at least once in some subjects over the two-year period. But I managed to get 'very good' in English and arithmetic in each of the four reports.

Our teachers in the Primary department were mainly elderly (as they seemed to us) spinsters although I expect they weren't quite as old as we may have thought – perhaps in their forties or fifties. Their main style of dress seemed to be what my mother called 'a costume' (a suit consisting of a matching skirt and jacket), with 'sensible' shoes and 'conservative' hairstyles. Some, but not the infant teachers, also wore academic gowns. Miss Tannock, one of the teachers in the annexe, later became the official head of these early classes as Infant Mistress. There was no segregation in the classes, and throughout my school-days we were a mixed–sex group. Much better, really.

In the autumn of 1950 we moved from the annexe to Primary 3 in the main Primary block, and from then on we were in X or R right up to Primary 7. I was in the X section. I think it was the top one although I was always nearer the bottom of the class than the top – quite literally, which meant that I was usually in the front or second front row. This actually suited me as I couldn't see the blackboard properly from the back of the room although it was some time before it was noticed that I might have some ocular deficiency. Our teacher in Primary 3X was Miss Lindsay, but she had a serious illness that year (possibly cancer of the throat), and she was absent for much of the time. This resulted in our having a number of other teachers, few of whom I can remember. One I do remember was Mrs Russell, and I seem to recall one of her own children paying an occasional visit to our class. We also had writing lessons in Primary 3 from the one-armed Mr Allan who was known as Daddy. We assumed that he had lost the arm during the First World War as he looked old enough to have served in that conflict. He would write something on the board, and we were supposed to copy it. But we were very mischievous, and we would take toys or other articles out to him saying "Look what I've got, Mr Allan". "Yes, very nice. Just sit down please". Miss Lindsay eventually came back, but her voice was now very harsh, and it remained so while we were in her class.

The Primary 3 and Primary 4 classes were at the west side of the building, overlooking the playground. The seating in these, as elsewhere in the school, was tiered. My Primary 4 class (1951-52), was with Miss Macdonald. The classroom was at the Finnart Street end of the building, but you had to go through the adjacent classroom to get to it. This was Miss MacKechnie's class, and it must have been tiresome for her to have another set of pupils tramping through her room every so often and disturbing her own lessons. Miss MacKechnie, presumably because of her gait, rejoiced in the nickname Bouncer.

Soon after I started in Primary 4, we had another visit from my Uncle John – 'Mappy'. We always looked forward to his visits, but this one was followed by my first trip to Edinburgh. We drove there in the Hillman, a huge treat. The distance from Greenock to Edinburgh was reckoned to be 66 miles: 22 from Greenock to Glasgow, and double that again from Glasgow to Edinburgh. With today's motorways you can do this in less than two hours, but it took us most of the day. But that time wasn't spent just driving: Mappy had planned that we stop off at places of historic interest.

We left Greenock on Friday, September 21 (it may have been a public holiday as my father was there too), and I was in seventh heaven: this was the greatest adventure so far.

We travelled first towards Glasgow, and we crossed the River Clyde on either the old Erskine ferry or the Renfrew ferry before stopping at a small town, Buchlyvie, where we tried to get some refreshment at an inn called The Cyclists' Rest. We ordered something, and my mother went off to find a toilet. On the way, she happened to pass the kitchen, and she thought that it looked very dirty. When she came back, she mentioned this to Mappy, who then said "All right, we won't stop here. We'll move on". He made some excuse, paid for what we had ordered, and we left. We then arrived at Stirling where, amongst other things, we spent some time in the castle. From an early age, I have always been fascinated by castles, and this was the thrill of a lifetime. A guide book, *Ancient Monuments & Historic Buildings – Ministry of Works/The Castle of Stirling/Price One Shilling'* (5p in today's money), was purchased and later given to me. Mappy had written in it (in green ink) "From Uncle John to David. On Friday 21st Sept 1951 – Shortly after Glasgow, Milngavie, Balfron and Buchlyvie – and its renowned Cyclists' Rest – and the "rest". The first of our famous visits – on a day full of incidents and interest – The Castle, the town, the Field of Bannockburn & the Bore-stone, and Scottish Flag-staff".

From Stirling, we travelled on to Linlithgow. There, we visited Linlithgow Palace: I was enthralled by its seemingly endless rooms, stairways and passages. There is a large fountain in the courtyard, and having either read somewhere or perhaps been told that it had flowed with wine at some major event, possibly a royal wedding, I volunteered this information to the custodian. He was suitably impressed, and turned on the fountain for us. Another guide book was purchased, and Mappy duly inscribed it "From Dad to David on the trip with Uncle John and his car. The second visit of Friday 21st Sept 1951. The Portcullis here is the central interest – and the Fountain played".

And so to Edinburgh where I met my Aunt Mina for the first time. Their home seemed enormous to me, but it was, by

Edinburgh standards, a perfectly normal three-bedroomed house in a short terrace – no. 6 Learmonth Grove in Comely Bank, fairly close to Fettes College. But I was still awe-struck by the house, particularly as they had a grand piano. I was also impressed by the fact that Uncle John garaged his car with a local firm, Moir and Baxter: most cars today are simply left outside. Next day, I had another thrill when we visited Edinburgh Castle and acquired yet another guide book. Mappy's inscription here read "Mum to David on first day's visit to Edinburgh. Uncle John's car today – 22nd Sept 1951 – does the work & we are conducted round the outer monuments of the Castle by a Black Watch S.M. [Sergeant-Major] who might be our own Winston's twin – dry humour & "rapier" thrusts of comments – on Mons Meg etc". ('Winston' is a reference to Winston Churchill, and Mons Meg is the famous 15th century canon that stands high on the ramparts.)

During the course of the week-end, we met Maurice Durlac, a very tall man who was a lawyer and WS (Writer to the Signet). He lived two doors away at no. 2 Learmonth Grove, and he had become a good friend of Mappy and Aunt Mina. He was a great character, and very amusing. I met him again on future visits. But this magical week-end was soon over, and we headed back to Greenock. I can't recall how we got home, but we probably travelled by train. It had been the highlight of my life so far; now I was returning to Primary 4 with Miss Macdonald.

Not long after this, I was back in Edinburgh for the wedding of my cousin June, Mappy and Aunt Mina's younger daughter, to Surgeon Lieutenant Ronald Millar, a dentist who had done his National Service in the Navy. I hardly knew June at that time, let alone the Millars, but the two families had long known each other in Dundee. Ron's father, Arthur, was a capable amateur musician: he had been the conductor of the Dundee Operatic Society, and he later became president of NODA, the National Operatic and Dramatic Association. Arthur's brother, Norman, was at one time Sir Thomas

Beecham's Secretary, and he married the harpist Sidonie Goossens of the famous musical family. Ron had also known Alexander (later Sir Alexander) Gibson, who became the conductor of the Scottish National Orchestra and was the founder of Scottish Opera. I believe that thanks to the Millars' impressive musical connections, the famous contralto Kathleen Ferrier was persuaded to come to 6 Learmonth Grove during her time at the Edinburgh Festival in 1952. She died the following year aged just forty-one.

June and Ron were married on Saturday November 17, 1951 in St Cuthbert's Parish Church at the west end of Princes Street. The Greenock contingent consisted of my parents and me, my Aunt Alice and my cousin Alison; this time we stayed at the Cockburn Hotel near Waverley Station. Maurice Durlac, whom I had recently met, was an usher. I also met Wilma, my first cousin once removed (the daughter of June's elder sister Muriel), who at a year older than me was one of the bridesmaids. There was a reception afterwards at the Adam Rooms in George Street: it seemed a very grand affair. I spent much of the time pestering guests for their autographs.

It was about this time that I began to have piano lessons. Growing up in a working class background in the East End of Greenock, my mother had never had the opportunity to have music or dancing lessons, but after their marriage she persuaded my father to get a small upright piano: he, of course, already had his violin. My mother then started to have lessons with Sybil Tate, a well-known teacher in the town, who was also an accompanist at the local Renfrewshire Musical Festival. And so I grew up in a practical musical environment, all the better as we had no television until I was much older. It must have been a stimulus hearing both my parents play, but I don't know if I persuaded them to let me have piano lessons or if they simply decided that I ought to be able to play an instrument. Sybil Tate may have stopped teaching by that time as she didn't take me as a pupil, but she recommended another lady, Mrs Scrymgeour, equally well-known in the district, who lived in Gourock, a few miles away. I therefore had to get there once a week, and at the end of that school day I would get the school bus to Gourock. But I had to get a public service bus home again. The school bus, a double decker, was an old one, probably pre-war, and the seats upstairs were wooden-slatted (no upholstery) which gave you a very bumpy ride – another lasting memory. Mrs Scrymgeour was an excellent teacher, but in appearance she was rather forbidding to a young child: she wore pince-nez glasses which even then seemed old-fashioned. She gave me a thorough grounding although I never liked practising scales and arpeggios. But I discovered early on that I was a quick sight-reader, something I have put down to having been a good reader even before I started school: perhaps there is a similar process at work in the rapid identification of symbols, either alphabetical or musical. It can be both a blessing and a curse – a blessing in that you can pick up a piece and play it fairly easily at a first reading, but a curse in that you tend not to devote much time to it and move on quickly to another piece. But an ability to sight-read has been a great asset to me as a professional musician.

The next major event during my time in Primary 4 was the death of King George VI on February 6, 1952. We were already at school when the news filtered through, and we were all sent home. A more personal incident occurred when I was sitting in the second front row behind a girl who was bigger than I was. She kept moving about, and I had to move too in order to see the blackboard. With my poor eyesight, I was also squinting at the board, and I appeared to Miss Macdonald to be jumping around and making faces for no obvious reason. She then stopped whatever she was teaching us, and brought me out to the front. "If you can't behave yourself", she said, "you will have to go back to Primary 1". She then dragged me out (not exactly screaming, but still somewhat alarmed) through Miss MacKechnie's room and across the playground to the annexe where I was brought before Miss Tannock, who dutifully tut-tutted at my appalling behaviour. Of course the threatened new beginning didn't materialise; I suspect that Miss Macdonald simply had to see Miss Tannock about something or other (they did converse for a while afterwards), and felt that the mere threat of starting again would improve my manners. As to my inability to see over the head of whichever girl it was, I have an *Eagle* diary for 1952 (the earliest one to survive) in which my height is recorded as being 4 feet 11 inches, my weight as 5 stone 8 pounds and my size in shoes and boots a mere 2. Like the eponymous hero in the film *Geordie* (1955), starring Bill Travers, I might have benefitted from a body-building course. In that film, Geordie, as a wee boy, has a girlfriend; the girl who was chosen to play the part, Anna Ferguson, came from Gourock and was a pupil at Greenock Academy. I think she was in the class above me.

Later in 1952, I moved up to Primary 5. Our teacher there was Miss Law who, like Miss Lindsay, was absent for some time during the year, and of whom I have few memories. Again, we had a succession of other teachers, but the one who stands out was not a teacher but one of the senior pupils: her name was Marelan Neilson, and she was a very good pianist. She had been drafted in to assist with the teacher shortage, and she taught us some songs, one of which immediately caught my attention. It was called *Orderly Day,* and it was a comical description of the duties of an orderly, beginning "At six o'clock of a shiny morn we start our little day/We wash the mugs and wipe the jugs and clear the pots away...", and so on over four verses, set to a bright and jaunty tune. At that age, I'm not sure that I quite understood what it was all about, but it was very catchy, and I never forgot it. Many years later, I discovered that the words had been written at an army camp at Catterick during the First World War to the tune of an old Victorian song called *Solomon Levi.* The author, Captain G.E.H. Keesey, was killed on active service in 1916, but the song was eventually published in one of the many anthologies of 'National Songs' that were popular between the two World

Wars. Much later, the text appeared on the internet, and it occasioned a flood of responses from people of my generation and younger, from literally all over the world, who had also sung it at school in the 1940s and 1950s, and even in the 1960s, and, like me, had found it equally catchy and memorable.

Following the death of King George VI in 1952 came the Coronation of Queen Elizabeth II on June 2, 1953. Although we were almost at the end of term (our Scottish schools finished a month before the English ones and started again a month earlier), the day was a holiday enabling people to listen on the radio or, if they were lucky, to watch it on television. We didn't have television then, but the parents of one of my classmates, Colin Wright, had acquired one, and as Colin's father worked beside my father in the office of the RNTF we were among several people who were invited to watch the ceremony at their home in Johnston Street in the West End. Despite the historic occasion, and the novelty of television, Colin and I didn't watch it all: every so often we went out to play in the garden. It was, however, the first time that I had seen anything on television. Then it was back to 'the wireless', and this gave me my first taste of the operettas of Gilbert and Sullivan: during that same Coronation week, Act I of *The Gondoliers* was broadcast. I was captivated by the bright colourful music although it was some time before I fully appreciated Gilbert's lyrics. I had no idea then that this *genre*, and particularly Sullivan's music, would play such a large part in my musical career.

In the early 1950s, people were still emigrating by sea to the United States and Canada, and even to Australia (among them Mappy and Aunt Mina's elder daughter Muriel and her family, including her daughter Wilma whom I had met at my cousin June's wedding). The liners coming into the Clyde, anchoring at the 'Tail of the Bank', just off Greenock, would be tendered from Princes Pier by the steamers of the CSPC (Caledonian Steam Packet Company). The Cunard liners sailed to the United States, and the Canadian Pacific liners sailed to Canada. A cousin of my mother was emigrating to Canada, and my mother had written to the Canadian Pacific Railway Company to ask if she could come on board to say a final farewell. She then received a permit that enabled her to board the liner, the *Empress of Scotland*, the tender leaving Princes Pier at 07.30 hours. This was on August 13, 1953, around the time that I was starting in Primary 6. Much as I would have liked to do so, I didn't accompany my mother on this occasion, but sometime in the early to mid-1950s I *was* on a large ship anchored at the 'Tail of the Bank': this was no less than an American battleship, the USS *Wisconsin*, which was paying a good-will visit to the Clyde. My friend Allan McEwan's father was a council official, and he had a couple of tickets for a reception on board the ship, but he kindly let the two of us go. At Princes [sic] Pier, as we were boarding the launch for the *Wisconsin*, two other people managed to join us on the strength of these two tickets, one of whom was another Greenock Academy pupil, Ian Jackson. It was certainly a great thrill being on board this massive ship: the foredeck, rising up to the bow, seemed to go on forever. But I don't recall much of the actual reception.

My final two Primary classes were in the older original building, and there, for Primary 6, I had Mrs Brown (married ladies were quite rare in the school at that time). The other Primary 6 teacher was, confusingly, *Miss* Brown (whose room was in the main Primary building), and she was definitely one of the school's characters. Her Christian name was Anne, and she was known as Queen Anne. I used to hear stories of her, and I often wished that she had been my teacher. But *Mrs* Brown was nevertheless perfectly capable and pleasant. Her room was in the north-west corner of the top floor, and, like Miss Macdonald's room, it had to be entered through another room. That was Mr McIntosh's room (if married ladies were few and far between in our Primary classes, male teachers were as rare as hen's teeth). Mrs Brown had a way of dismissing the class by calling out the row numbers –"one, two" and so on. She also used to have little quizzes near the end of the period. During one of these, she asked a question to which the answer was London's Whitehall. No-one seemed to know the answer. At that point the bell rang, and so she said "Quick now, anybody?" As there was still no answer she provided it herself, and she followed it immediately with the familiar dismissal. But as there was a sluggish response she repeated the dismissal so that it all came out as "It's Whitehall. One, two…one, two" which I recognised as being the telephone number of Scotland Yard. This amused me greatly. Strange the things that stick in the mind.

During my first term in Primary 6, we paid another visit to Edinburgh, and while we were there we went to Blackness Castle, just west of South Queensferry, and Holyrood Palace. Yet another guide book was purchased at Holyrood and inscribed as follows: "A glorious day of sunshine at Edinburgh – with the sincerest wishes of Mappy/After a fine run via Blackness Castle. 12/IX/53". All of these guide books are still treasured possessions.

I had my next great adventure at the Easter break in 1954. This was a trip to London. My Aunt Alice and Uncle Barney's eldest child, my cousin Winifred, was married by this time and living in a flat in central London, and my mother and I went down there for a holiday. Winifred's sister, Alison, ran a travel agency in Laird Street in Greenock, and she arranged the trip for us: we went down, overnight, by bus. We had to go to Glasgow to get this bus which left at about 6.00 pm (1800 hours, although we didn't use the continental clock then) from the now demolished St Enoch Station. There were stops along the way, but with no motorways it was a fairly tedious journey, and we didn't get into London until noon the following day. I must have fallen asleep during the night, but in the morning, as we got closer to London, I became aware of scenery that was distinctly different to anything I had hitherto seen in Scotland – much less hilly, and very much greener and more pastoral. Winifred and her husband, Peter, lived in Gerrard Street, near Shaftesbury Avenue, right in the middle of London's Chinatown. They had a penthouse flat at the top of a jeweller's premises. It would probably be worth a fortune today although I think they were only renting it. One of the big hits of that year was *The Little Shoemaker*, sung by Petula Clark, and we heard it constantly on the radio (or wireless, as we would have said) during our stay.

I was eager to see as much as I could, and we managed to get into Westminster Abbey, Madame Tussaud's, (now, like the famous Bettys [sic] tearoom in Harrogate, spelled without the apostrophe), the famous roof gardens at Derry and Tom's, and the Tower of London. We used the Underground at times, but we were also given the number of a bus that would take us to the Tower: that way we would see more of the city. We got the appropriate bus, but even before the conductor came round for the fares I had an idea that we were going in the wrong direction – and so it proved, and we had to get off and start again. We also paid a visit to the famous toyshop Hamleys (supposedly the oldest in the world, and now also spelled without an apostrophe). As I was still collecting Dinky Toys, I persuaded my mother to buy me one – a Foden lorry with chains: it came under the category of Dinky Supertoys and was more expensive, costing the princely sum of 8/9.

In the summer of 1954, I went to Aberdeen with both my parents (a rare 'family' holiday) as my father wanted to visit old haunts. He also wanted to see my Uncle Walter and Aunt Edna as we seldom saw them. Having survived the First World War, Uncle Walter now suffered from 'trench foot', as did so many who likewise survived that conflict apparently unharmed. Among the 'old haunts' was the Duthie Park where my father said he had smoked his first cigarette. He told me that after inhaling he thought the bandstand had turned upside down. My parents bought me a book in Aberdeen – Henry Gilbert's re-telling of the Robin Hood legend in the once-famous Nelson's Classics series. Following Uncle John's example, my father inscribed the book "To David/From Mum and Dad/9th August 1954/frae 'Aiberdeen [sic] Awa'" – a phrase associated with 'the granite city'.

Of the two Primary 7 teachers, I now had Mr McIntosh – a tall man who was, to me at least, quite intimidating. (The other Primary 7 teacher was Miss Kirkwood. Her room was on the ground floor near the main entrance, next to an area with rows of coat pegs that served as a cloakroom.) Again, my memories of that year are few and far between, one of them being of Mrs Brown's Primary 6 class tramping through ours, just as we had done ourselves the year before. I now realised how disrupting this was. It was in this class that we were 'tried out' with Latin as this was going to be a subject in the Secondary department. I don't count linguistic ability among my strongpoints, and I didn't do too well with it.

Another memory, specifically of Mr McIntosh himself, is of winter with snow on the ground. We were outside during the morning break, and we were throwing snowballs at each other. Unfortunately, my aim was somewhat erratic, and one of my missiles just missed Mr McIntosh. His towering presence then bore down on me, and he gave me quite a dressing down. But I managed to escape 'getting the belt' (i.e. the strap, or tawse) which at that time was the common punishment, certainly for boys, for any such misdemeanour. Girls were seldom, if ever, belted.

On a more positive note, it was Mr McIntosh who first noticed that I had difficulty in seeing properly, and so it was in Primary 7 that I had eye tests and began to wear spectacles. The first of these had the dreaded wire legs that hooked round your ears: they could become very uncomfortable if the wire started to unravel. I have also become increasingly hard of hearing over the years, and I think this too may have started when I was in Primary although it wasn't so obvious at the time.

It was also during Primary 7 that I had what must have been my first appearance in print when I wrote a short piece (or maybe had it written for me) for our school magazine: this appeared in vol. XLIII, December 1954 (price 1/6 – or seven and a half new pence). In it, I described an incident that had happened a couple of years before on a visit to nearby Largs with my mother. On returning to the shore, after a trip in one of the small boats that used to take people round the bay, I stepped on to the jetty, turned round, somehow lost my footing and fell back into the water. Luckily, it wasn't very deep, but of course I was completely soaked. A lady who was there, and who lived nearby, took pity on me and offered to take me home, dry me out and provide me with a change of clothing before we got the bus back to Greenock. My mother had to return to Largs shortly afterwards to retrieve my dried out clothes and return the borrowed ones.

While still in the Primary department, I joined the Cubs as a preliminary to joining the Scouts although I can't remember just how old I was at the time. The troop that I joined was the 5th Renfrewshire which met in the hall of the church that was then called the West Kirk, in Nelson Street, where Greenock Academy had its end-of-term services. But the hall was quite separate from the church and was situated at the end of Ardgowan Street (the Ardgowan Hospice now occupies the site). This was even better than getting to the Watt Library as I could literally get from our house to the hall without leaving the pavement. Despite those relatively traffic-free days, this was still something of a bonus, and it was doubtless a relief to my parents as accidents could still happen although these were sometimes the result of reckless behaviour. There was, indeed, just such an accident involving a boy in our group who had foolishly started to swing from the tailboard of a moving lorry (a not uncommon act of bravado for boys in those days) with, sadly, fatal consequences. The 'Akela' in charge of us was Moira MacElwee whose father, James, was the Scoutmaster of the troop that I joined when I was older. We called him Skipper.

A particular memory of my Cub days was the exhortation to 'dyb, dyb, dyb' ('do your best') to which we dutifully replied with 'we'll dob, dob, dob' ('do our best'), but I remember more of the Scouts than the Cubs. On early Cub memory, however, is of a fancy dress party to which I went as a crusader, dressed in an old sheet on to which my mother had sewn a couple of large red crosses. I also needed a sword to complete this costume, and I might have fashioned one from two lengths of wood, but with my love of swords I was bold enough to go to the McLean Museum (round the corner from the Watt Library) and persuade the curator, Mr MacPhail (whom I knew quite well), to lend me a real one. Being in possession of such a weapon today would almost certainly involve the arrest of the curator, and probably my parents too. But the crusader costume won 1st prize.

Another memory of the Cubs was a party to which we were invited to bring 'a friend'. I asked my classmate Dorothy Somerville (my first love), and I had to go to her house – in a tenement at the corner of Kelly Street and Finnart Street, more or less across the road from the Territorial Army Drill Hall – to collect her. Her father, who opened the door, asked me if my intentions were honourable, the significance of which, at that age, was completely lost on me. I don't recall how, if at all, I replied to this, but I must have remembered what he said and must have told my mother, who then took great delight in repeating it to all and sundry – to my everlasting embarrassment. The Cub pack was part of my time in Primary, but I joined the Scout troop on October 15, 1955, shortly after entering the Secondary department.

The year 1955 saw the centenary of the school, and, along with several events to mark this milestone, a hard-backed centenary booklet was produced. The only event that occurred during my time in Primary was a Centenary Concert in the Town Hall in June, most of the others taking place between October and November. These were a Centenary Dinner, again in the Town Hall, an 'At Home' in the school, a Public Thanksgiving Service in the West Kirk in Nelson Street, and a Centenary Ball, also held in the Town Hall. Of these, I can only remember the concert, but a further 'provisional' event, listed in the booklet, was to be a production of Shakespeare's *A Midsummer Night's Dream* given by school pupils in the Arts Guild Theatre in December. I remember attending this production, but it was held in the Lady Alice School in Inverkip Road, just opposite my Aunt Alice and Uncle Barney's house in Dunlop Street. Presumably the Arts Guild was not available at the time.

2. Secondary – 1955-1961

I entered Secondary IL at the end of summer 1955 (Secondary years were given in Roman numerals). Here, as in most schools, we had different teachers for every subject. For the first three years, these subjects were English, maths (geometry and algebra), science (physics and chemistry), Latin, French, history, geography, art, physical education (PE) and music, the latter just class singing. Again, as in the Primary department, the teachers all seemed pretty ancient to us, but this time there was a roughly equal mixture of men and women; even more than in the Primary they all seemed to have nicknames, some of them obvious, others much less so. French teacher Herbert Watson, who was quite dapper, was known as Tuppenny; English teacher Ian Macdonald, who was tall, was known as Big Mick. Hugh McFarlane (another French teacher) was Biscuit as there was once a biscuit firm in Scotland called Macfarlane Lang, art teacher John Brown was Face, and science teacher Allan Macphail, who had an artificial leg, was inevitably called Hoppy (children can be cruel). Maths teacher Allan Becket was known as Bucket. But perhaps the cleverest nickname was reserved for Latin teacher J.H. Cameron Love. He was quite a small man, or 'wee' in Scots, and his nickname was Amamus, which is the Latin for 'we love'. I wonder how many children would (or could) come up with such a nickname today.

Harold McNeill, who taught chemistry, had at one time been known as Soapy, but he later acquired the nickname Pot, perhaps for one very obvious reason. He had a ponderous way of speaking, constantly muttering 'mm-hm, mm-hm' and referring to everyone in the third person. "What's he doing there?" was an oft-heard bellow to anyone not paying attention. Pot's classroom was at the head of a flight of stairs, and there was invariably much noise as pupils waited on the stairs to go in. He would then come out of his room and shout "What are they doing there? If they can't behave themselves they'll be sent to German Reserves for a culture course – with a capital K!" It was, of course, not too long after the end of the Second World War (during which he had been a GIO – Gas Identification Officer), but it was still a somewhat bizarre outburst.

The ladies also had nicknames. May Johnston, who taught history, was known as Sally, and both Isabel Lyle (English) and Sarah Hughes (maths) were called Biddy. Mrs Cameron (maths) was Ma Cameron; Margaret Landles (art) was Peg. Christina MacGregor (maths) was Daisy (there was an art teacher, Miss Russell, whose Christian name *was* Daisy) and Catherine Stoddart (science) was known as Salome. Her room was in the first addition to the original building, and the old blackboard there was fixed to the wall. When she wrote on it, she would start at the left side, stretching up as high as she could reach. But she couldn't sustain this, and so it started to come down as it went along; this became known as the Ann Street writing after a very steep street in Greenock. We watched her efforts with great amusement and muffled giggling. It's a wonder anyone ever learned anything.

Physical education wasn't one of my favourite subjects as exercise equated in my mind with sport for which I had little aptitude, particularly as I lacked the competitive spirit. With poor eyesight, I was no use to any side, either in cricket or rugby, but neither of my parents took any active interest in sport, and so there wasn't much incentive at home to do well in this area: my parents were more interested in the arts. My father did the football pools every week, but his choice of draws was purely arbitrary. I never heard him comment on any side – not even on Morton, Greenock's own team. Later, I became the scorer for one of the school cricket teams, but that was my closest involvement with sport. However, in my last years at school I often joined classmates on visits to Edinburgh to see the rugby international matches at the old Murrayfield stadium.

There was also a single period of religious education (RE), this class being taken by various teachers: I believe it was taught on a voluntary basis. Depending on who took the class, it could be very boring or quite entertaining. One of the teachers, a lady who was not a permanent member of the staff, took this class in Daisy Russell's art room. Here, there were individual desks with stools, two rows of each on three sides of a square, with the blackboard on the fourth side. Jotters were handed out each week, and we were supposed to write down in them what was being written on the board: these jotters were handed in again afterwards. But although we may have looked as if we were assiduously writing things down we would 'write' with pens whose tops were still on so that nothing actually appeared on the page. Presumably the jotters were never checked when gathered in as I don't recall any recrimination.

On one occasion, someone thought of a prank which amused us all greatly, but which is difficult to describe without a diagram. At a given signal from the organiser of this ploy, when the teacher was writing on the board, each pupil on the front row directly behind her (and out of her vision) moved one place to the right with the person on the extreme right moving to the back row. At the same time, those on the back row moved to the left with the person at the extreme left moving up to the front row; so you had a set of people moving round in a circle (this had to be done quietly!) After a while, one of the boys involved in this said something loudly, and the teacher turned to where she last saw him only to find that, inexplicably, he was now in quite a different place. We were all in fits of laughter. I don't think we learned very much about religion in that class.

At Christmas 1955, I received a present from Uncle John. This was a book called *In the Wake of da Gama* by Genesta Hamilton. It was, in fact, a book from his own library, and it came with an explanatory letter. He had recently bought it, had read it, and had decided that he would buy a copy for me. But he found that it was now out of print. The letter was to tell me this, but it was also to say that he had found it exceptionally interesting, had been to many of the places mentioned, and hoped that one day I too might see them. Sadly, despite having travelled widely in some parts of the world, I have yet to see most of the places mentioned, particularly those on the east coast of Africa.

They say that school days are the happiest days of your life, and that could well be true as you don't have the responsibilities of adulthood, but most of my happiness came from activities outside the school curriculum as I didn't shine at many subjects: history was my favourite followed by English. We studied Shakespeare, of course, but also Scottish authors such as Scott and Stevenson, who were perhaps studied less in England. Hector Munro, who taught geography, would occasionally get films, and this would effectively take the place of any teaching. If you arrived at Hector's room (upstairs in the Primary building) and saw that the large green curtains had been drawn you knew that you were in for a treat. Some of these films were from the American documentary series *The March of Time*. I remember once, in one of Hector's classes, looking at a map of America and thinking how odd some of the far west states looked – how could they be more or less square? It didn't seem natural to anyone from Europe. It was many years before I learned how these boundary lines had come about.

Films did indeed constitute one of the few areas of school life that I positively relished as we had a film club that met on a Saturday night in the school hall. The club was run by several of the teachers – 'Hoppy' Macphail, 'Biscuit' McFarlane and Hector Munro – and it was very popular, but it could be very noisy, particularly before everyone had settled down. The film would be often be stopped after a short while, and we were told to be quiet before it continued. Many a childhood romance blossomed during these evenings, including another one of my own. Among the films we saw were *High Society*, *The Ladykillers*, *Reach for the Sky*, *Henry V*, *High Noon* and *The Court Jester*.

Sometime during my later Primary days, I acquired my first bicycle. It had belonged to the son of a local doctor, and it was advertised for sale in the *Greenock Telegraph*. It took me a little while to get the hang of cycling. At first, my father would take me out, holding on to the saddle to steady the bike as I got used to it. I clearly remember the day when, unbeknown to me, he took his hand off the saddle as we went along. "Are you still there?" I shouted, as the bike seemed to wobble slightly. "Yes", he replied, and on we went. But of course it eventually dawned on me that he was now some way behind, and I had finally mastered the art. My father seemed to have acquired a bike himself around this time as we sometimes went out together. One day, we cycled along the old road from Port Glasgow to Langbank and Houston, but we got soaked when the rain came on unexpectedly: living in Greenock we should have been better prepared.

There was no room for two bicycles in our little flat (barely room for one), and we kept them in a large cellar in one of the Ardgowan Street tenements nearer Nelson Street. This was by courtesy of a Mr McFarlane whose daughter Katrina, older than me, was also at Greenock Academy. (My father may just have borrowed Mr McFarlane's bicycle to keep me company: not long afterwards, he gave up cycling.) At the end of my first year in Secondary, I gained a Cycling Proficiency Certificate, dated 19.6.56, which was awarded jointly by The Royal Society for the Prevention of Accidents, The Cyclists' Touring Club and The National Cyclists' Union. To get the certificate, I had to satisfy these organisations by demonstrating an 'ability to ride and control a bicycle on the roads safely and proficiently'. We also got a badge with the certificate, but mine has not survived.

Then I acquired a new bike – a splendid green Raleigh with butterfly handlebars and a four-speed gear: several of my school-friends had similar bikes (I still have mine). I managed to keep this one in our small flat. It cost £26, which doesn't sound much today but which was quite a tidy sum in the mid-1950s, and it was acquired from the well-known cycle shop of John S. Phillips at the foot of Kilblain Street where the bus station is now situated. The shop occupied the ground floor of a tenement (next to it was another well-known Greenock firm, Clark and Selkirk – Plumbers), but it had acquired a little single storey showroom that jutted out on its own. I think the area was known, unofficially, as 'Phillips' Corner'. John S. Phillips also ran a Motoring School. Just opposite Phillips' shop was a corner shop that would happily sell customers just a couple of eggs and a rasher of bacon, and would even open a packet of cigarettes to sell you just three or four.

Cycling around the West End of Greenock was safe and easy in those days as there was very little road traffic. One particular pleasure was to cycle to the foot of Campbell Street and then directly on to Princes Pier with its wonderful Italianate railway station, at one time the terminus of the Glasgow & South Western Railway. Sadly, this magnificent building was later demolished.

The Crawfords, with whom we had had holidays at Arrochar, were now working on a farm at Stair in Ayrshire, and they invited me to go there for a holiday. I persuaded my parents to let me cycle down on my new bike, telling them that I would be fine. My father had a set of Bartholomew's road maps of Scotland – half inch to the mile – and I studied the relevant ones ('Firth of Clyde' and 'Ayrshire') and was confident that I knew exactly how to get there. This was in 1957 when I was still just thirteen, and although the roads were much quieter than they are now it was still quite a dangerous thing to attempt, a Cycling Proficiency Certificate notwithstanding. Parents who allowed a child of that age to set off alone on a forty-mile journey today would almost certainly feel the full force of the law. But I duly set off on July 1, and arrived at Stair without any mishap. We didn't yet have a phone, and so all I could do was to send a postcard on July 2 to say that I had arrived safely. My parents never said how they felt about my potentially dangerous journey, but they must have been quite anxious, and would have breathed sighs of relief when the postcard arrived. Two weeks later, on July 15, I sent a letter to say that I would be coming home on either July 28 or 29.

The farm's owners were Mr and Mrs John Lockhart, members of a well-known Ayrshire family. John Lockhart was a brother of Howard M. Lockhart, of BBC Scotland, whose voice was familiar from *Children's Hour* programmes. The Crawfords lived in a lovely little house called Burnbank Cottage, and the holiday there was bliss. I was often up at the farm getting involved in various things, including watching the cows being milked by hand. The milk was warm, but it was cooled by being poured over a metal frame. I was also allowed to sit on one of the huge mudguards of the old Ferguson tractor when it was out in the fields – something you couldn't do now with today's enormous tractors, even if you were allowed to do so. I enjoyed being on the farm, but I also explored further afield. Nearby was the village of Tarbolton with its little house where Robert Burns co-founded the Tarbolton Bachelors' Club. I spent a full month at Stair, leaving on July 29.

My Scout troop (5th Renfrewshire, with Skipper James (Jimmy) MacElwee in charge) met, as did the Cubs, in the hall of the West Kirk. Jimmy had a party piece that we always asked him to perform if there was a quiet moment. He would take a chair, turn it upside down and balance it on his chin – to rapturous applause. I never saw it fall. Another regular ingredient of those Friday evenings was marching; this often involved cross-marching, a difficult manoeuvre that required your full attention if disaster was to be avoided. There was also Bob-a-Job week when we offered to perform some task for a 'bob' (a shilling – now 5p). One such task I remember was removing what seemed a vast number of bottles and jam-jars from the home of Herbert Henderson of the Watt Library: Herbert's house was, in fact, in the western wing of the library.

The Cub uniform included a school-style cap, but our Scout uniform included the old Baden-Powell hat as worn by the Canadian Mounted Police (many, if not most, of the Scout troops now wore a more modern beret). You were supposed to iron the hat's brim every week to keep it stiff and looking smart. Our troop also had a pipe band, and it invariably led the procession on Armistice Day in November, the rest of us trailing along behind. If it rained, which it often did at that time of the year, the hat would get wet, the brim would begin to droop (particularly if you had been a bit remiss with the ironing), and water would run down your face and the back of your neck: not at all comfortable. But, concurrently with becoming a Scout, another new interest had begun.

A notice appeared in school one day about something called a Club Night to be held in the gym: this was being organised by the Scottish Schoolboys' Club (SSC) that had been enjoying a recent and successful revival in the school. I didn't know anything about the SSC, but the evening sounded interesting, and so I went along. And it was indeed very enjoyable, with plenty of games including one called Pirates which involved climbing on the wall bars and staying on the equipment – mats, the ropes, a vaulting horse, and so on – while evading a pursuer: if you touched the floor while being chased you were 'out'. It was such good fun that I decided to find out what else the Club did. I then discovered that they held Sunday Meetings in a house in the West End – the home of an older man, Donald McL. R. Steel. I have already said that I am not religious, and I discovered that there was a Christian background to the Club. Founded by Stanley Nairne

OBE in 1912, its aim was "to help its members discover the full meaning of the Christian faith for themselves and the world". At first this set alarm bells ringing, but I went along to the house and discovered that although the meetings involved a hymn, a prayer and discussions about various topics, the Club didn't exactly force religion down your throat. There were boys there from every year including many from the rugby and cricket teams, and they were the boys that you tended to look up to, even if, like me, you were not good at sport. The older ones had already been to Easter and summer camps which they had obviously enjoyed and which sounded good fun. And so I joined the SSC. The Greenock branch also included some boys from Greenock High School, among them Campbell Snoddy, Donald Crawford and Donald Harrison, but their numbers in SSC were never as great as those from Greenock Academy.

My first camp was at Easter 1956, and it was held at Broomlee residential camp at West Linton near Edinburgh, a hutted camp with dormitories and a dining hall: it wasn't exactly 'camping' as I came to know it, but it was still very enjoyable. By now, I knew that as well as the Greenock branch, the SSC had branches in Glasgow and Edinburgh, and there was also a Counties branch with boys from Troon and Dundee, but I was surprised to see boys from Newcastle upon Tyne. What were they doing in a club for Scottish schoolboys? The answer was that this branch had been started by Charlie Hay, an Anglican vicar at Heddon-on-the-Wall just outside Newcastle, who had had some contact with SSC, and thought that boys that he knew would fit in very well with what was on offer. Most of them came from Dame Allan's School in Newcastle where I think Charlie was the school chaplain. And so they, with their (to us) strange accents, became a regular and much appreciated presence at the camps. Another feature of these camps was an evening sing-song during which the boys from Newcastle would often give a rendition of *The Blaydon Races*. One of the older boys, Ian Matthew, became a good friend whom I saw later from time to time when I lived in England.

Then, in the summer of 1956, came my first summer camp at Bruar, near Blair Atholl, in Perthshire. The camp was a tented one on a small neck of land between the rivers Garry and Bruar, just across the road from what is now the up-market House of Bruar shopping centre. There were some inconveniences, such as the somewhat primitive latrine arrangements, but to be in the country, so far away from home, was wonderful. You would often hear a steam train puffing its way up the valley (no diesel or electric trains in those days), and indeed that is how we arrived at the camp – by train from Perth, alighting at the nearby station of Struan which has long since closed. It was while we were waiting on the platform at Perth for our train that I acquired the first book that I bought with my own money, and which I still have. This was the very first Agatha Christie – *The Mysterious Affair at Styles* – in a Pan paperback (all of 2/6 or ten and a half new pence) whose cover carries an artist's impression of Hercule Poirot that is not unlike the actor Sir David Suchet who later became synonymous with the role in the television adaptations. This was the start of a life-long addiction to Agatha Christie, and to books generally. Soon after this, I was regularly visiting a second-hand bookshop in the East End of Greenock where I began to acquire what is now an extensive library, starting with many of the classics: Scott, Dickens, Dumas and others in the famous Collins' Classics or Nelson's Classics series; also a neat six-volume edition of the complete works of Shakespeare. The collecting mania continues to this day.

We shared the SSC camps with boys from all over the country (but mainly from Glasgow and Edinburgh), and many life-long friendships were made – and not just with boys of your own age: one of my lasting Greenock friendships has been with Stewart McMillan, who was several years above me at school. I met him initially through SSC, but we also had a mutual interest in theatre. The singer Peter Morrison, also from Greenock, is another friend that I met through SSC. One of the older campers, called officers, would be the Camp Chief. The first one that I knew was Norman Hutchison, who lived to the ripe old age of 102. Norman was the Club's Organiser. His successor, David Sinclair (from Edinburgh's Royal High School), became another good friend. Matt Neilson, also from Greenock, turned up at my first Bruar; he too became a Camp Chief. I learned later that Matt was a cousin of Marelan Neilson who had taught us *Orderly Day* just a few years previously.

Sport played a big part in many of these boys' lives. At that time, rugby was still an amateur game, and it was often said at the camps that most international teams would contain at least one SSC boy. One player whom I knew well, Ian S.G. Smith (from Heriot's school in Edinburgh) was capped eight times for Scotland. He wrote a book about his experiences – *A Full Back Slower Than Your Average Prop* – which he kindly autographed for me at its launch in 2019: 'To David/The Piano Man'.

I went to Bruar for most, if not all, of my Secondary summers from 1956. There were two camps of a week each (you could go to either one or to both), but there was also an advance guard to set up the camp, and a rear-guard to take it all down again. I was often at all of these – an almost three-week holiday. One year, when I was with the advance guard, the large marquee that served as a dining room and venue for the evening sing–songs was being erected. Once it was up, an old upright piano was brought in, and as I was one of the regular pianists at these sing-songs I sat down at it to try it out. Suddenly, the marquee collapsed round about me. Luckily, none of the poles hit me or the piano, but as the other helpers could still hear the piano tinkling as the marquee fell – and then silence – there was a frantic rush to make sure that I was all right. Another interesting experience.

Any initial worries I had about my lack of serious religious feelings were soon dispelled by the fellowship of these camps and the other activities we indulged in during the school year; I later found that other boys, and even some senior officers, also felt as I did. But there were others for whom religion did mean something, and several of the older Greenock Academy boys entered the ministry of the Church of Scotland – John Cook, John Nicol, Malcolm Richardson and Leith Fisher. Another older Greenock officer who entered the ministry was Murdoch McPherson, who was also a well-known sports commentator. Murdoch died young following an accident at his home.

The Greenock branch had a reputation for putting on shows for which we also wrote songs, sketches and even spoof versions of musicals such as *Oklahoma!* In our version, this became *Fort Matilda!* (a railway station in Greenock): with similar scansion this enabled us to write a parody of the original title song – "Fo – – – rt Matilda, it's the best halt reached by any train, Fort Matilda!" Another spoof musical was *Our Dark Gent* – a parody of *My Fair Lady* that had recently come out in 1956. We used to spend hours together writing these shows, and howling with laughter at our inspired efforts, but when we presented the shows in Greenock's Arts Guild Theatre we were lucky if we got a mild titter at what we thought had been wildly funny and original lines. But the fun had been in the writing.

In 1957, I went to my second SSC Easter camp, but this was not at Broomlee. The year 1956 had seen the Hungarian uprising, and Broomlee was now housing refugees; so we went to another site at Dalguise in Perthshire. This was a tented camp in the grounds of Dalguise House, but it did have a permanent dining hall. (There was one Easter when we camped at Dalguise in snow.) In August, I was back at Bruar for two weeks: that was just after my month's holiday at Stair. One feature of the Bruar camps was an excursion to either Ben-y-Vrackie, near Pitlochry, or Schiehallion in Perthshire (more properly hill walks rather than dangerous mountain climbs), and on the Wednesday of the first week we climbed

Schiehallion: incredibly, I was first at the top. Where has that energy gone?

The founder of SSC, Stanley Nairne, now in his seventies, would often make an appearance at the camps, and during the sing-songs he would sometimes take part in the sketches, one of these being 'Hitler never forgets!' The rudimentary curtain would open showing Stanley, as Hitler, sitting at a table (covered by a blanket) sentencing a succession of underlings for forgetting to do something, and ending each time with "Hitler never forgets!" He would then leave the table, at which point it could be seen that he had forgotten to put on his own trousers. Another sketch was his version of the Dead March from Handel's *Saul* where he stood at the lower end of the piano with his back to it while the pianist (sometimes me) played the piece. At the appropriate moments, when there are loud bass chords, he would sit down on the keyboard to gales of laughter. These sketches sound rather silly, but they showed a lighter side to our revered and often very serious leader.

The Greenock and district Scout troops also had a campsite, Everton, at Inverkip. This was much nearer home, and I did go there from time to time, but these were week-end camps. Extra-curricular activities such as Scouts and SSC were the happiest times of my schooldays, but soon I was involved in a school activity that was to have the most far-reaching effect on my life.

Greenock Academy's music teacher, Dr Percy Elton, retired in the early 1950s, and at first we had a temporary replacement in a young man, Cameron Johnston. But then we acquired a permanent replacement in Donald B. Miller (already in his early sixties), who soon left his mark on the school.

He too was given a nickname – Minty – after the popular Millar's mints (the name had a slightly different spelling, but that didn't matter). He lived in Rothesay on the island of Bute, and he travelled up to Greenock every day – a journey that involved an early steamer to Wemyss Bay on the mainland and then a bus to Greenock – and back again in the evening: a long day, and he too, like Hoppy Macphail, had an artificial leg. But he was seldom, if ever, unable to make this daily journey. (I remember sitting a school exam at which, at first, either Minty or Hoppy was invigilating, and during which the one was relieved by the other. While it may seem unkind to say so, the sight and sound of their progress as they hirpled across the room – one coming in, the other going out – was undeniably amusing if also somewhat distracting!)

Unlike Percy Elton, whose musical interests seemed to be choirs and playing the organ (he also composed an attractive setting of *The Lord's Prayer* that we sang at school assemblies), Donald Miller's background was in musical theatre – opera, and operetta – and he soon decided that it was about time that the school put on a Gilbert and Sullivan opera. He chose *HMS Pinafore*, and this was to be presented at Greenock's Arts Guild Theatre at the end of my third year in Secondary. When I first heard about it, I was keen to take part, but when rehearsals started in 1957 my voice had not yet broken, and Minty decided that I couldn't appear in the show. But my piano playing was now good enough for me to be able to play for some of the rehearsals, often after school, which I much enjoyed and which also helped to improve my technique. During the run of the opera (June 18-21, 1958) I also acted as call-boy. Among the performers were Peter Morrison and Ian McCrorie, each of whom would later make his mark on music in Scotland. The orchestra consisted of just twelve players – four violins and a cello, two flutes and a clarinet, one trumpet, one trombone, a timpanist and our own geography teacher Hector Munro 'filling in' at the piano for any missing material. Hector was also the official rehearsal pianist throughout the year.

As I got to know *HMS Pinafore,* I realised that one of its principal characters, Sir Joseph Porter, had the same name as my Uncle Barney whose full name was Barnard Henry Joseph Porter. I also came to realise that my father shared a birthday with Arthur Sullivan (May 13), and he lived to be the same age as W.S. Gilbert – seventy-four. Strange coincidences indeed, but, as I found out later, by no means the only ones connecting me with G&S: were these early ones pointers to what was to come? That never crossed my mind at the time, but I loved *HMS Pinafore*, and I was able to borrow vocal scores of some of the other G&S operas from Greenock Public Library.

I was still having piano lessons with Mrs Scrymgeour, sitting the Associated Board examinations each year and taking part in the annual Renfrewshire Musical Festival. I don't like performing solo in public, preferring to accompany singers or play for shows, and I was always nervous when I was on a platform alone. But I still managed to do quite well at the Festival, and often came second in the solo classes although I never managed to get top marks. Mrs Scrymgeour would usually also enter two of her pupils for the piano duet classes, and in January 1958, playing with John Bell (a Greenock High School pupil who later became a very fine organist), we did take first place. The adjudicators on that occasion were Sydney Northcote from South Croydon and Herrick Bunney, the organist of St Giles' Cathedral in Edinburgh.

In April 1958, after an SSC Easter camp at Dalguise, I went to Edinburgh to stay with Uncle John. While I was there, I was taken to the King's Theatre to see an amateur production of Sigmund Romberg's famous operetta *The New Moon*. When I left, he gave me another book from his library – *The Life and Adventures of Valentine Vox the Ventriloquist* by Henry Cockton, a Victorian novelist I hadn't heard of. Cockton was obviously fond of alliteration, and this had clearly appealed to Uncle John, who, as he had done with the guide books, wrote an inscription inside – "To the new Valentine Vox of the vociferous villainy of the vulgar Mackies – but never vainglorious or vilifying – only laughter-provoking. To all that venture on the Via Dolorosa – To the last but not least of the Mackies – David – the little beggar – with very very [sic] good wishes – Uncle John – April 1958". (He may also have enjoyed the book as there is a character in it called Uncle John.) There is another character in *Valentine Vox* called Grimwood Goodman, and Cockton also wrote a novel called *Sylvester Sound the Somnambulist*. With my burgeoning interest in G&S, I began to realise that W.S. Gilbert too was very fond of alliteration. Vox lived from 1807-1853, and Gilbert must surely have known his novels. Perhaps much of his own alliterative writing, like the names of the officers in *Patience* (Colonel Calverley, Major Murgatroyd and the Duke of Dunstable), can be traced back to Henry Cockton.

Back in Greenock in May, I saw another famous show (more accurately a musical comedy) *The Arcadians*, music by Lionel Monckton and Howard Talbot, which was again an amateur production: it was given by Greenock Players in the Arts Guild Theatre. Most of the local musicians who took part would be performing in our *HMS Pinafore* the following month. Shortly after that, my mother took me to Glasgow to see a Saturday matinee of Lehar's famous operetta *The Merry Widow* at the King's Theatre. This time, it was a professional production by Sadler's Wells Opera whose Musical Director was Alexander Gibson, but as this was a matinee it is likely that the performance was conducted by one of the other conductors, Michael Moores or William Reid. Then in June came the school's performance of *HMS Pinafore*. In just three months I had seen four classics from the world of light opera, but I had no idea that my life would eventually encompass much of this repertoire, and that I too would one day conduct operetta in the King's Theatres in both Glasgow and Edinburgh.

At the end of Secondary III I had to choose which subjects I would take for the final two or three years. With my abiding interest in old buildings, I thought that I would like to become an architect, but it hadn't occurred to me that I wouldn't be designing old castles or country houses that I always found so fascinating. Nevertheless, still with this idea in mind, I opted to take art as a subject, thankfully dropping science. I also dropped geography in favour of history, and Latin in favour of French, but I continued with English and maths. I didn't take music as a subject although I now played for the SSC Sunday meetings and the shows that we put on regularly. But as well as playing for the shows, I sometimes performed onstage, particularly in a cross-talk act with another friend, Malcolm Cook, as 'Weelie and Jeem' (these names were contrived from 'Willie' and 'Jimmy', which is how men in Glasgow and Clydeside were often addressed if their real names were not known). Our act was a succession of corny jokes such as "Waiter, would you ask the orchestra to play *Clair de Lune*" – "I'm sorry sir, they're only a three-piece orchestra, and *Clair de Lune* isn't one of them", and "Waiter, there's a fly in my soup" – "Yes sir, the chef used to be a tailor".

Now in Secondary IV, I had fewer subjects, but I still struggled to cope with some of them, particularly French and, in maths, algebra. For some reason, I didn't find geometry so difficult, and I could even rattle off the theorem of Pythagoras – 'the square of the hypotenuse of a right-angled triangle is equal to the sum of the squares of the other two sides'. It was the drawing in geometry that appealed to me. From an early age, I was always drawing plans of imaginary castles and houses, and that was what had given me the idea of becoming an architect (I might have made a passable draughtsman). In art, I was good at the history of art and quite good at still life, but I could not draw figures – they really looked like beings from another planet; so I struggled with art too.

Just around the time that I started in Secondary IV, word reached Greenock that Herbert Henderson, former librarian of the Watt Library, had died while on holiday in Scarborough. He once gave me a copy of a poem *The Green Oak Tree* which I believe he wrote himself: although type-written he had signed it at the bottom. Unlike the better-known version of this supposed origin of Greenock's name (more likely to be a derivation from the Gaelic), Herbert's version also concerns the erecting of a fountain in Greenock's Cathcart Square to take the place of the oak tree that had been cut down. Unlike the 'green oak tree', the fountain 'still is there'.

For 1958's Christmas present, Uncle John gave me the combined *Scottish Psalter and Church Hymnary (revised)* of 1929 (words and music). Although successive volumes have discarded many of the excellent Victorian tunes for some of the hymns (including a number by Sullivan), I still use it occasionally when playing for church services.

January 1959 saw the bi-centenary of the birth of our great national poet Robert Burns (1759-1796), and the Corporation of Greenock hosted a Burns Supper for the town's senior and junior school pupils which was held in the Town Hall on Thursday January 15 with the then provost, David Gerrard, in the chair. We did have Burns Suppers at the Academy, held in the school dining room (one of the 1950 buildings facing Nelson Street), but these were just for our own staff and pupils. This was a much more elaborate affair, and it was very enjoyable. There was musical entertainment by a local singer, May Gilmour, and a group called The Cronies, with accompaniment by William (Bill) Hardie: Bill's daughter Jacqueline would soon be taking part in our school G&S productions, followed later by her brother Roger. One of the speakers, giving the reply to the toast of 'The Lasses', was our English teacher Miss Lyle. Shortly after this, Greenock Players presented a new play about Burns – *There was a Lad* – by Joe Corrie, again in the Arts Guild Theatre. At the end of the month came the 34th Musical Festival where I took part in the duet class with Dorothy Hendry, another of Mrs Scrymgeour's pupils, who was also in my class at school. This time we came second.

My voice had now broken, and Minty Miller let me sing in the chorus of the next opera *The Mikado*. Prior to this, in October 1958, a group of us went to the King's Theatre in Glasgow to see the D'Oyly Carte Opera Company perform this most popular of all the G&S operas. Many schools and amateur societies at that time regularly performed G&S: apart from being great fun, they are fairly easy to put on, particularly for young people, and much of today's repertoire had not yet been written.

Peter Morrison, who had played Sir Joseph Porter in *HMS Pinafore*, had now left school, but Ian McCrorie was still there (he played Pooh-Bah), and it was through his influence that I acquired another interest. Ian was a multi-talented individual, and even as a schoolboy he was an authority on the Clyde river steamers. I got to know him during the rehearsals for *The Mikado,* and he persuaded me that I should get a season ticket for the steamers in the summer: this gave you limitless travel on any of the ships. There were still quite a number of older steamers at that time as well as the more modern motor vessels and the first of the new car ferries. A week's season ticket cost 42/6 (two pounds, two shillings and sixpence) – 70/- for two weeks. One goal of steamer enthusiasts is to try to sail on as many ships as possible in one day, and Ian would work out ways of doing this. You catch such and such a steamer at, say, Gourock, get off at Dunoon and catch another steamer to, say, Rothesay, and so on: I still have two plans that he worked out, one of them involving seven vessels, the other, eight. Ian left school in 1959 and took a summer job as an assistant purser with the CSPC (Caledonian Steam Packet Company). This was a common summer vacation job for students, and I began to think that maybe one day I might get a similar job.

It was around this time that we moved from no. 12 Ardgowan Street to no. 7a Houston Street, the top half of a mid-nineteenth century villa; this time my parents bought the property, a step into the unknown for many people at that time. It didn't cost much even then, but my father still thought that it was a step too far and that he would never be able to keep up the payments. The house was much larger, and it had an attic. With just our furniture from Ardgowan Street, it seemed half empty, and my parents set about trying to find suitable items to fill it. Few things, if any, were purchased new (my parents couldn't afford them), and most of what we got came from salerooms: with plenty of large villas in Greenock there was never a shortage of suitable items. If the contents of a particularly large house were being disposed of, the sale would often take place in the house itself. My mother went to these house sales even before we moved to Houston Street, and she would sometimes take me with her. I remember going to one of the grandest houses in the town, *Balclutha*, before its eventual demolition to make way for the new Greenock Academy – itself now demolished. Another mansion, further down the coast at Wemyss Bay, was Castle Wemyss, the home of Lord Inverclyde. After his death in 1957 there was a sale of household effects *in situ* before this mansion too was demolished. My mother and I went down by bus to the sale; this time she acquired a set of hand-painted coffee cups that I still possess.

Our new house had a very large lounge in which our little upright piano looked like a matchbox placed against the wall. But it wasn't long before we acquired a much larger instrument. My mother was working in a ladies' dress shop in Largs, altering garments as required. She would chat to the customers while she was doing this, and she discovered that one lady and her husband ran a small preparatory school, Clyde College, in the town. They were retiring and moving to a smaller house, and they wanted to get rid of a number of items including a grand piano (they actually had two); as my mother expressed an interest, she was invited to have a look at them. I was also invited to come with her and choose which one I would like. Both pianos were in one very large room. One was a comparatively modern 'baby' grand and the other was a much larger, and seemingly much older, instrument – a Broadwood. I thought it was much the better of the two, and I assumed that they would want to take it with them, but they said that they would prefer to take the smaller one, and so we acquired the Broadwood with its lovely walnut case. It didn't look at all out of place in our large lounge. It cost my parents £20 (plus more for delivery) which, again, doesn't seem very much now. I discovered that the piano dated from 1881, and I still have it although it is showing its age: it is hard to keep it in tune as the tuning pins are now somewhat worn. It is 'straight strung' which accounts for its length of some seven feet (most modern grand pianos for domestic use are 'cross-strung' which helps to keep them somewhat shorter).

Greenock Arts Guild, where we presented our school productions of G&S, was founded just after the Second World War. For many years, its indefatigable Secretary was Annette Johnson. The first building in Campbell Street was later replaced by new premises on Greenock's waterfront, but I spent much time in the old building, sometimes 'out front' but often backstage or even onstage, during my school years. The Guild presented a wide range of performances throughout the year, both professional and amateur. Among the former were numerous chamber music concerts, but there was also local talent regularly on display. Greenock Players presented their annual productions, including pantomimes, and there was also George Square Players with whom I was more closely involved: this was mainly thanks to Stewart McMillan, who did much work on sound for the group, and another friend, Robert (Bob) Richardson, who was also an SSC officer.

Greenock Academy presented *The Mikado* at the Arts Guild Theatre from June 17-20, 1959, and after this came the summer holiday. I then had a very pleasant week on the steamers with my season ticket, and this was followed by another SSC camp at Bruar, with its games, sing-songs and hill walks. When I was younger, family holidays like the one in Aberdeen in 1954 were rare, and, apart from my month in Stair and one or two shorter periods away from home, I relied mainly on the SSC Easter and summer camps for holidays. At the end of summer 1959 I entered Secondary V.

Tickets for concerts and shows must have been relatively cheaper then as I seem to have been at many performances during my school days, not only in Greenock but also in Glasgow; that involved the additional expense of a train journey. The Scottish National Orchestra (SNO), forerunner of today's Royal Scottish National Orchestra (RSNO), came to Greenock regularly. Most of their concerts were given in the Town Hall. One of these was in September 1959, the conductor being the newly appointed Alexander Gibson, now back in his native Scotland. The soloist in the Schumann piano concerto was Phyllis Sellick. She was married to the pianist Cyril Smith, who had recently lost the use of his left arm. Having previously worked together as piano duettists, they eventually transcribed many pieces for three hands and continued to perform duets together.

Visits to Glasgow were not confined to 'serious' concerts, and a popular outing was to see one of the famous *Five Past Eight* revues at Glasgow's Alhambra Theatre. I saw one of these shows later in 1959 with Jimmy Logan, Jack Radcliffe and Eve Boswell. Sadly, the Alhambra was later demolished: it was greatly missed. Also in 1959 there was another school trip, this time to Glasgow's Citizens' Theatre to see Shakespeare's *Othello*; shortly after this I was in Glasgow again to see the famous Evelyn 'Boo' Laye and Stanley Baxter in *The Amorous Prawn*, a play that was soon to be filmed with Joan Greenwood and Ian Carmichael. In February 1960, Greenock had another visit from the SNO. Its then leader, Sam Bor, was the soloist in Mozart's violin concerto no. 4. We still didn't have television at home, but there was no shortage of quality live entertainment.

I was keen on cycling, and I often took my bike to school if the weather was favourable (as did many others: there was a quadrangle in the middle of the main complex where we parked our bikes) so that I could go off somewhere with my classmates immediately after school. At Easter 1960, as well as attending the SSC camp at Dalguise, I went bicycling with a number of my school friends on a youth hostelling trip that lasted several days and took us to Killin in Perthshire.

There were no motorways then, but the roads were busier than I remember on my lone journey to Stair three years earlier. But as there were several of us this time we felt that there was safety in numbers, and I don't recall any accidents. Youth hostelling was very popular at that time; you could join the Scottish Youth Hostelling Association for the princely sum of 2/- (two shillings) if you were under 16, or 5/- if you were aged 16-20.

It was now time to sit the dreaded 'Highers' and 'Lowers': it depended on your prowess which one you sat in any given subject. I didn't do particularly well, but I managed to get a Higher English, Higher history, Lower maths, Lower art and arithmetic: in those days arithmetic was a compulsory separate paper. My French was so bad that I wasn't even allowed to sit a Lower. But while we may not all have been multi-lingual scientific boffins, most of us left the Academy reasonably literate, numerate and, thanks to old Daddy Allan in Primary 3, with fairly legible handwriting. (When I got my first cheque book, the bank manager told me that I had to cultivate a distinctive signature that would be hard to copy – a far cry from today's 'signatures' that are often just indecipherable squiggles or can be generated electronically by someone else.)

But after the Highers and Lowers of 1960 came the next G&S opera; this time it was *The Pirates of Penzance*. As luminaries such as Ian McCrorie had now left the school, new principals had to be found, and I stepped into the role of Major-General Stanley (strangely, my father's middle name – yet another coincidence!) It took most of each academic year to familiarise ourselves with these roles. This was just as well: not only does this character have dialogue, but he also has to sing one of W.S. Gilbert's famous patter songs "I am the very model of a modern Major-General, I've information vegetable, animal, and mineral"; this did take some time to learn. It was, nevertheless, a very enjoyable experience to be on the stage when we came to the performances (June 15-18, 1960), again at Greenock's Arts Guild Theatre. I was getting more and more hooked on these operas, but I had not even considered the possibility that one day I might have a full-time career in helping to present them professionally. Just prior to the opera, on June 2, Malcolm Cook and I took part in a concert with several of our school friends to raise funds for Greenock Cricket Club. Once again, we did our 'Weelie and Jeem' act – more corny jokes.

Shortly after the opera, I was performing again, but in a somewhat different capacity. At that time, instrumental tuition in schools was in its infancy, but a Renfrewshire County Youth Orchestra had been formed by the County Music Organiser, F.W. (Freddie) Ladds, and letters had gone out inviting pupils to join. As there was yet no instrumental tuition at Greenock Academy I could only play the piano, but there were vacancies for percussionists: it was assumed that if you could read music you might be usefully employed in the 'kitchen department' (as the percussion section is often called): timpani and side drum require a somewhat more advanced technique. And so I applied, and I found myself, with several others, taking part in the orchestra's first performance in the George A. Clark Town Hall, Paisley on Wednesday June 22, 1960. It was another very enjoyable experience, and it gave me an insight into orchestral playing, particularly (in the percussion department) of having to count through endless silent bars ('tacet') in the hope that you would eventually come in at the right place with your single clash on the cymbals or 'ping' on the triangle. After the concert, we had a nice letter from Freddie Ladds, who said that the performance had been well-received. He ended the letter with "Have a good holiday!"

And I did have quite a good holiday that year. First of all, I went down to Hampshire to stay with my cousins. I went into Portsmouth and saw several of the steamers that operated on the Portsmouth-Ryde service including the ill-fated *Shanklin* that was later to sail on the Clyde as *Prince Ivanhoe* but was wrecked in Port Einon Bay in Wales in 1981. Then there was another SSC camp at Bruar, and after that I entered my last year at school – Secondary VI, 1960-1961.

I had realised by now that there would be more to a study of architecture than just drawing ground plans, and I had to think again about what I would do when I left school. Not having shone at many school subjects, this was at first a rather frightening thing to contemplate, but with another school opera on the way, and with music as one of my better subjects, I wondered if I could become a school music teacher myself. Perhaps I might finish up in a school where they also put on G&S, and I could get involved with that; like Minty Miller I might even be able to conduct the operas. To this end, I now took music as a subject, and I managed to get a Higher in a year. These exams were graded in eight ranges, upwards from 50%, and I was in range two that was 80%-84%.

That wasn't as much of an achievement as it might sound as I now played the piano quite well, could read music quickly, and had passed several of the Associated Board exams including the grade V theory exam that you had to pass before you could continue with the piano exams. And with history as one of my best subjects I also knew a lot about the history of music. But a Higher music was my only scholastic achievement that year as despite continuing with French, and finally sitting the exam, I didn't even manage to get a Lower, a failure that would have some consequences later. I continued with English lessons, and two of us continued with history lessons in which we had an in-depth look at Operation Sealion, Hitler's planned invasion of Great Britain in 1940 – a mere twenty years before, and almost not quite 'history', but still fascinating. In October, we paid another visit to the Citizens' Theatre, this time to see *Hamlet*, but an altogether more entertaining outing was to the Alhambra to see the 'all Scottish pantomime' *A Wish for Jamie* with Kenneth McKellar (as the eponymous 'Jamie McHaver'), Fay Lenore, Reg Varney and Rikki Fulton.

Early in 1961, I paid two more visits to the Arts Guild. The first one was in February, and it was to hear an all-Chopin recital by the Russian pianist Julius Isserlis. He was now in his seventies, and his eyesight was obviously very poor as he was wearing spectacles with very thick lenses. He seemed to grope his way from the wings to the piano, but he eventually got there and played a difficult programme beautifully from memory. The following month, I was back at the Guild, this time to see something rather different – 'B.B. Frolics', a mixed programme by the Greenock battalion of the Boys Brigade. Strangely, this too involved spectacles although in a somewhat surprising way. The second item on the programme was music by the local Silver Band. Halfway through their performance, part of the backcloth collapsed round about them. The music ground to a halt, and while the backstage crew tried to deal with the backcloth a hand suddenly emerged from the wings, stage-right, holding a pair of spectacles. These were quickly put on to a small child who had been playing a very large instrument. Being so unexpected, it was extremely funny. The backcloth was soon back in place, and the programme continued as originally planned.

Although stamp collecting was not one of my interests, I had now joined the school's stamp club which was run by Harold 'Pot' McNeill. Meetings took place in Harold's laboratory, room 24, at 4.00 on Friday afternoons, but several of us, ostensibly part of the club, met in an adjacent laboratory, room 22, and seldom showed our faces at the actual meetings. The reason for this was that we were the tea committee who prepared tea and/or coffee for the serious stamp collectors next door. Harold kindly provided biscuits. Among our number was a younger boy, Iain McLean, who had acquired the nickname 'Ig'. It was, apparently, an abbreviation of Ignatius, and specifically from Ignatius Loyola, founder of the Jesuits, but quite what the connection was is as much of a mystery as why the tea committee became virtually a separate institution.

Ever mindful of the fact that we appeared to show no interest in stamp collecting, I hit on the idea of preparing a spoof exhibition of items relating to the tea committee: this included labels from a tin of instant coffee and the numerous packets of biscuits that we consumed. There was also one stamp, highlighted to show that it was bad taste to produce one in room 22 (home of the tea committee), and several old coins – three pennies and one halfpenny – 'the amassed fortunes of the tea committee'. There was even a piece of metal, the sole remaining part of a kettle that had been left, unfilled, on a bunsen-burner. These 'exhibits' were on sheets of foolscap paper, and they were written up in a philatelic style such as pointing out damage to a biscuit label that would greatly reduce the value of the item. The spoof exhibition was shown at a stamp club meeting, and it elicited a few smiles from the genuine collectors – including Harold, who took it in good part.

The school's next opera production was *Iolanthe*, and, having played Major-General Stanley the year before, I now took on the role of the Lord Chancellor, who has yet another of Gilbert's famous patter songs, possibly the most difficult of them all – the famous 'nightmare song' "When you're lying awake with a dismal headache, and repose is taboo'd by anxiety". If the Major-General's song was difficult, this was almost impossible, but again I had a year in which to learn it, and these numbers take such a time to get into one's head that once you have learned them you seldom forget them. Perhaps if I had spent as much time on my French I might have managed to pass that exam too.

But one thing I did pass in 1961 was my driving test. Although neither of my parents could drive, they realised that with increasing car ownership it might be useful if I learned to drive, and so I was given a course of lessons at Phillips' Motoring School. Many of my school friends were able to practise driving on their parents' cars; some of my older friends, having passed their tests, even had cars themselves – usually, in those days, what we would now call 'old bangers', often pre-war and picked up for something like £20. Another SSC friend, Neill Cook (brother of Malcolm, and several years older than me), had an old Morris – a late 1930s model with running boards. As my parents didn't have a car, he kindly let me practise driving around Greenock's West End with its broad streets and relatively little traffic. Life was a lot easier and restriction-free in those days.

Having decided on a career as a school music teacher, I applied to become a student at the Royal Scottish Academy of Music (RSAM), forerunner of the Royal Conservatoire of Scotland. (Like Trinity College in London it was, strictly, the Royal Scottish Academy of Music and Drama (RSAMD), but in printed matter relating to us it was just the Royal Scottish Academy of Music.) I had an audition on Thursday July 6, and I was lucky enough to be accepted. At that time, the Academy had a course that was designed specifically for teaching music in Scottish schools, giving you a diploma that had ordinary degree status. It had the somewhat cumbersome title of 'Diploma in Musical Education of the Royal Scottish Academy of Music' – mercifully shortened to Dip Mus Ed, RSAM. When I started in 1961, the projected salary for a school music teacher with this qualification (and after a short teacher-training course at Jordanhill College) was the princely sum of £750 per annum.

We performed *Iolanthe* at the Arts Guild Theatre from June 14-17, 1961, and on June 28 there was an end-of-term service in the West Kirk (now Westburn Church) in Nelson Street, almost across the road from the school. We invariably disrupted traffic for some time to allow everyone to get from the school to the church, walking there in the traditional 'crocodile'. Our geography teacher, Hector Munro, always played the organ at these services. I then bade farewell to my schooldays. When we left school, we were presented with a little booklet, prepared by the County of Renfrew Education Committee, with advice on how to conduct our lives as we entered the big wide world – looking after our mind, body, soul and money amongst other things. Well-intentioned, and quite sensible on most topics, it does seem a little old-fashioned

now, but it may have been an off-shoot of Greenock's *Citizens'
Code* of 1950, apparently the first of its kind. There was also a
more substantial *Youth Handbook* that contained much useful
information about activities; also an introduction addressed
'To the Youth of Renfrewshire' by the Director of Education,
John Crawford.

I didn't go to the SSC camp at Bruar that summer as I had
my first paid job as an assistant purser working for the CSPC,
who ran the steamers for British Railways. This was thanks to
my introduction to the river steamers by Ian McCrorie, who,
now at Glasgow University, was himself regularly an assistant
purser during the holidays. With quite a large fleet consisting
of four paddle steamers, three turbine steamers, four modern
motor vessels, four car ferries and other smaller vessels there
were many vacancies for assistant pursers: some of the ships
had two assistants to help with the increased summer traffic. It
was a popular job for students, and there was no guarantee
that just by applying for a job you would automatically get
one. But I was lucky, and I found myself on the paddle steamer
Waverley with another student, Brian Jamieson. Built just
after the Second World War, as a replacement for the LNER
steamer of the same name that been had been sunk at Dunkirk,
Waverley was the youngest of the four remaining paddle
steamers. Famously 'bought for £1', she is now the last ocean-
going paddle steamer in the world, sole survivor of the many
steamers, both paddle and turbine, that once sailed on the
Clyde. There had also been many other steamers around the
shores of Great Britain, among them P. & A. Campbell's large
White Funnel Fleet in the Bristol Channel.

It was fun having a job working on the river, rather than
being stuck in an office. It was invigorating, and it gave you an
appetite for the four meals that were offered during the day –
breakfast at 08.00, lunch at 12.00, a high tea at 4.00 pm and
an evening meal at 8.00 pm! As junior officers, we had to wear
the appropriate uniform. This consisted of dark trousers with
either a proper merchant navy jacket or a dark navy battle

dress (I had the latter): the CSPC provided a cap. Our captain that year was David McCormick, and the chief engineer was Bill Summers, who had been with *Waverley* from the beginning. The purser was John Brewster, who had earlier appeared in a short British Transport film *Coasts of Clyde* (1959) narrated by the Canadian actor Bernard Braden.

One of our duties was to collect, sort and tie up the tickets as these had to be sent back to the head office. We also had to go round the ship checking that passengers did have tickets; that could be in all weathers so we also had oilskins. Some of the ships, such as the Gourock-Dunoon and Wemyss Bay-Rothesay car ferries, had a somewhat restricted roster, but *Waverley* had a very interesting one that was different every day. We covered much of the Clyde area, our destinations including Inveraray at the head of Loch Fyne, Campbeltown at the foot of the Kintyre peninsula, and Tighnabruaich via the famous Kyles of Bute. There was even an up-river cruise into the heart of Glasgow, a particularly interesting trip as shipbuilding was still a major industry at that time.

Another cruise that was popular was the 'Three Lochs Tour'. This started at Craigendoran pier, the former home of the LNER steamers, just east of Helensburgh on the north bank of the river. With a rail link from Glasgow, passengers could join the steamer there. She then sailed via Loch Goil to Arrochar at the head of Loch Long where passengers disembarked. They made their way by road to Tarbet pier on Loch Lomond where they joined the paddle steamer *Maid of the Loch* that sailed to Balloch pier. A train from there to Craigendoran (and further on if required) completed a round trip – one of the more unusual outings among what was still a very comprehensive list of day excursions.

Many of the ship's deck crew were from the Highlands where they tended their crofts during the winter: Gaelic was often a first language, and this sometimes caused a few difficulties. One day, we were on a round trip from Gourock to Inveraray. This gave time ashore at Inveraray, and we were lying at the pier with one of the Highlanders, Calum, manning the gangway. (If it was a busy day, and there were two gangways, Calum might be heard saying, in his Highland sing-song way, "Use the both gangways, please".) A couple came on board and asked where the ship was going. "Och, it's a round trip" says Calum. "And where is she going?" "Och, she's going to Gourock now". So, thinking that we were *starting* a round trip at Inveraray, they got on board, and only found out that we were on the homeward stretch when they came to the purser's office to get their tickets – *after* we had left. We had to put them off at Tighnabruaich from where they got a taxi back to Inveraray – a very long and tortuous journey at that time. Of course the CSPC had to pay for this.

The weather on the Clyde can be difficult, even in summer, but I can only recall one day when it was so bad that we were not able to complete our scheduled run. We were heading for Campbeltown one Monday, and even in the comparatively sheltered waters of the inner Firth it was very stormy. But when we passed Garroch Head on the island of Bute and headed into the outer Firth we began to feel the full force of the gale. It was impossible to continue, and the captain announced that because of the inclement weather we would not be going any further. We turned round, and were virtually blown back into the inner Firth. I can't remember how we spent the rest of the day with our disrupted timetable.

Another problem, even in the inner Firth, was simply docking at a pier in bad weather. We sometimes had several attempts, often not quite getting there, if the captain was being too cautious, or sometimes being blown by the wind and effectively smashing into the pier. Luckily, this didn't happen too often. Throwing the line to the handlers on the pier, which can be difficult enough at the best of times, was particularly tricky in poor weather conditions. But despite these problems we nearly always managed to stick to our schedules: the mail had to be delivered.

There was also a cruise round the island of Bute with before-and-after calls at Rothesay. On the first call, one of my duties was to hand over a package to someone at the pier (I think it was film that had to be developed), and when we called again later in the day I had to pick up a package that might have been the film that had now been developed, or perhaps an earlier batch of film. This procedure worked well enough for most of the summer, but one day I forgot to hand over the package on our first call, and I spent the rest of the afternoon wondering if I was going to be dismissed for gross negligence. Of course this didn't happen, but I wasn't too popular with John Brewster.

Assistant purser, P.S. *Waverley*, 1961.

Another memory concerns the famous Cowal Games that were held in Dunoon. At the end of that day, I think we were the last steamer calling at Dunoon before heading for Gourock and Craigendoran, and the crowd on the pier was enormous. The ship had an official passenger capacity of some 1350 (greatly reduced today), and we had little counters to keep track of how many passengers were on board. But on that occasion we simply lost track of the numbers boarding, and we may well have had more than 1350 on that last stretch. After most people had left the ship at Craigendoran we could still hear the skirl of pipes coming from the lower bar. The piper was, not surprisingly, somewhat the worse for wear, and it was with some difficulty that he was persuaded to come up on deck to be gently assisted on to dry land.

On another occasion, the ship was chartered for an evening 'Showboat Cruise' organised by the *Evening Citizen* newspaper. John Brewster dreaded this event, and he told us to lock ourselves in the purser's office. In those days, tumblers were made of glass, not plastic, and so by the end of the evening there was a lot of broken glass everywhere. It was quite a mess.

At one time on the Clyde, when there was much competition for custom between those who ran steamers (the railway companies, private companies or individuals), it was common for steamers to indulge in racing: the first steamer to arrive at a pier would obviously get the pick of the passengers. Racing was dangerous, and it was officially frowned upon – but it still happened. If not excusable, there might at least have been a reason for it at one time, but with all the steamers currently under one management (the CSPC) there would seem to be no reason for it now. But 'old habits die hard', and I remember one occasion when *Waverley* and her older quasi-sister *Jeanie Deans* were both returning up-river to Craigendoran – I think we were ahead, but we were definitely indulging in a race for home. One of the piers that we were due to call at was Innellan, but it seemed unlikely that there would be any passengers boarding there; also, there were few people on board, and it seemed equally unlikely that anyone would be disembarking, and so an announcement was made – "Would any passengers for Innellan please come on deck immediately". No-one had appeared by the time we approached the pier, and while we slowed down we could see that there was no-one there apart from the rope handlers, and so we didn't stop (the rope-handlers were somewhat bemused) but just continued on our way. I can't remember if we did win this 'race', but it was an unusual experience (effectively from a bygone age), and particularly unusual in that both *Waverley* and *Jeanie Deans* had been built for the same railway company, the LNER (based at Craigendoran, and whose steamers' names all came from the novels of Sir Walter Scott), and had never been rivals in that respect.

As employees of the CSPC, and therefore also of British Railways, we were entitled to what were called 'privilege tickets', and so on August 24, 1961 I was able to visit Northern Ireland for the first time. I didn't organise this myself: that was left to Ian McCrorie. There were several of us, including Ian's classmate and friend Russell Davidson (also an assistant purser) and Russell's sister Lynne who, although younger than me, already had a very good voice and had taken the principal roles of Katisha in *The Mikado*, Ruth in *The Pirates of Penzance* and the Queen of the Fairies in *Iolanthe*. Ian was working that day and wasn't with us. To get to Belfast we had to get a train to Paisley Gilmour Street, and then another train to Ardrossan where we embarked on the M.V. *Irish Coast*. We had a short time in Belfast (which didn't allow us to see very much) before getting a train at York Road to Larne where we got another ferry to Stranraer, a train to Paisley and finally another train back to Greenock and (for the Davidsons) Gourock: a long but memorable 'away-day'.

I had now acquired my first camera. Although new, it was of a much older design, and it opened out like a concertina. My first attempts at photography date from August 1961, and they are all of the river steamers. But it took me some time to realise that you have to wait until the subject you want to photograph is really filling your viewfinder: in nearly all of these shots the steamers seem very far away. Eventually I got used to it. The roll of film that I used could only take eight shots although very occasionally you might get a ninth. All of these early photographs are in black and white. You could get a roll of colour film, but for me then it was too expensive.

I enjoyed my summer on the river, but at that time I was not quite as interested in the history of the steamers as I later became, and it was the only summer in which I became an assistant purser. Other more interested aficionados spent all of their student summers 'on the boats', and some of them, like Ian McCrorie, wrote extensively on the subject. I did eventually become a member of the CRSC – the Clyde River Steamer Club – but only after I came back to Scotland in 2007. But, having already started to collect postcards, I concentrated on acquiring postcards of the steamers and the Clyde area during that summer of 1961. Many of these were still the old sepia ones, but others, such as the famous J. Arthur Dixon series, were in colour. Diligent searching through racks of cards in stationers' shops often resulted in finding interesting older cards at the back, the remnants of previous batches; sometimes these were of steamers that had been broken up years before. Such a 'find' was always exciting. Knowing of my interest in cartology, the Librarian in the Watt Library, who had taken over from Herbert Henderson, once gave me a number of cards of the steamers dating from the 1930s for which I was very grateful. At the end of the summer, on Tuesday September 26, 1961, I became a full-time student at the Royal Scottish Academy of Music.

Chapter 3: The Royal Scottish Academy of Music and Drama – 1961–1964

Year 1 – 1961-1962

The history of the RSAMD goes back to the Glasgow Athenaeum of 1847. Later, in 1890, it became the Glasgow Athenaeum (Limited) School of Music, its first Principal being a Greenock man, Allan Macbeth (remembered today, if at all, by one attractive piece of Light Music – an intermezzo called *Forget-Me-Not*). Later still, in 1929, it became the Scottish National Academy of Music (SNAM), concurrently with a Chair of Music being established at Glasgow University. At first, these were combined under a joint Principalship (although apparently this created many problems) which was held at first by W. Gillies Whittaker, who was succeeded in 1941 by Ernest Bullock. It was during Bullock's time (In 1944) that the College became the Royal Scottish Academy of Music, with the College of Dramatic Art being added in 1950. Ernest Bullock was knighted in 1951, and he retired in 1953. The two posts at the Academy and the University were now separate, and Bullock's successor as Principal of the RSAMD was Henry Havergal; it was 'Henry' (as he was affectionately known to everyone) who was Principal when I became a full-time student in 1961.

Henry was definitely a character – his eccentricities were numerous. He belonged to the world of the (mainly English) public school system that few of us knew much about, and he seemed a rather grand figure. (His son, Giles, became artistic director of Glasgow's Citizens' Theatre.) A graduate of

Oxford and Edinburgh Universities (he was later awarded a Hon D Mus from Edinburgh), Henry had taught first of all at Fettes College in Edinburgh, and then at Haileybury, Harrow and Winchester. Like my Uncle John, he invariably wore a bow tie, but, contrasting somewhat with this image, he often sported rather loud socks. But he was an impressive figurehead, and he made a number of welcome changes at the Academy. One was the introduction of a diploma, the DRSAM, which was for those students who wished to pursue a professional career as a singer or instrumentalist: the Dip Mus Ed, RSAM (formerly SNAM) had already been established by Whittaker. (Although now technically the RSAMD, the two music diplomas were still Dip Mus Ed, RSAM and DRSAM – without the final 'D'.) Our fees for the course were paid by the Scottish Education Department, and I had a maintenance allowance for the 1961-62 academic session of £160: £54 for the first term, and £53 for each of the second and third terms. My parents' contribution was £25. The Academy session was of thirty-six weeks' duration, running from about the third week of September until the end of the following June.

The building was on the corner of Buchanan Street and St George's Place (since renamed Nelson Mandela Place), the main entrance being in the latter. There were three separate blocks, the main one containing the office, two halls and the individual teaching and practise rooms as well as the Principal's study and a Board Room. A second block was the old Athenaeum Building in Buchanan Street that contained the Athenaeum Theatre. A tall, thin building, it appears, from old photographs, to pre-date the main block. As well as the theatre, which was underground and close to the Underground Railway, it also contained the organ room, at the top of a flight of stairs that wound round a lift shaft, and, at ground floor level, the buffet. At first floor level, a door connected this building to the main block. Compared with the number of students at the present Royal Scottish Conservatoire, our

The Royal Scottish Academy of Music.

numbers were few indeed, and the buffet, small as it was, could usually accommodate most people who wanted to use it at any one time. The third block, in St George's Place, had a more classical façade; it housed the Academy's music library and the drama department.

As well as soft drinks, tea, coffee, and biscuits such as 'jammie dodgers', you could also have 'lunch' in the buffet, but the menu was limited to a pie, a sausage roll or a bridie (a sort of Scottish-style Cornish pasty) with peas, beans or spaghetti (tinned). You could ring the changes on the main course with various combinations, but it wasn't exactly a healthy diet, and after a while I came out in a rash of spots and carbuncles that took some time to clear up. There were other eating places locally including a little tearoom called Wendy's which was in a basement a few blocks away in, I think, West Regent Street. You could at least get a decent bowl of soup there. But there was one restaurant that was very much healthier, and that was the newly opened Ceylon Tea Centre in Buchanan Street, just a few doors down from the Academy. Salads and rice dishes were on offer there along with a range of teas. I think it was very much ahead of its time, but I'm sure we didn't fully appreciate it then.

The Scottish Milk Marketing Board had a restaurant in Gordon Street, directly opposite Glasgow Central Station. Pie and chips was a favourite meal there, but the pies were cheese pies, and they were certainly a little healthier. Further up Buchanan Street was the Ivanhoe Hotel where we often had a drink or two (sometimes more than two), all part of our blossoming adulthood, and next door to the Ivanhoe was a 'greasy spoon' café that we also visited regularly. But perhaps the highlight of the week was to have a meal at an Italian restaurant, Dino's, on the opposite side of Buchanan Street from the old Athenaeum Building and next to the original entrance to Buchanan Street Underground, where a Spaghetti Bolognese cost the princely sum of 3/9 (or just under 20p in today's money). But this was the early 1960s, and eating out was all very new to us. We felt very grown up indeed. Riotous living with my term's £54 maintenance allowance!

Most of my classmates from Greenock Academy who were also studying in Glasgow, either at the University (there was only one then) or at one of the many colleges of further education such as the RSAM, continued to live at home and travel up daily by train rather than find digs in the city, and I did this too. In those days, and particularly for university students, there was a tendency to choose the one nearest to you – Edinburgh, Glasgow, Aberdeen or St Andrews – and many of these students could continue to live at home. But the RSAM students came from all over Scotland (sometimes from even further afield), and they had to find student digs of one sort or another. As I was returning to Greenock at the end of each day, I didn't experience much of the normal student life beyond whatever one was studying, and I began to wish that I too was living in Glasgow. I did eventually live there, but that came later. The advantage of living at home was that I could continue to attend concerts and other performances in Greenock: the SNO still came regularly to the Town Hall, and in January 1962 George Square Players presented Shakespeare's *Twelfth Night* at the Arts Guild.

The Dip Mus Ed course was very much an 'all-round 'affair in that you were supposed to be reasonably proficient at everything without necessarily being as good as you needed to be as a performer for your main study in the DRSAM course. As well as sight-singing, harmony and counterpoint, keyboard harmony and history of music you had three main practical subjects. The piano was the obvious one as a principal or first study for anyone becoming a school music teacher although this could just as easily have been singing or perhaps the violin. But most of us were first study pianists, partly because there had been little or no instrumental teaching in schools for our generation. It was just starting as we left. My piano teacher was Lawrence Glover, a delightful Irishman who died relatively young some years later. According to the syllabus, there was even a David Mackie (no relation) on the staff who taught piano. It would have been interesting if he had been my teacher, but I never met him, and I don't recall ever seeing him in the building.

Those of us who were first study pianists had to take singing as a compulsory second study. Most of the singing teachers at the Academy were women. Among them were Winifred (Winnie) Busfield (another great character) and the formidable Marjorie Blakeston, who also taught class singing and was a wizard at finding her way round the tonic sol-fa charts, including modulation. (By now, tonic sol-fa was seldom used in schools although it was still part of the RSAM syllabus.) My vocal studies were with Wilfred H. Phillips, the only male singing teacher on the staff, who taught several of the second study students like myself. He was a Fellow of the Royal College of Organists (FRCO) and, like Dr Elton at Greenock Academy, I think the organ was his main interest.

Our third study was an orchestral instrument, but as few of us could play one when we came up to the RSAM we had to choose one and start from scratch. My father played the violin, and I might have chosen that, but he wanted me to play the flute as he told me that my grandfather had played one (I never found out what happened to it), and so I chose the flute. The Academy provided us with instruments, and I had a very good wooden flute that had belonged to a professional flautist: it had been made by the firm of Rudall, Carte & Co, and the Academy had acquired it after his death. I was familiar with these names although at that time I had no idea that the Carte side of it would mean so much to me in later years. My flute lessons were with John Wiggins, who played in the BBC Scottish Symphony Orchestra. He was very patient with me as it took a long time for me to get any sound out of the instrument. Unlike the reed instruments (oboe, cor anglais, clarinet and bassoon) you have to make the sound on a flute (and piccolo) by blowing across the hole – finding an embouchure – and at first I just couldn't do this. I would come out of lessons feeling quite dizzy after a session of puffing and blowing, and I would stagger down to the buffet to recuperate. I even considered asking to change to another instrument, but eventually I began to get the hang of it.

My harmony teacher was Albert Heeley, who was the organist of St Mary's Episcopal Cathedral in Great Western Road. I remember him as a kind, gentle man, but I hardly got to know him as he died very suddenly during my first term: he collapsed at the entrance to the Academy on his way in one morning. Those of us who were his pupils now had to be farmed out to other harmony teachers, but as they had their own pupils this was tricky, and for a while I found myself with the college's second-in-command, Dr Kenneth Barritt, who rejoiced in the nickname of Dr Glum. He was quite a different character from the exuberant Henry Havergal, being outwardly rather severe, and at first I was very wary of him, but I soon realised that he was really quite shy. As Director of

Studies (his official title) he had plenty of work to keep him busy, and we were soon re-allocated; I found myself with someone quite unexpected, and not actually a member of the staff – the conductor Bryden Thomson, then the assistant conductor of the BBC Scottish Orchestra. A fellow-Scot, and known as Jack Thomson, he was a former graduate of the college and one of the few to hold a Dip Mus Ed, RSAM (Hons). Later, he became the music director of the Scottish National Orchestra. An ebullient personality, and a formidable score-reader at the piano, it was a great privilege to have had some lessons with him. I still have harmony exercises with his corrections. I then found myself with a new member of the staff, Tom Messenger, a graduate of Glasgow University. Albert Heeley also taught musicianship, and these classes too had to be taken by one or other of the harmony teachers.

We had history lectures from Christopher Grier, who was the music critic of *The Scotsman*. A tall, elegant figure, his lectures were always very entertaining. Once, when leafing through a magazine, I discovered that he also modelled clothes – equally elegantly. Life is full of surprises.

One other subject that we heard about from older students, but which had recently been deleted from the course, was Dalcroze Eurhythmics. This was a group class during which, supposedly, you were required to bounce a ball in 2/4 time or be a butterfly in 6/8 time. We got the impression that few students took this very seriously!

Apart from getting to know our various teachers, there was the pleasure of making new friends. The first of these was Alexander (Sandy) Oliver. Originally taking clarinet as a first study, he later changed to singing and had a very good career as a tenor, much of it in mainland Europe. I first became aware of Sandy when I saw him chasing one of the new female students round our common room, both squealing with laughter. Here, I thought, was someone who might be fun to know. Later, I realised that Sandy and the girl, Liz Sinclair, already knew each other as both had been pupils at the old High School of Stirling. Sandy actually came from Bridge of Allan where his parents ran a pub called the Bridge Inn. I would get to know it well over the next three years.

Another fellow-student was Harry Stevenson, who also became a good friend. We enjoyed playing piano duets, often arrangements of Haydn and Beethoven symphonies and the like, and this was a good way to get to know the standard repertoire. Clarinettist Ken McAllister was another good friend. I didn't have a steady girlfriend at that time, but we went around in a mixed group. Among the girls were Wilma Craighead, Marjorie Smith and Sandra MacRae. I also discovered people who had played in the Renfrewshire County Youth Orchestra, among them Dip Mus Ed student Ronald Walker, clarinettist Andrew Brockett and Freddie Ladds' son Roger, a cellist. Another student was singer Carey Wilson. Carey's father was the famous Scottish tenor Robert Wilson, who was known as 'The Voice of Scotland', and I was once invited to their home in Ayr to meet him. He had been in a serious car accident from which he never fully recovered, and he was very quiet and withdrawn. He died not long afterwards. I discovered later that Robert Wilson had been in the D'Oyly Carte Opera Company from 1931 to 1937.

As well as our three main studies, we were all required to sing in at least one of the various choral groups. Most of us were in the Mixed Choral Class, but there was also the Bach Choir that had many former students and others; with so many female students, there was also a Female Choral Class. It was decided that I was a tenor although I always felt that I was just a high baritone. The tenor sections in the choirs were always the smallest in number, and so it was sometimes quite a strain singing what were often very high lines: with so few of us, you felt very exposed. There was one older man who used to come to the Bach Choir rehearsals. He stood beside me, but he rarely opened his mouth while the rest of us were struggling to cope. We called him 'Keep death off the road'. My first concert with the Bach Choir was in St Mary's Cathedral in November when we gave Bach's *Magnificat* and parts II and III of *The Christmas Oratorio*. The orchestra for the Bach Choir and other concerts was drawn from the Academy's own students. One of these was horn player Joe Currie whose party piece was an impersonation of Hitler. Joe had dark, lank hair. He would comb it to one side, put the comb under his nose to represent the moustache, and then climb up on to a table in the common room and start ranting and raving and spouting unintelligible gibberish. It was a star turn, and it was very funny.

Throughout the year, there were numerous concerts given either by professionals or by the students themselves. There were Friday mid-day concerts in the Stevenson Hall, many of these given by members of the staff such as Wight Henderson (piano), Louis Carus (violin) and sisters Joan and Hester Dickson (respectively cello and piano). My flute teacher, John Wiggins, gave one with the oboist Deirdre Lind and a string trio. There also were artists from outwith the RSAM, and sometimes there was a lecture instead of a concert: the last of the series in my first year (on March 9, 1962) was a lecture by Dr Boris Blacher, the Director of the Berlin Academy of Music. The Mid-Day Concerts were listed on our timetables, and attendance was thus deemed obligatory.

The various choral groups would come together for certain concerts, and the first of these that I was involved in came just a week after the St Mary's Cathedral concert. It was held in Glasgow's Barony Church; the programme included Britten's *Saint Nicolas*. Then came the annual Christmas Carol Concert that took place in St Andrew's Hall behind the Mitchell Library near Charing Cross. For this concert, Henry used the Scottish National Orchestra. It was the first time that most of us had sung with a major orchestra, and it was a wonderful experience. The sound was thrilling (the hall itself had wonderful acoustics), and I think that quite a few of us just listened to that without giving much input as choristers, but there were so many in the choir that that hardly mattered. The programme opened with the delightful *A Children's Overture*, by Roger Quilter, cleverly put together from a number of the nursery songs in Walter Crane's *The Baby's Opera* published in 1877 (co-incidentally the year of Quilter's birth). There were also marvellous arrangements of Christmas carols by one of the staff, Dr Frank Spedding, who, despite being a rather shy man, had a wonderful sense of humour. Another fellow-student, Fergus Malcolm, had taken the double bass as his third study, and Frank Spedding, Fergus's harmony teacher, wrote a quirky piece, *Brontosaurus*, for him. He had to play this for his final exam, and I played the piano part. Frank Spedding was on the examining panel, and he sat at one end of the table, smiling shyly to himself and obviously enjoying the performance.

At the end of the first term, there was another annual event – the Christmas Ball. This was held in the larger of the Academy's two halls, the Stevenson Hall, named after a former Lord Provost of Glasgow, the millionaire Sir Daniel Stevenson, who had been a significant benefactor to the Academy. My partner for this event was another student, Marion Brodie. I think many of the girls made their own dresses for the Ball, something I suspect few would do in today's throw-away society, even if they did wear what might be termed 'Ball gowns'. But this was sixty years ago; times and fashions change. The music was provided by a little band under the direction of the father of one of our students, James (Jimmy) Murray. This, again, was at a time when things were very different, and most music for dances was live before discos became the norm. Jimmy Murray was a very fine violinist. After further study in Brussels he came back to Glasgow to the number three position in the BBC Scottish Symphony Orchestra; he then went to Manchester as assistant leader of the Hallé Orchestra. He died far too young at forty-nine.

The Academy Ball finished in the 'wee small hours', and there was no way in which I could get back to Greenock. But

Sandy Oliver had invited me to come to Bridge of Allan, and as there was a milk train that ran to Stirling from the now long-gone Buchanan Street Station we joined other late night revellers on this unusual mode of transport. We then had to get a taxi from Stirling to Bridge of Allan, arriving at the Bridge Inn at around 06.30 where we were welcomed by Sandy's mother and her husband Jimmy. This was the first of many enjoyable visits for me. The pub had a large public room, and Mrs. Oliver, who played the violin and the mouth organ, would often entertain the customers on a Saturday night; sometimes she would ask Sandy to sing. If I was staying there, I usually played for them. On subsequent visits, I met other people including George McVicar, latterly the music adviser for Stirlingshire, whom Sandy knew well. He too was a Dip Mus Ed. Later, at the Academy, there was another student, David Frame, who also came from Bridge of Allan.

One enjoyable feature of student life was the annual Glasgow Students' Charities Appeal during Charities Week,

Sandy Oliver at Bridge Inn, Bridge of Allan, 1962.

my first experience of this being in January 1962 when I was given a card that entitled me to be a 'House to House Collector' on behalf of the Appeal. Open lorries were used as 'floats', usually decorated in some way, with students, including myself on at least one occasion, on board attired in various costumes. Another memorable occasion was when the Academy gave an orchestral concert in Glasgow's Central Station. I took part in this, the actor Duncan Macrae conducting us with a french loaf, and I remember playing one of Eric Coates' marches, possibly the one from the film *The Dam Busters*. I think that must have been later in my student career as I doubt that my flute playing in January 1962 would have been up to taking part in an orchestral concert.

During yet another Charities Week, probably during my last year or perhaps when I was at Jordanhill Training College, I took part in an escapade that involved a number of us driving through to Edinburgh in a borrowed van, intent on stealing a stag's head from the students' union building at Edinburgh University. My job on that occasion was to act as the driver. With no mobile phones, we had to keep in touch with each other by using public telephones – just as you see in films of that period. The others managed to get the stag's head, and we set off home. We were fully expecting to be caught, and prepared to spend at least one night behind bars, but we got away with it. The M8 between Glasgow and Edinburgh was being constructed at that time (it opened officially in 1965), and I seem to recall that a short section of it was already in use, facilitating our getaway. But when a ransom was demanded for this object it was refused, the Edinburgh students apparently saying that they were glad to be rid of it.

My first year continued with a regular diet of lessons in my three practical subjects – piano, voice and flute – and the other classes that were part of the course including harmony and counterpoint, history of music, and musicianship; in that first year we even had a class in rudiments with the tiny, bird-like Winifred Parkes. During my time at the Academy, in my studies with Lawrence Glover, I covered a wide range of keyboard music from Scarlatti and Bach through Mozart, Beethoven and Schubert to Debussy, Bartok and Rawsthorne. In my second study, singing, my first lessons with Wilfred Phillips consisted mainly of vocal exercises before I moved on to songs such as Schubert's *Who is Silvia?* and Schumann's *The Walnut Tree* – both, frankly, beyond my vocal capabilities, particularly in terms of artistic expression. Once I had achieved an embouchure, my flute lessons included many scales, arpeggios and exercises by the famous flautist Marcel Moyse, but I did eventually manage to play an unaccompanied sonata by J. S. Bach and a Mozart concerto. We were certainly kept busy although the regimen was less strict than that of our schooldays.

As well as the concerts at the Academy, there was a wide range of concerts and other productions in the city from the ballet *The Sleeping Beauty* at the King's Theatre to a jazz musical *King Kong* at the Empire Theatre. (The Empire was called 'the graveyard of English comics' as shipyard workers at variety shows there were reputed to have handfuls of rivets in their pockets to throw at any act from the south that they didn't like.) Although I enjoyed operetta and musical comedy, I had not yet acquired a taste for grand opera. I could enjoy the music, but my poor showing with languages, coupled with poor hearing, meant that I could seldom follow what it was all about. But, in company with other students, I found myself going to more and more opera performances; when Sadler's Wells Opera (forerunner of English National Opera – ENO) came to the Empire in November 1961 I saw Wagner's *Tannhäuser* and Rossini's *La Cenerentola*. This was broadening my musical horizons, if still mostly failing to broaden my understanding of the plots. More to my liking were Bernstein's *West Side Story* at the King's in December, the *Fol-de-Rols* in February 1962 and *The Yeomen of the Guard* – an amateur production by Glasgow's Orpheus Club – at the Alhambra in March.

At that time, Glasgow had a small cinema, properly a News Theatre: these were once common throughout the country. This one was in Renfield Street, just around the corner from the Central Station, in the same block as the famous up-market store of R.W. Forsyth (my mother used to save up to buy me 'a good pair of shoes' there) and just before Renfield Lane. These News Theatres showed only newsreels, cartoons and 'shorts' such as the comedy films of Laurel and Hardy or The Three Stooges; I also remember seeing the Goons' *The Running, Jumping and Standing Still Film* there. A number of us would go in regularly as a relaxation from our serious musical studies.

Then came another concert in St Andrew's Hall, again with the combined choirs and the Scottish National Orchestra. We were originally supposed to be doing a mixed programme consisting of Stanford's *Stabat Mater*, Holst's *Hymn of Jesus* and Bruckner's *Te Deum*, but for some reason this was changed, and we did Verdi's *Requiem*. This was on Thursday March 15, 1962. Once again, I don't think I contributed very much to the performance as I was overawed by singing with the SNO, and particularly in such a spectacular work as the *Requiem*. It was a very enjoyable part of our musical education to be singing in so many of the great choral works: it is a very different experience from listening to a work as a member of the audience, particularly when singing with an orchestra.

In May, there was an unusual departure from the norm when the next choral concert took place in St Giles' Cathedral in Edinburgh. This was a slightly different programme to the one in November although it included a second performance of Britten's *Saint Nicolas*. Following this, we had our annual exams, and I managed to get through everything although there were a number of far better pianists than I was, and I am certainly no singer despite Wilfred Phillips' efforts in that direction. I did best in the written papers – harmony and counterpoint, and history. The only prize I ever got at the

RSAM was for keyboard harmony, but I think that is an intuitive skill. However, it can be cultivated and improved, and it is something that has been very useful to me throughout my career.

Following the exams, in June 1962, I took part in an opera performance. The RSAM put on an opera (or operas) every year, but this one was unusual in that it was a joint production with the drama department. We hardly ever met the drama students, and normally I would not have been in the opera class, but a notice had gone up asking for volunteers for the chorus, and, along with Sandy Oliver and others, I decided that it would be fun to take part: I had already enjoyed being in Greenock Academy's G&S productions. I now got to know some of the drama students. The opera was Smetana's *The Bartered Bride,* and the programme stated that it was 'Presented by The Opera Class in collaboration with The College of Dramatic Art'. The music school produced virtually all the principal singers and chorus; among the latter was Patricia MacMahon, who later became a well-known singing teacher. But there were some drama students in the chorus. One of these was Gay Hamilton, who later had a brief career in films and television. I think that Tom Conti, who had graduated in 1961, was also involved in some capacity backstage. My partner in the chorus was Irene (known as Kate) Foster who was in third year in the music school.

The production was in the hands of Colin Chandler, the Director of the drama department, and Muriel Dickson, who taught singing in the music department. Miss Dickson (known as Poppy) had sung at the Metropolitan Opera in New York, and this was often stated, with some pride, at the Academy. Far less often mentioned was the fact that she had had an earlier career as a principal soprano with the D'Oyly Carte Opera Company in the 1930s. I don't think I ever spoke to her during all my time at the RSAM, even during rehearsals for the opera, but I did get to know her later when I joined D'Oyly Carte in 1975.

In the third act of *The Bartered Bride*, a circus comes to town, and here the drama department really came into its own, providing all the various 'acts', from comedians to tight-rope walkers, that you would expect in a circus. Of course, there weren't any animals, but one of the characters, the stuttering Vasek, has to appear in a bear's costume. It was all great fun although, sadly, it was the only time during my years at the Academy that there was such a collaboration.

And so my first year came to an end. A letter, dated June 6, 1962, informed me that the examiners had decided that I could proceed to the second year of the course. This was a relief as there were several students who either didn't pass or who dropped out for one reason or another. There was now a break of almost three months. What was I going to do with it? Having left Greenock Academy, I wasn't expecting to be involved again with their now well-established school operas, but a surprise awaited me. The orchestra for each of the first four productions had consisted of the same local players, but the timpanist wasn't available this year. Donald Miller, knowing that I had played in the Renfrewshire County Youth Orchestra as a percussionist, contacted me to see if I would stand in which, with some reserve, I did. This year's production, again G&S, was *The Gondoliers*, and it ran from June 20-23, 1962, once again in the Arts Guild Theatre. The regular timpanist, Alec Bremner, was back the following year.

I had enjoyed my summer job on the paddle steamer *Waverley* in 1961, but as I thought that it might be interesting to have a variety of summer jobs while I was a student I didn't apply again to be an assistant purser. But in fact I didn't have a job at all in 1962. I was still living at home, and I had kept in touch with my classmates. Several of us (we called ourselves 'the chums') had decided that we would be very adventurous and have a holiday abroad on the Costa Brava, one of the first really popular destinations of the then burgeoning 'package holidays'. In the end, some of the group dropped out, but a few of us stuck to the original plan, and in July we went to Tossa de Mar.

This was my first visit to a foreign country, and we went nearly all the way by train. It must have taken two or three days although I forget exactly how long the journey was. We travelled first to the south of England from where we embarked for France although, again, I don't recall from where, or where we landed. We then arrived in Paris where we got a train all the way down to the Spanish border. There, we got yet another train (an old-fashioned one with wooden-slatted carriages) to the nearest station to Tossa de Mar, finally boarding a coach for the last leg of the journey. With the subsequent increase in air travel, I don't think anyone would willingly undertake such a journey today, but that was quite common in the early 1960s. However, it was still very tiring, and as we were now young adults, and felt very grown up, we fortified ourselves on this epic journey with bottles of Newcastle Brown Ale that we had brought with us. I don't like lying on a beach for days on end when I'm on holiday, and so I spent quite a lot of the time exploring the town and taking some photographs: by now, I was getting more used to the camera after my not very successful early attempts the year before. I also found some interesting records of Spanish military band music. But soon it was time for the gruelling return journey to Greenock. Once home from Tossa de Mar, I went to Bridge of Allan where we attended the Bridge of Allan Games which included an interesting Veteran and Vintage car rally.

The year 1962 saw a couple of memorable celebrations. The first of these was the Golden Jubilee of the SSC, founded in 1912. This was marked in several ways. There was a service in St Giles' Cathedral in Edinburgh, and the well-known BBC programme *Songs of Praise* was recorded at the summer camp at Bruar on August 5 (transmitted on September 30). On August 18 there was a Jubilee Garden Party in the grounds of

Dalguise House in Perthshire where, apart from my first camp at West Linton, I had attended all the Easter Camps since 1957. Stanley Nairne, the founder of SSC and still vigorous at eighty-one, was present at Dalguise as were others of that vintage including Eddie Bosomworth from Edinburgh and John Kerr from Greenock – founder of the Greenock branch and also a famous cricketer in his youth. A strange-looking lady in dark glasses, calling herself Mrs Grace Jefferson Davis, was also to be seen wandering around. "Who is she?" everyone was asking. It turned out that 'she' was in fact Norman Hutchison who had held the position of Organiser for the SSC. The disguise fooled most people. During the summer camp at Bruar, several of us went to the nearby Pitlochry Festival Theatre to see the play *The Hasty Heart* (previously filmed with Richard Todd), a cultural outing that had been suggested by my friend Ian Matthew from Newcastle, now an English teacher.

Shortly after this, at the beginning of September, there was a particularly interesting event at home to celebrate the 150th anniversary of the paddle steamer *Comet*, the first successful steam vessel in Europe, dating from 1812. A mere tiddler at just over 40 feet in length (*Waverley* is almost 200 feet longer), it was possible to build a full-size replica which made a commemorative journey across the Clyde from Port Glasgow (where the original ship was built) to Helensburgh on the north shore. Unfortunately, it was a rather murky day, but I did manage to get a photograph of the historic event. After this, the replica stood in the centre of Port Glasgow for sixty years, but it was allowed to deteriorate to such an extent that what was left of it was finally removed. This called forth a vigorous correspondence in the local press condemning what was considered by many to be an inexcusable act of cultural vandalism. But in 1962 such an end could not have been foreseen. I was now about to embark on year 2 of the Dip Mus Ed course.

Year 2 – 1962-1963

The second year continued in much the same way, with regular piano, singing and flute lessons. Rudiments was dropped, and musicianship was now with Owen Swindale, but two new subjects were introduced – choral conducting with Dr Barritt and accompaniment with Mary Firth. I have always preferred being an accompanist or being 'in the pit' for our SSC shows in Greenock and, later, for many other similar productions; so this was a class I particularly enjoyed. At that time, there was no tuition at the RSAM for repetiteurs: anyone who showed any interest in that area would be sent off to London or elsewhere on completion of the Academy course. In the light of my later career, such a course would have suited me very well although it would almost certainly have included language study for opera and lieder, and I would have found that difficult. Foreign languages have never been my strong point.

Living at home in Greenock, I was still able to get involved in our SSC shows, and shortly after the term started we had another one. We had previously called these *All-Weather Revels*, but as it was the Club's Golden Jubilee year we called this one *Jubilee Revels*. The programme for this event sported an attractive cover designed by Chris Buntain, who was a year above me at school. Chris was training to be an architect. There was also a letter from Stanley Nairne. Stanley had previously attended the Greenock branch's centenary dinner in February, and both then and in his letter he expressed his appreciation for the contribution the Greenock branch had made to the Club. Ian McCrorie and I both acted as accompanists for the show, but I also took part in one number with Stewart McMillan and Peter Morrison. Dressed in borrowed gym slips, and listed in the programme as 'Guise n' Dolls', we performed "Three little maids from school are we" (*The Mikado*) – another pointer, had I known it, to my later involvement with G&S and D'Oyly Carte.

At home, if I wasn't practising, I usually had time at weekends to keep up with my school friends. I also started taking a series of photographs of the older parts of Greenock as a lot of demolition was taking place, mainly in the central part of the town. I used to go out on Sunday mornings when it was quiet, and while my black and white photographs were not of any outstanding quality they were at least recording parts of the town that would soon be gone forever. In 1980, Inverclyde District Libraries published a booklet called *Greenock from old photographs*, and I wrote to the librarian to say that I had a number of similar photographs of older parts of the town. The librarian then asked if she could make copies of these, and I was happy to let her do this. In 1983, a second volume of photographs appeared, and I was pleased to see that it contained two of mine.

In the early 1960s, the country still had steam trains although diesels were now being introduced on most lines. On our Glasgow-Gourock line there is a very long tunnel between Greenock West and Fort Matilda (immortalised in our SSC parody of *Oklahoma!*), the stop before the terminus at Gourock. I believe it is the longest tunnel in Scotland. Anyone travelling to or from Gourock would hardly be aware of any discomfort on just one journey, but the drivers, who were doing several runs a day, said that they were aware of diesel fumes collecting in this tunnel, and so these new engines were used only occasionally on our line. This meant that while the rest of the country was slowly converting to diesel we continued to have not only steam engines but also the older carriages that went with them: these would otherwise have gone to the scrapyard. There is a great deal of nostalgic interest in steam railways, but there was a down side to steam locomotion, namely soot. Clothes suffered as a result, and you could get a little piece of grit in your eye if you leaned out of the window. It was easy to do that in the old carriages as the window in the door could be let down by means of a strap. There were warning signs that read 'Do not lean out of the window', but these were generally ignored, and they were invariably altered to 'Do not clean soot off the window'.

We referred to the carriages as 'horse boxes' as they consisted of a number of separate compartments, the full width of the carriage, with a door at each side and two long bench seats. Each compartment was self-contained, and there was no corridor – and therefore no toilet – so it was always wise to make sure that you wouldn't need to go during the run to Glasgow which could be almost an hour if the train stopped at every station. (If I was coming back at the end of the day, and had something in Greenock in the evening, I would try to get the famous business flyer, the 5.20 pm (no continental times then), which only stopped at Paisley Gilmour Street before Greenock West which it reached just before 6.00 pm.) Travelling regularly to Glasgow with many of my school friends, we would try to get a compartment to ourselves. This was not always easy, but there was a trick of sitting by the window and putting your foot on the door handle, and this would stop anyone else opening the door. But even if there were other people in the compartment there were still usually several of us, and we passed the time by playing cards, invariably a form of whist.

Almost before leaving school, I had started to smoke. Most people seemed to smoke then, even if they didn't inhale. (Watching old films now, it is interesting to see so many people smoking, but it is also easy to spot the real smokers – those who did and those who did not inhale.) Cigarettes were quite cheap, but I also started to smoke a pipe; that too was quite common although it did tend to make young people look much older. I was very fond of scented tobacco (Dutch, I think) which was popular but more expensive. Many of the students at the RSAM were smokers although it didn't seem occur to anyone that not only was it not very good for the body, generally, but, particularly for the singers, it might not be good for their voices. Some older male singers even relished the darkened tone that smoking seemed to give their voices.

Not long into the second year of the course we had the Cuban missile crisis. Having been brought up in the 1940s and 1950s, with the Second World War behind us, we were very lucky in not having had to fight, and we thought that never again (surely) would we be called up to do so: even National Service had finished by the time I left school. But, with the prospect of a nuclear war, this was a very different situation. I went up to the RSAM one day when the crisis was at its height. It must have been mid-morning as it was unusually quiet and I had the carriage to myself. I sat there thinking about what might happen – even if I didn't have to fight we might yet all be killed. Luckily, the worst scenario was averted, but it was a particularly scary time.

While this was going on, Glasgow had another visit from Sadler's Wells Opera, and perhaps to take our minds off the crisis we went to as many performances as we could during the week of October 15-20 – *The Magic Flute, Rigoletto, The Bartered Bride* and, on the Saturday, *Iolanthe*. With Sadler's Wells, of course, the operas were in English, which was useful for me, and I had even been in the last two, *The Bartered Bride* just months before. *Iolanthe* was particularly interesting, not just because I had recently played the Lord Chancellor in our school production in 1961 but because the copyright on performances, strictly guarded by the D'Oyly Carte Opera Company, had expired at the end of 1961. Any professional company was now at liberty to perform these operas in any way that they wished, and Sadler's Wells was the first company to do so with its production of *Iolanthe*, the first performance being given at Stratford-upon-Avon. There had been worries (sometimes later justified) as to how these operas might now be presented, but this production was still fairly 'traditional'.

College life continued as before, and even my flute playing began to improve. The combined choirs and the Academy's First Orchestra were due to give Haydn's *The Creation* on Thursday, November 1 in the St Andrew's Hall, and everyone was looking forward to it. Henry Havergal was to give a lecture on the work, scheduled for the mid-day concert on Friday October 26, 1962, but no-one could have foreseen what happened. St Andrew's Hall was the venue for a number of different events, and on the previous evening there had been an international boxing match between Scotland and Romania. This finished without any indication that anything untoward might happen, but during the night the Hall caught fire and burned down. Part of the façade was saved, and, luckily, the fire didn't spread to the adjacent Mitchell Library. I can't remember what Henry said the following lunchtime (the lecture may have been cancelled), but we now had to look for another venue. More significantly, Glasgow had lost one of the finest concert halls in the country; this was a real tragedy.

Temporary venues for concerts now had to be found; one was Green's Playhouse, said to have been the largest cinema in Britain, if not in Europe. I went to a concert there on my birthday in November to hear Ingrid Haebler play Beethoven's second piano concerto. Another venue was an old cinema in the Anderston district of Glasgow, but with very little dressing-room accommodation it was far from satisfactory. With few suitable venues in the city, this old cinema, originally the Tivoli Variety Theatre before becoming the Gaiety cinema in the 1930s, soon became the Glasgow Concert Hall for a number of years before being demolished in 1968 to make way for the M8 motorway. Among those who performed there were the Beatles. We were able to give our performance of *The Creation* in Glasgow University's Bute Hall on Nov 1, with the soloists on that occasion being Patricia Clark (soprano) and William (Bill) McCue (bass) (both former students of the Academy) and John Wakefield (tenor) from Sadler's Wells Opera. The programme listed the Academy chorus as having no less than ninety-three sopranos, sixty contraltos, twenty-four tenors and thity-five basses! I still have a flyer for the concert that gives St Andrew's Hall as the venue: it may well be a collector's item now. Our Christmas Carol

Concert this year was again in the old Gaiety Cinema at Anderston Cross.

There would also have been another Ball at the Academy, and it may have been on that occasion that I was involved in an embarrassing situation with Fergus Malcolm and his girlfriend (and later wife) Marion. Fergus, who lived in Holytown near Bellshill (east of Glasgow), an area I didn't know at all, had a car that he called Della, and I had been asked to drive it. After the Ball, we set off, first of all to take Marion home. Fergus and Marion were in the back seat, and Fergus gave me directions –"left here," "next right," and so on. When we got to Marion's house, we sat for a bit before the back door opened. The next thing I remember was the back door closing and Fergus saying something that I took to be "right, off we go" or words to that effect – and off I went. Not being familiar with the area, I just kept going, every so often asking "right here?" "left here?" or whatever – but without receiving any reply. Not having the best hearing in the world, I assumed that he *had* replied but I hadn't picked it up – and most of the decisions at junctions seemed reasonably obvious. But we finally came to a junction where a clear decision had to be made, and I said "where now, Fergus?" to which, again, there was no reply. This time I needed an answer, and so I stopped the car and turned round – no Fergus! What he had obviously said earlier was something along the lines of "I'm just seeing Marion in: I won't be too long" before closing the car door – from the outside!

Not only was it a shock that he wasn't there, I now had absolutely no idea of where I was. What was I going to do? – and what would he have thought of me driving off in his car and leaving him stranded? Not so many people had cars then, and at that time of the night (or morning) there were few cars in sight and no-one around to ask, not that I even knew where Fergus or Marion actually lived. I then did the only thing I could think of which was to try to retrace my steps. At first, this didn't appear to be achieving anything, but I kept driving around until, mercifully, I suddenly spotted Fergus standing on the opposite side of the road. I could only utter the most abject apology and refer to my less than perfect hearing as the culprit. We then drove to his home. He had previously agreed to put me up for the night, and despite this embarrassing incident I was still welcome there. Happily, we have remained friends.

Back at the college after the Christmas break, there were more concerts including students' concerts and the Friday mid-day concerts. For Friday February 22 the concert syllabus stated only 'under negotiation', and this may have been the day when we had yet another lecture, this time from the famous French composer, conductor and teacher Nadia Boulanger (1887-1979). It was a rare chance to see and hear one the most distinguished musicians of her time, but she was at great pains to insist that her younger sister Lili (1893-1918) was much more talented, her early death being much regretted. In March, again in St Mary's Cathedral, the Bach Choir gave a performance of Bach's *Mass in B minor*. The orchestra on this occasion, led by Louis Carus, consisted of students, staff and visiting professionals with Henry as the *continuo* player. Dr Barritt conducted the performance.

There were still plenty of things to do and see in Greenock. In January, George Square Players presented Shakespeare's *A Midsummer Night's Dream*; shortly after this the Arts Guild played host to Intimate Opera, a company whose artistic and musical director was Antony Hopkins, well-known as a broadcaster with his long-running programme *Talking about Music*. As the name implies, Intimate Opera toured small-scale works with usually just two or three performers (no chorus) accompanied by a pianist (not Antony Hopkins here). These small-scale presentations were ideal for a venue like the Arts Guild although, despite very little space in the wings, it had also played host to ballet and even the SNO, albeit with reduced numbers. On this occasion, there were three one-act pieces from the 18th, 19th and 20th centuries – Samuel Arnold's

The Enraged Musician, Offenbach's *The Bachelor's Bond* and Gian-Carlo Menotti's *The Telephone*. Many years later, I worked for a similar opera group, London Opera Players, for whom Antony Hopkins wrote several short operas.

In May, we had another visit from the SNO, this time with James Gibb as soloist in Beethoven's fourth piano concerto. Preceded by Mozart's symphony no. 34 and followed by Dvorak's symphony no. 7, this was a typical programme of the time with standard repertoire and no modern or unusual works. The analytical notes for these SNO concerts were written by our history lecturer, Christopher Grier. In those days, the concerts always began with the National Anthem for which everyone stood. Not so in the cinemas, where the National Anthem invariably came at the end of the last showing, and there was usually what amounted to a stampede by most people to get out before it began!

Scottish Opera had given its first season in 1962, and as part of its second season it now gave Verdi's *Otello*: I saw this at the end of May, widening my experience of grand opera. On June 4, I received a letter (as in June 1962) informing me that the examiners had allowed me to proceed to the final year of the course – another relief and with no re-sits. I could now relax. Later that month, the college presented more opera, this time 'Il Trittico', Puccini's three short one-act operas – *Il Tabarro, Suor Angelica* and *Gianni Schicchi* – the latter being the best-known with its famous soprano aria "O mio babbino caro" ("Oh, my beloved father"), sung on this occasion by Patricia MacMahon as Lauretta. With little chorus work in these operas (other than for Sisters and Novices in the all-female *Suor Angelica*), there was no call for male volunteers for the chorus as in the previous year's production of *The Bartered Bride*, and so I had to content myself with being part of the audience. Sitting in the Academy's Athenaeum Theatre, you became very aware of the Glasgow Underground (often referred to as 'The Clockwork Orange' from its diminutive size – compared with, say, the London Underground – and the

distinctive colour of its carriages) which runs just underneath
Buchanan Street: every time a train passed you felt the
vibrations. Before the term finished I managed to see yet
another *Five Past Eight* at the Alhambra, this one starring
Max Bygraves.

This year, I did have a summer job, starting on July 1. I was
working for a licenced grocer, Duncan Shaw, whose premises
were at 81 Albert Road, Gourock in the short range of
buildings on the shore side of the road after the open-air
swimming pool and almost opposite the former Ashton
Church (later demolished to make way for flats). The shop is
now a private house. Such a work experience would seldom
appear today on anyone's CV as there must be few, if any,
licenced grocers anywhere, supermarkets with their range of
products, including a readily available supply of alcohol,
having effectively become the normal outlets for all one's
needs. Also, with so many rules and regulations in today's
world, it is more difficult for students to find temporary
summer jobs: many now seem to work in bars and restaurants
during term times to earn extra money.

Duncan Shaw had been in a serious car accident some years
before, and he had suffered facial damage including the loss of
an eye and damage to his jaw. I found him somewhat
intimidating although his gruff manner may have been an
understandable result of his injuries. But he had a delightful
female assistant whose name was Frances (her surname
escapes me now), and she certainly brightened up the shop.
Her husband worked for a company that was experimenting
with a form of Jaffa cakes. But they couldn't get the recipe
quite right, and so he would take home batches of these trial
runs as they couldn't be sold. Frances would then bring some
into the shop for our tea breaks. The jam filling was either too
soft or too hard, but they were always very tasty.

Duncan Shaw had had a diary printed. It included
interesting information such as race meetings (horse racing
was presumably an interest of his), early closing days in

Scotland and times of trains to and from London. In those days, these journeys took about seven hours.

As well as any passing trade, the shop had a number of regular customers who placed orders that we made up in cardboard boxes; the main part of my job was to deliver these in a small van, registration DVS 806. I covered quite a lot of ground from Gourock through Greenock to Kilmacolm, some miles away. Furthest west in Gourock was *Levan House*, now divided but then still just one large house; another large house (in Greenock) was *Alt-Na-Craig* on Lyle Road: it is now a care home. I used to help in making up the orders; these would sometimes include ground coffee. If we had coffee at home, it was invariably from a small tin of 'instant'. I had never come across 'proper' coffee before; the aroma of freshly ground coffee beans was a new experience, and I found it quite intoxicating.

Having packed all the day's orders in the van, I would then set off to deliver them. This could take some time, particularly when I had to go to Kilmacolm, but once I got back there would always be something to do in the shop. And so the summer passed very pleasantly – with one exception; that was the day I was involved in a slight accident. I was sitting at traffic lights when someone ran in to the back of the van. Luckily, there wasn't too much damage, but Mr Shaw wasn't very pleased.

The job finished in September, and Sandy Oliver and I went down to Liss in Hampshire to stay with my cousins June and Ron Millar in their lovely thatched house called *Oakdene*. Having been stationed at Portsmouth during his National Service, Ron was quite happy to remain in this part of the world, and he set up his dental practice in nearby Petersfield, later having a second practice in Waterlooville. June and Ron now had three children – Shona, Dugal and Fiona. Uncle John was living there too (in a separate part of the house that he called 'the bottle and jug department') having eventually moved from Edinburgh after Aunt Mina died in 1957. We had a pleasant time at Liss, including trips to Portsmouth, but, again, the holiday was soon over, and it was time to start the third year of my Dip Mus Ed course.

Year 3 – 1963-1964

L ooking back on those years, I can hardly remember any of the new first year students when I was in second year. Perhaps as new students we made friends mainly with those in our own year and, having done so, didn't feel the need to make new friends – or did we just feel superior? This was rather like school where you tended to look up to those above you and look down on those below you (as in that famous sketch!) But now, in my third year, I did make a number of friends among the new first year intake. Among the men were Sandy Leiper and Bob Harvey, but I also made friends with several of the girls as I started a relationship with one of them, Juliet Robertson, and therefore got to know several of the friends that she was making, most of those from the new intake. Among them were Elizabeth Woodward, a flautist, whose father was Professor of Spanish at St Andrews University in Fife, and Emma Jack who also came from Fife. Juliet was from Edinburgh, and her father was a lawyer and WS (Writer to the Signet) like Uncle John's friend Maurice Durlac.

I was still living at home during my final year, but by now, and particularly with a new relationship, I was finding it tiresome to have to travel back to Greenock every day although there were times when I stayed overnight in Glasgow, often (unbeknown to various landladies) in digs where we had been having a party. One memorable affair was a fancy-dress party to which I went in Juliet's clothes and she went in mine. Harry Stevenson was dressed as a bishop. Another student, Sara Symondson, was a farmer's daughter, and she had borrowed a small pick-up truck from the farm. Several of us went to the party in the truck, huddled together in the open space behind the cab. During the journey, we had to stop at traffic lights, and we were approached by a policeman who evidently thought that this motley collection of individuals required some investigation. A mild situation by today's standards, it was, nevertheless, somewhat embarrassing, particularly if you were cross-dressing, and we hastily explained that we were just on our way to a fancy-dress party.

In this final year, the course followed much the same pattern. My piano, flute and singing teachers remained the same, but musicianship was now with Herrick Bunney, who had adjudicated John Bell and me in 1958 when we got a first in the duet class at the Renfrewshire Musical Festival. John was now also a student at the RSAM. My singing never reached a professional standard, and although my flute playing had certainly improved, it too was never good enough to enable me to play even in the Academy's Second Orchestra. But my best work was again with the written papers, and in 1964 I passed the advanced harmony and counterpoint paper which was not part of the course. With the Bach Choir, we performed three Bach cantatas in the Stevenson Hall in November; our Christmas Carol Concert, again with the Scottish National Orchestra, was held in the temporary Glasgow Concert Hall. In March 1964, once more in St Mary's Cathedral, the Bach Choir performed Bach's *St John Passion*, and at the end of April, in Paisley Abbey (a new venue for us), the combined choral classes gave Tippett's oratorio *A Child of Our Time*.

Concert-going continued as usual throughout the year. The SNO was back in Greenock in September 1963, again with Phyllis Sellick who played the Schumann piano concerto although she had played it in Greenock just four years earlier, proof that at that time programme planning catered for the standard repertoire (and the artists) that audiences wanted to hear. The conductor was Leon Lovett. In November, Sadler's Wells Opera (Musical Director now Colin Davis) was back in

Glasgow, and I saw their production of Offenbach's delightful *La Belle Hélène*. The lighter side of music – operetta (including G&S), musicals and shows like the *Fol-de-Rols* or pantomimes – was rather sniffily looked down on at the RSAM as we were there to study 'serious' music, but when any of us performed at local concerts (often church concerts) we invariably included lighter items.

Also in November, I got involved with one of George Square Players' productions in Greenock. This was Jean Anouilh's three-act play *Ring Round the Moon*, the second act of which takes place during a Ball. The producer wanted background music throughout the act, and Stewart McMillan was asked to provide this. Stewart then asked me to advise him on what might be suitable, and I suggested a number of items that he put together on his Grundig tape recorder: these were played as the second act progressed. Stewart was credited in the programme with 'Sound Effects', which wasn't altogether unexpected, but I was surprised and delighted to see that I was credited as being 'Musical Director'.

Shortly after this, on November 22, John F. Kennedy was assassinated. My parents still didn't have television, but I remember watching news coverage on sets that were in the window of a radio and television shop in Greenock. Several other people, presumably without sets at home, were also watching: standing outside, of course, we couldn't actually hear anything. From time to time, as I progressed through Secondary school, classmates would, say "Oh, we've got television now", and when I visited friends I would invariably see something 'on the box'. When I asked my parents when (or if) we were going to get one they always said that it would be a distraction for me as I was supposed to be practising the piano and the flute. However, early in 1964, just months away from my final exams, they decided to get one. They might have waited just a little bit longer, but fortunately it didn't prove to be too much of a distraction.

The Alhambra's seasonal pantomime had now become *A Love for Jamie*, and it had some new faces – Jill Howard replacing Fay Lenore, and Terry Hall with 'Lenny the Lion' replacing Reg Varney – although still with Kenneth McKellar as 'Jamie' and Rikki Fulton as his sister 'Lizzie McHaver'. While I enjoyed my serious studies at the RSAM, I had always felt a leaning towards, and affinity with, the lighter side of music and the stage, and if I had known what eventually lay ahead I would almost certainly have tried to get into that side of 'the business' much sooner. But that was for the future.

A sad family event was the death, on February 10, 1964, of Uncle John 'Mappy'. His elder daughter Muriel came over from Western Australia and stayed for some time to attend to various family matters. Muriel, her husband Jimmy (a doctor) and their children Wilma, Peter and Harry, had emigrated in 1954: it took them almost a month to get there, sailing on the SS *Strathnaver*. By 1964, it was possible to fly back, but this might still have taken anything from 24 to 30 hours (if it had been a jet aircraft), with a number of stop-overs perhaps at Singapore, Karachi, Beirut and finally Rome or Frankfurt. If the plane had been a prop aircraft, the journey would have been longer, maybe even 30 to 35 hours. Not for the faint-hearted. As the funeral was in England, I wasn't there myself, and I don't think my father was there either. In the course of her stay, Muriel came up to Scotland, and she was with us for a few days in March. I hadn't seen her since June and Ron's wedding in 1951.

When I became a student at the RSAM I stopped having piano lessons with Mrs Scrymgeour, but I hadn't lost touch with her, and she sked me if I would accompany at a concert given by the St John's Woman's [sic] Guild Choir in St John's Church in Gourock on March 18 which I was happy to do. Mrs Scrymgeour conducted the choir, and there were solos from two well-known local singers, Eileen Witherow and William (Willie) Rodger. Another lady, a Mrs Johnston (listed as an elocutionist) gave, according to a report in *The Gourock*

Times, 'entertaining and versatile readings'. The report also said that I was 'a most proficient accompanist' throughout the evening. Afterwards, Mrs Scrymgeour wrote to thank me for my 'willing and kind help' and wished me luck in my final exams.

April was another busy month. During the first week, I was in Bridge of Allan again where on Monday 6 we witnessed a major fire at the 'Kork 'n Seal' factory. The following night I was back in Glasgow to see Britten's *Peter Grimes* performed by Sadler's Wells Opera at the Alhambra: it was conducted by Leonard Hancock, who would soon be with the new Scottish Opera. Sandy and I then went down to London with Gordon Anderson, a school friend of Sandy who had borrowed his father's car, a little 'Baby Austin', for the trip. We stopped off in Knutsford, Cheshire, to see Sandy's sister Margaret, her husband Jack and their young children Douglas and Graham. They managed to accommodate us, and the following day we went in to the old part of the town and saw the Royal George Hotel which is mentioned in the famous Victorian novel *Cranford* by Mrs Gaskell: there is a plaque on the hotel wall to this effect. We then set off for London, Gordon and I taking turns to drive. It all went quite smoothly until we had an accident. It wasn't serious, but there was some slight damage to the car. Like Duncan Shaw, Gordon wasn't very pleased.

We finally got to London, and found accommodation in an old hotel near Hyde Park. We spent a few days in the capital and saw Lionel Bart's *Oliver*; also a novel form of cinema projection called Circlorama in a cinema at Piccadilly Circus. The auditorium was small and round, and there were no seats, the idea being that you had to keep looking round to get the effect of the numerous projections on the completely circular screen. There were several short episodes, one of which was, I think, a bus or car journey: looking ahead, you could see where you were going, and when you turned round you saw where you had just come from. It was a clever idea, but it was really just a gimmick and wasn't suitable for regular film-making. Indeed, it had a very short lifespan.

The biggest event during my third year was a visit by Her Majesty Queen Elizabeth the Queen Mother on Tuesday April 14, 1964. Her Majesty was Patron of the Academy. As a full-time student, I sang with many others in a performance of Hubert Parry's *Blest Pair of Sirens* (words by John Milton), supposedly one of Her Majesty's favourite pieces. There were several rehearsals for this, and there were instructions concerning dress and admittance to the building. This was by ticket only, and those of us who were performing received our tickets at one of the rehearsals: anyone wishing to be in the audience had to collect his or her ticket from the office.

On the day itself, no-one was to be admitted to the building after 1.00 pm without a ticket, and any students remaining in the building after 1.00 pm would be required to show a ticket to the police who would then clear the building. We, the performers, had to be in position by 3.30 with Her Majesty due to arrive at about 4.15. During this time, there was a piano recital by Raymond O'Connell, a member of the teaching staff. On her arrival, the Queen Mother was received by Dr W.M. Cumming (Chairman of the Academy's Board of Governors) and his wife. Henry Havergal was then introduced. Next, the Queen Mother visited the drama department's television studio where a rehearsal was in progress; after this, she entered the Stevenson Hall to a fanfare followed by the National Anthem. *Blest Pair of Sirens* was now given with two-piano accompaniment, and after this, at around 5.00, the royal visitor was entertained to tea in the Board Room. We then had to leave the Stevenson Hall and file out into the street as no-one was to be allowed on the stairs when the Queen Mother emerged from the Board Room. Just before she left the building, the head janitor, William Dick, was presented. It was an interesting and memorable day.

At the end of April, Greenock had yet another visit from the SNO, the conductor this time being Bryden Thomson who had given me some harmony lessons in my first year on the sudden death of Albert Heeley. The soloist was Joan Hammond, who sang arias by Verdi, Dvorak and Puccini – again, familiar territory. The one unusual item on the programme was the *Suite Française* by Darius Milhaud. Born in 1892, Milhaud was still alive in 1964 (he died in 1974), and a piece by a living composer was rare at these concerts. Then, at the Kelvin Hall Arena in May, came the first Scottish performance of Britten's *War Requiem* after its premiere in Coventry Cathedral in May 1962. It was considered to be the most important new work produced in Britain during my time at the RSAM.

After this came the final exams, following which I received another letter, dated June 2, 1964, this time informing me that I had satisfied the examiners in all subjects and would be awarded the Dip Mus Ed, RSAM, the certificate being presented at the Annual Prize-giving on June 30 in the Athenaeum Theatre. Again, Dr Cumming and his wife did the honours, the former addressing the students, with Mrs Cumming presenting the diplomas and awards. We were not required to wear academic dress for this, just to be smartly dressed. The next step was a two-term course of teacher training at Jordanhill College of Education before embarking on my planned career, but before that came yet another summer job, perhaps the most memorable of all, at Butlin's Holiday Camp at Ayr.

I hadn't thought very much about a summer job this year until the final exams were over, but Sandy Oliver and I then had an idea that as music students we might be taken on as Redcoats at Butlin's. We didn't realise that most of the Redcoats were almost certainly young entertainers who were already in the lighter side of the music business (Des O'Connor was one) which in those days was still known as Variety although even then this was beginning to come to an end, partly due to the rise of television. But we wrote off, fully expecting to be welcomed with open arms, only to get letters back saying "Sorry, we have no vacancies for Redcoats, but we can offer you jobs as pan washers at our Ayr camp". This was a bit of a disappointment, but as we had left it a bit late to start applying for other work we decided to accept the offer, and we duly turned up at Ayr. The job turned out to be what can only be called a 'once in a lifetime experience'.

We were allocated a chalet that was on the upper storey of a two-tier row. Unfortunately, it was quite a long way from our place of work. We were woken up every morning by a song coming through the loudspeakers which were placed at various points throughout the camp. This ditty ended with the somewhat optimistic line "Whether wet or fine/The sun will always shine/On your But-lin's ho-li-day!" What had we let ourselves in for?

The pan wash ('wash' invariably pronounced as in 'bash') was in part of the kitchen block, a rather grim building whose windows, prison-like, were high up in the walls. We worked in shifts that were either 7.00 am-2.00 pm or 2.00 pm-9.00 pm. These operated in rotation, so that if you did the 7.00 am-2.00 pm shift one day you did the 2.00 pm-9.00 pm one the next day. That was good as you had a whole day between them, but after the 2.00 pm-9.00 pm shift you had virtually no time off with the next shift starting at 7.00 am the following morning. If you were late for the early shift, despite the morning serenade blaring through the loudspeakers, someone was soon round to bang on the door to see if you had overslept. We didn't have a proper uniform like the Redcoats, but we were supplied with an outfit consisting of a jacket, trousers and a pair of wellington boots: you certainly needed the latter as there was always water splashing about – even indoors: there was an open drain under the sinks. Our task was to clean the trays that the food was prepared on, and also the large pots and pans that had contained perhaps soup or custard. The sinks were very large – so large, in fact, that I could only just reach the taps by stretching over.

Pan washer at Butlin's, Ayr, 1964.

There were several of us engaged in pan washing. Some were students like ourselves, but others were presumably recruited from the Labour Exchange (known as 'the Burroo' in the West of Scotland: apparently some people there couldn't pronounce Bureau when it was called the Employment Bureau) and, like us, were engaged only for the summer seasons. We thought that one man's name was Paisley, but we found out that he was known by that name as that was where he came from: we never did find out what his real name was. Some of them could barely read or write, and there was one woman who signed her pay slips with a X. The pay itself wasn't very good – about £4.10/- per week – but we didn't have to spend much money as food was provided, and the entertainment was free. There was a post office in the camp, and I opened a savings account and managed to save almost £30.00 – quite a good sum then.

There were some very unsavoury, not to say dangerous, characters among the pan washers, one of whom was known as Mad Jack. He had a violent temper, and he would always react strongly if antagonised. Sometimes, when he was standing at the sink, another character would appear at the door and shout abuse at him. He would react to this by picking up the nearest utensil, often a large pot, and hurling it wildly – not even carefully aimed at his tormentor – so that you had to be on your guard in case you were the one who was hit. Jack was also reputed to have smashed up furniture in the camp with an axe. Coming from a sheltered background, and with a grammar school education, this introduction to the seamier side of life was quite a revelation: it was certainly nothing like the fictional Maplin's Holiday Camp portrayed in the television sit-com *Hi-de-Hi!*

In the pan wash, the trays came to us on a series of mobile frames – effectively shelves on wheels – on which the trays were stacked. If the meal had been a salad, the trays were usually quite easy to clean, but if it had been something like steak pie then we had a much harder job, particularly if the trays hadn't come in immediately after use. Often, by the time we got them, the pie crusts and whatever else had been left on them were beginning to harden; you literally had to scrape most of it off before the washing began. All of this took time, often resulting in an alarming build-up of dirty trays, and there always seemed to be more people on duty when the trays were relatively clean than when they were really dirty and you needed as many people as possible to get through the work. I'm sure that half of these trays were never washed properly as there was always pressure to get them ready for the next meal: every so often a face would appear at the door of the pan wash and we would hear the inevitable "Hurry up wi' they trays". We did our best, but it was often almost beyond us. There were times when there wasn't any hot water, and occasionally we would also run out of detergent. This meant a long walk to the store (which was, typically, at the other end of the camp) to get some more, but sometimes we found that even the store had run out of supplies.

When we had time off, we investigated what entertainment was on offer. A feature of these camps (there were several throughout the country) was a series of competitions such as 'Glamorous Grannies' (someone under forty could win that) or 'Knobbly Knees' although it was often just out of desperation to find something to do that we watched them. There was also a staff talent competition, and Sandy and I decided to enter. Some of the performances were quite bizarre, and as music students we had a very obvious advantage. But the judges were well aware of this, and so we only got a second prize. There was also a cinema. It showed a different film each night, but as campers came for just one week the same films were shown to each new intake. This was a bit limiting for us, but there was one film that I really enjoyed, an off-beat murder mystery called *The List of Adrian Messenger*. It had a wonderful cast – George C. Scott, Kirk Douglas, Herbert Marshall, Clive Brook, Gladys Cooper and Dana Wynter, with a number of guest appearances, in disguise, from Frank Sinatra, Burt Lancaster, Tony Curtis, Robert Mitchum and Kirk Douglas himself. It was easily the best thing on offer, and I looked forward to seeing it every week while we were there.

One thing I didn't realise until we started at Butlin's was that as well as Redcoats there were other groups – Bluecoats, Browncoats, Greencoats, Yellowcoats – the colours indicating either different functions or different levels of seniority. We saw them mainly in the other washing-up area in which we worked from time to time. This was a long room, cleaner than the pan wash, with a few sinks at one end, this area being partially hidden by a screen. The sinks here were quite as large as the ones in the pan wash, and one very small lady who was regularly on duty couldn't reach the taps and had to stand on a box to do so. Quite why she was given the job was anyone's guess, but this was just one of many unanswered questions at the camp. We were in this washing-up area one day, and there was a large pile of boxes near the sinks. One of the colour-coated figures then appeared and said "See they boxes? Get them doon the other end". We duly obliged, but not long afterwards someone in a different coloured coat appeared and said "There's a pile o' boxes doon the other end. Get them up here". We said, politely, that the boxes *had* been at this end but we had been told to move them to the other end. "Don't argue! Get them up here!" This was typical of the way the place was run. Every so often, amidst the chaos, someone would appear and tell us that there was to be an inspection by 'the sanitary'. Panic would then set in, but this was just a ploy to get the place tidied up quickly: I was never aware of an inspection in all the time I was there. The man in charge of the temporary staff said that if it wasn't for the students they would find it almost impossible to run the camp.

Back in the main pan wash, our work continued for some time until, one day, Sandy Oliver was given a chef's hat and was told "You're a cook now" (no previous experience required). He then started working in the kitchen. He told me that life there was even more of an eye-opener than in the pan wash, and if I wasn't working I would sometimes go in to the kitchen to see what was going on. One of the other cooks was 'big Davy', and Sandy asked him one day what he did during the winter. Davy's reply was "Och, ah jist hive a long lie".

Eggs for breakfast were fried on a very large hotplate – maybe a couple of dozen or more at a time. Chefs were supposed to crack the shells with one hand while removing those already on the hotplate with the other hand. But the happy campers were not allowed to have eggs with broken yolks, and if the yolk was broken during cooking the egg was immediately put into a dustbin that stood nearby: this nourishment was eventually given to the pigs of Ayrshire. It was hardly surprising that Ayrshire bacon was so highly thought of. That was perhaps unnecessary waste, but what was even worse was when food that fell on to the floor was not disposed of but was picked up, dusted or even blown on, and then found its way on to some unsuspecting happy camper's plate.

Trays of food were put into the mobile frames that were taken through to the serving area where the food was put on to the plates. The frames were open at one end to allow the trays to slide in, but there was an upright bar at the other end to hold them there. However, as the frames were manhandled so much this bar was sometimes missing (something that wasn't always noticed), and a tray would often be pushed in at one end of what had become an open-ended frame, sail right through and straight out at the other end, scattering its contents on to the floor. Again, the food would simply be picked up, dusted down, and put back on the tray, to be served later to the happy campers. If they had known what went on behind the scenes, I expect many of the campers would have terminated their holidays immediately.

There were hundreds of people at the camp each week, and preparing a meal for each camper was like a production line. Each server had a tray of food, and as the plate came along he or she would put a portion of whatever was on the tray on to the plate. When the tray was empty, the technique was to yell out what was required followed by 'up', and (hopefully) another member of the kitchen staff would then bring a replacement. At meal times there would be a cacophony of strident voices yelling "mince up", "peas up" or (at breakfast) "back bacon!"

When we signed on at Butlin's it was for an agreed length of time. If we stayed the course we would get a bonus. We could leave at any time if we wished, but if this happened before the agreed time (even just a day before) we would forfeit the bonus. Soon after becoming a cook, Sandy was offered a job singing in a production of Kurt Weill's *Happy End* at the Edinburgh Festival. This was obviously going to be more congenial for him, and he had no difficulty in deciding what to do; so he left Butlin's: I don't think the loss of the bonus worried him too much. I stayed on to the end of my agreed time, washing seemingly endless trays and pans (and making sure that I didn't upset Mad Jack), and I finally left with a reasonable bonus to add to what I had saved in my post office account. It had been quite an experience, and it really was 'something else'. For some time afterwards, I had recurring nightmares about the pan wash in which I was sometimes lying in the open drain under the sinks.

It was now time to embark on the next stage of my career, and I duly enrolled at Jordanhill College of Education on Friday October 2, 1964.

Interlude: Jordanhill College of Education – 1964-1965

Jordanhill College of Education was in the north-west of Glasgow, roughly halfway between Great Western Road to the north and Dumbarton Road to the south: the entrance was in Southbrae Drive, off Crow Road, near Jordanhill Station. The buildings later became part of Strathclyde University. Compared with the RSAM, five minutes' walk from Glasgow Central Station, it was more difficult to get to despite the fact that I had now left home and had my first digs in Glasgow which I shared with Sandy Oliver. This was at 22 Westminster Terrace at the western end of Sauchiehall Street and near the Kelvingrove Art Gallery and Museum. It was a very large flat, like so many Victorian houses in Glasgow, and being on the top floor of the building it also had an attic. Sandy and I had rooms at the front, overlooking Sauchiehall Street: our landlady, the enigmatic Mrs Duncan -"I like to take theatrical people, you know" (delivered in a cultivated 'Kelvinside', or pseudo-posh, 'pan-loaf' accent) – called this part of the house 'the flatlet'. Gordon Anderson and Harry Stevenson, and even Sandy's other sister, Sheena, and her husband, Ronnie, also stayed there at one time or another. I don't recall a Mr Duncan, but there was a brother–in-law, Fergie, who seemed to be kept a virtual prisoner in the attic like a character in a Victorian novel. We rarely saw him, but we had an idea that the demon drink played a part in his isolation: he was obviously an embarrassment to Mrs Duncan. Lurid tales of landladies have often been told by people in the theatrical profession, and ours had her share of eccentricities. One of these was to half cook eggs in the evening and leave them overnight in fat before finishing off the cooking process in the morning for breakfast – something we didn't really look forward to. She also had a black cat called Luther.

Sandy, fresh from his experiences at the Edinburgh Festival, was still at the Academy, and so we didn't see much of each other. But other friends, such as Harry Stevenson and Marjorie Smith were also at Jordanhill, and I was very glad of their company at the time. My relationship with Juliet Robertson, who was just going into her second year at the Academy, was still ongoing although that had its problems, and these were exacerbated by my experiences at Jordanhill. Some bold-spirited couples may have lived together at that time, but most of us had been brought up in a rather strict Calvinistic Scotland that still considered this to be unacceptable, and so I didn't really see all that much of Juliet either, except at week-ends.

Having had three enjoyable and more or less carefree years at the RSAM, I wasn't quite prepared for what came next; the two terms at Jordanhill were possibly the lowest point of my entire career. Apart from the RSAM graduates, there may have been a few university graduates with a B Mus, or others with diplomas from the various colleges: the Royal Academy of Music, the Royal College of Music, Trinity College of Music and possibly even the Royal Manchester College of Music (Lawrence Glover, my piano teacher at the RSAM, was an ARMCM). But if there were any such graduates and diplomates, I can't remember them, and that in itself may be an indication of how withdrawn I became during this time. Those of us from the Academy were in the majority, and so we didn't really have to make new friends unless we wanted to. The maintenance allowance was now double what it had been in my first year at the RSAM – £106 a term.

The music department was on the first floor of the Crawfurd [sic] Building; the man in charge was Wilfred Norris. Doubtless a competent musician, he seemed very remote, and few of us took to him. Indeed, the general atmosphere of Jordanhill seemed remote. It was so different from the RSAM, with bells sounding every forty minutes – "to get you used to being in a school". But as I had found much of my own schooling irksome I didn't find this very helpful. It was indeed like being in a school, but once again as a pupil. From day one at Jordanhill I had a sinking feeling in the pit of my stomach that I wasn't going to enjoy the course, and that turned out to be the case.

The timetable was much fuller than the more relaxed one at the RSAM. On Mondays and Tuesdays we were in schools, both Primary and Secondary, and from Wednesday until Friday every forty-minute period was taken up with something – Psychology, Education, Special Methods and even a period of Religious Education; one period was also given over to the lunch break. We had to write essays, and we were even required to give a lunchtime recital, something I had managed to avoid at the Academy. When I did my recital, I was extremely nervous and uncomfortable, but I did have Harry Stevenson beside me to turn pages and give some moral support: otherwise, I don't think I would have got through it. I remember finishing the recital with the *Four Bagatelles* by Alan Rawsthorne, pieces I had studied at the Academy with Lawrence Glover. The last one ends quietly on a chord of C major, and just as the chord was dying away the ubiquitous bell sounded – I was never more pleased to hear it! The College also had an orchestra in which I played as a flautist; that was perhaps the only thing I did enjoy at Jordanhill.

Also on the music staff were William (Bill) Irvine, Margaret (Nellie) Wallace, Tom Johnson and Walter Scott. There may have been others although I don't recall any more. Each tutor supervised several of us for teaching practice, and they would come to watch us taking a class. I was one of Walter Scott's group. He wasn't too impressed with my efforts, but I can't say that I found him particularly sympathetic either. The first schools I was sent to were Rosemount Primary in the Royston district of the city and Oakbank Primary in Maryhill although I have virtually no recollection of either of them. But I do have clear memories of the next school, Bernard Street Secondary in Bridgeton. When I first went there, it was to watch the teacher taking a lesson. It wasn't a very auspicious beginning. There was evidence of a fair amount of vandalism as many of the windows in the music room had been broken. These were boarded over, and the lights were on all day: it was a rather depressing atmosphere. But that was nothing to what went on during the lesson as the poor man (it would be unkind to name him) attempted to get some very unruly boys to sing.

In those days, there was little attempt to tailor a music class to what the children would be familiar with: for many, this was probably only the latest pop songs. The Scottish Education Department's idea of what should be taught seemed to be just a watered down academic course, and this was of no use to children from poorer areas with little or no background in the arts. Trying to teach young boys to sing in two parts when they had little or no interest in the subject or any aptitude for it, and who treated it all as a huge joke, was quite depressing. But as the music teacher struggled with his task during that lesson at Bernard Street two of the boys were literally chasing one another up and down the rows of desks, cheered on by the others. The teacher then tried to restore order by threatening to belt the culprits (using the belt or strap, officially called a tawse but which was known as a Lochgelly as they were made in this small Fife town, was still very much a standard punishment for excessive misbehaviour), but this was treated with derision by the others. He then tried to separate the boys, but their classmates kept moving the desks around to stop him getting near them: at one point the boys were actually climbing over the desks. I couldn't believe what I was seeing, and I was glad to get away at the end of the period.

As the first term neared the Christmas break, I felt more and more that this wasn't the job for me. It had finally dawned on me that teaching is something you really have to want to do: merely being competent in your particular subject is not enough. I had enrolled at the RSAM as music was one of my better subjects, and I thought that I might end up in a grammar school environment similar to that of Greenock Academy. But I now realised that I had no burning desire to teach. Such a situation as I had witnessed at Bernard Street might have been a challenge to a good teacher, but I doubt I would have fared any better had I been in charge that day. I got more and more depressed about the future, so much so that on December 10 I had a meeting with Wilfred Norris at which I told him that I had made a big mistake in taking up teaching, and I wished to leave. But he managed to talk me out of this, and so I stayed on in the hope that I might still get my certificate which would at least be worth having: mercifully, it was only a two-term course that finished at Easter. I still wasn't sure if this was the right decision, but I couldn't think what else I could do. I wasn't good enough to be a solo pianist, but I had never wanted to do be one. I was temperamentally unsuited to it, my experience with the lunchtime recital at Jordanhill proving this beyond all doubt. But it was still an unsettling thought that I might have to spend the next forty years in a job that I basically disliked, and that would have been bad for promotion prospects, no matter how much music itself meant to me. It hadn't occurred to me that I might possibly get a job as a repetiteur, but if I had left Jordanhill at that time, and had found something else, I might never have had the chance to join the D'Oyly Carte Opera Company (albeit some years in the future) when I just happened to be in the right place at the right time when the Company needed somebody to fill a vacant position.

As something of an antidote to my current problems, I was getting more interested in doing arrangements, and for the Christmas concert at Jordanhill I made my first full-scale orchestration in November 1964, an arrangement of *While humble shepherds watched their flocks*. Later, in March 1965, I made an arrangement of the Welsh song *All through the*

Night, also for the Jordanhill orchestra. As I was still involved with the SSC in Greenock, I made an arrangement of the Beatles' song *She loves you, yeah, yeah, yeah* for their next show. I was having harmony and counterpoint lessons with Tom Messenger, and as this involved a lot of fugal writing I turned *She loves you* into a little fughetta and called it *She loves fugue, yeah, yeah, yeah* with the first line as the subject.

When I was young, I seemed to show some aptitude for the stage: I was always dressing up, and I had won the prize as a crusader at the Cub party. My grandmother apparently once said to my mother "That boy will end up on the stage" (although without the usual tag to my mother's "Oh really?" – "Yes, sweeping it"). But as I got older I seemed to lose much of whatever confidence I apparently showed in this thespian proclivity, and, particularly with my piano-playing, I shrank into myself much more. This was why I preferred accompanying to solo playing, and was always happier playing for other individuals or for our SSC shows in Greenock. I did cope with principal roles in the G&S productions at school, and I was able to sing the famous patter songs without too much difficulty, but there were other people on the stage as well, and that may have boosted my confidence. But as far back as I can remember, certainly from Secondary school onwards, I have always had elements of self-doubt and a lack of confidence, and these certainly came to the fore now. This also had an effect on my relationship with Juliet although there had already been problems before I came up to Jordanhill.

Juliet's parents seemed to inhabit a world that I hadn't come across before. Her father and brother had been educated in England, at Shrewsbury School, and both had been to Oxford University; Juliet had also been educated in England, at East Grinstead. Having grown up in a rather different world, this did make me feel somewhat inadequate. The family even lived in a bigger house in Edinburgh than Uncle John's – a large detached villa in Morningside – and they all spoke with English accents (Juliet's mother was actually English). Even at the RSAM this wasn't doing much for my self-confidence, but I think Juliet was very much aware of it, and she often made a conscious effort to sound more Scottish. At the time, however, I definitely felt that I was a bit out of my depth. From a later perspective, and having lived and worked in England for many years, I can see all of this in a different light. But it was new territory then, and I found it quite difficult. Now at Jordanhill, and not doing very well, what little confidence I had in myself had reached rock bottom, and the relationship suffered even more although for the moment it kept going.

Having been persuaded to finish the course, I started the second term at Jordanhill on January 7, 1965, and I soon found myself in a school in the extreme south of the city. This was Glenwood Secondary in Castlemilk, a large housing estate (one of the biggest in Europe with originally some 34,000 people) that had been built in the 1950s, along with several other estates, to house people from inner city areas like the infamous Gorbals that were now considered to be sub-standard. Glenwood Secondary School was built in 1958. To get to it I had to get a 43 or 44 bus to Queen's Park and then a 5 or a 14. I had to leave Mrs Duncan's house no later than 8.00 am – and I was never good at getting up in the morning. At Glenwood, I was again faced with classes of young boys who had little or no interest in the subject (the girls were less of a problem), and although there wasn't quite the same mayhem I still found it a struggle. The head of music was Iain Turpie. I didn't realise it at the time, but Iain would become a large part of my life for the next four years.

The course at Jordanhill continued with classes, concerts, essays to be handed in, and, of course, the dreaded 'crit' lessons: I had one of these on February 8, 1965 with a class of second year boys, with Walter Scott sitting at the back of the room. The structure of the lesson is interesting in seeing what we had to do sixty years ago. First of all, there was voice training with exercises in sol-fa leading to simple bass parts, and although I can't remember if I achieved anything with this (I was using a song called *Buttermilk Hill*) there couldn't have been many boys of that age whose voices would already have settled into either tenor or bass. This was followed by ear training and use of the modulator. I could barely cope with this myself, and so I don't know what these boys thought of it all, but with the presence of an external examiner in the room at least there weren't any discipline problems. Finally, I had to teach a unison song. As always, I was glad when these lessons were over. But shortly after this, despite all the problems and anxieties, I was relieved, and somewhat surprised, to find that I was awarded a certificate which allowed me to teach music in schools. The term ended on April 9, and I was equally relieved to be finished with Jordanhill. That evening there was a party in Edinburgh at the home of one of Juliet's friends. One memory of that event was our collective delight at the latest Beatles' numbers. I was still involved with the SSC, and the following week-end there was another Easter Camp – not at Dalguise this time but at Wiston in Lanarkshire.

Shortly after that, the schools started again for the summer term on Tuesday, April 20, and my brief teaching career began.

Chapter 4: The teaching years – 1965–1969

1 – 1965-1966

Greenock Academy was a grammar school, and most of the pupils came from backgrounds with at least some experience of the arts. We had put on the G&S performances that had been the impetus for me to pursue a career teaching music in schools, and I thought that one day I might be in a school where I could get involved in similar productions. Until I began my teacher training, I had little or no idea of what other schools might be like; Bernard Street Secondary, in particular, was something of an eye-opener. But of course I was never aware of any more positive things that might be happening in the school. My first experience of Glenwood Secondary wasn't as bad as that of Bernard Street, but I still saw little of what else the school might be doing. At Jordanhill, as I was already wondering if teaching was the right job for me, I was genuinely worried about the future before I had even got my first job. But I thought that although I had made mistakes in the initial training period I would hopefully be going somewhere else to make a fresh start. However, this was not quite how it turned out.

Having decided to stay in Glasgow, the way to get a job was to apply to Glasgow Corporation's Education Department, and I duly found myself in the office of Ian Barrie, the man in charge of placing music applicants in schools. He had a large book on his desk with details of vacant positions, and, to my dismay, he said that there was a position at Glenwood School. I can't remember if I said that I would prefer to be starting in a school that I hadn't yet been to, but the job at Glenwood was only for three days a week – Monday, Wednesday and Friday – with Tuesday and Thursday at Allan Glen's, a boys' grammar school in the centre of the city. This would mean that I wasn't in either school for two consecutive days which seemed to be a more satisfactory arrangement, and so I accepted the offer. When I went to the music college in 1961, the salary I could look forward to as a school music teacher with a Dip Mus Ed, RSAM was £750. Yes, that was an *annual* salary: many people currently earn more than that in a week. But now, in 1965, this apparent pittance had risen to £820, and during the four years that I taught it went up by increments until it reached the giddy heights of £1,000. That was a red-letter day.

As a new member of staff, both at Glenwood and Allan Glen's, I found that staff rooms had a hierarchy of their own. If you sat in the first available seat during the morning break, someone would invariably say "Oh, that's Mr so-and-so's seat". I soon got used to this, but the staff room was, nevertheless, a haven from the hurly-burly of teaching. Like many people, I was quite a heavy smoker at the time, and at the break, after the second period in the morning, I would make straight for the staff room, fumbling in my pocket for a cigarette that was usually in my mouth before I got there. It was only during those morning and lunchtime breaks in the staff room that I began to get to know some of the staff in each school. Norman McLeod, who taught Modern Studies at Glenwood, was the representative of the teaching union EIS (Educational Institute of Scotland), and he persuaded me to join. One young art teacher at Glenwood had acquired an old pre-Second World War car with running boards; the children had christened it 'the Eliot Ness special', a reference to a recent popular TV programme *The Untouchables* (1959-63) with Robert Stack as Eliot Ness, an American Treasury Department agent best known for enforcing prohibition in Chicago in the 1930s. The headmaster at Glenwood was James (Hamish) Gardner.

Despite now being a fully-fledged teacher, I didn't find the endless class singing, often with these young boys at Glenwood, any easier. Neither I nor the other assistants did any certificate work with the few students who were at that level: that would have been more interesting. But as well as class singing, we had to teach more serious music appreciation which involved listening to music and talking about European and Russian composers. We even gave them little written exams from time to time, and these resulted in some wonderful howlers, particularly in spellings such as Bathoven, Bramse, Hubert and Mendelsoski. One child's attempt to spell Tchaikovsky resulted in four efforts: Chikoski, Czicosi, Tycozki and Chicosi, all scored out and followed by "can't spell that one right"; on being asked to list sections of the orchestra, one bright spark wrote "Front, left side, right side, back". Another child gave Leningrad as a composer. But the pupils who took music at a higher level could also produce such gems as "Chamber music is music that is so quiet that it is played in a small room" and (describing the evolution of the violin from the older viol) "At first the viol was held between the knees, but gradually worked its way up until it was resting under the chin". An alarming prospect for any potential viol player!

These efforts did not always stem from low intelligence, but often just from a lack of any meaningful cultural background. Some of the children in Castlemilk were in the first stages of a new life away from inner city slums such as the Gorbals, and much of what they were now experiencing was new territory. The teaching programme as laid out by the Scottish Education Department was far from suitable for many of them, but we were stuck with it.

One piece of programme music that I played regularly at Glenwood was *Vltava* (the second of Smetana's cycle of six symphonic poems called collectively *Ma Vlast*), a musical picture of the River Vltava, or Moldau, on its journey through what is now the Czech Republic to Prague and then to its confluence with the River Elbe. I tried to get the children to

think of our own River Clyde with its beginnings near
Elvanfoot in Lanarkshire, flowing through Glasgow to its
emergence into the Firth of Clyde at Greenock's 'Tail of the
Bank'. I don't know if my efforts engendered any love of
Vltava (or classical music generally), but every time I hear this
piece it takes me back to that music room in the upper floor of
the building. I can still see myself gazing out of the window,
and wishing that I was a thousand miles away as the record
was spinning round on an old gramophone.

Another music teacher, Jimmy Geddes, also came in for one
or two days a week, and as he too only took these periods of
class singing we shared our feelings about them. But there was
one other lady who appeared occasionally, and she had some
discipline problems. She also had a curious way of addressing
any child whose hand went up – "Yes, what is it, this boy?"
One day, she was giving out books, and I expect hands were
going up more than usual – "Here, Miss!", "Please, Miss!"
and so on – probably a carefully orchestrated distraction as
the books were being quietly passed along to the pupils at the
windows and then thrown out. Despite this room also being
on the upper floor of the building, it clearly hadn't occurred to
the boys that there was another classroom directly beneath
them, and that there would almost certainly be a class *in situ*
witnessing this shower of books cascading down. The man
taking an English class there was Bob Lennie, who eventually
came up to see what was going on. Our lady music teacher
didn't last too long at Glenwood, and was eventually replaced
by a younger woman. Many years later when I was an organist
in a church in Glasgow I discovered that a lady in the
congregation had been married to Bob Lennie although they
had subsequently parted.

I now got to know Iain Turpie, the head of music whom I
had met earlier in the year, and I had become aware that there
was a lot of music going on in the school apart from the
obligatory one period a week of class singing for most of the
pupils. There were junior, intermediate and senior choirs, folk,

guitar and recorder groups, a string group (including a string quartet), and both a junior and senior orchestra. This was much more musical activity than there had been at Greenock Academy, but, unlike in my own schooldays, there were now instrumental tutors coming to schools regularly. Iain found out that I was keen on doing arrangements, and as early as February 1965, while I was still at Jordanhill, he asked me to do one. Unusually, for me, this was actually an original offering, a short piece for brass quintet called *Valse Lente*; it was followed by another short original piece, also for the brass quintet, called *Fanfare*. The majority of my arrangements have been of existing melodies – hymns, carols, Scots songs, other folk songs or whatever – arranged either for piano, some instrumental group or full orchestra. Later, I did many arrangements for Iain, and this was something that I really enjoyed. But I often had to sit up late at night doing them.

Iain Turpie will long be remembered by many Glenwood pupils in whom he fostered a love of music, particularly choral singing, but he will also be remembered by many, many more through an organisation that he founded in 1962 called the Glasgow Arts Centre. Meeting first of all in the old Girls' High School in Garnethill Street (off Sauchiehall Street) on Friday evenings, it was later expanded to include several Arts Centres: there was one in Easterhouse (another large housing estate in the east of the city) and one in Castlemilk itself. Open to all schools in the Glasgow area, the Centre's various activities included senior and junior choirs, an orchestra, an art section and a drama section, the latter run by Iain's wife, Kay. As I was now at Glenwood regularly, Iain persuaded me to get involved in this worthwhile enterprise, mainly as an accompanist but also to do further arrangements which were often on a larger scale. The Arts Centre was very enjoyable. It had a good social life, and I always looked forward to Friday evenings after a hard week at Glenwood and Allan Glen's. It was the one thing that kept me in teaching longer than I might have stayed. Among many tutors who joined the Arts Centre were Hector McLeod, who took the junior choir, my RSAM friend Sandy Leiper who took the orchestra, and another former RSAM student, Norman Adam: Norman and his brother Renwick were old school-friends from Greenock Academy. When an intermediate choir was formed, it was conducted at first by Hector. Norman then took the junior choir, eventually conducting the intermediate choir himself. Other members like Gordon and Dorothy Gunnee, David Roger and Andrew Muldoon, who all later helped to run the Centres, had themselves joined the Arts Centre when teenagers.

While most of my working week was at Glenwood, my Tuesdays and Thursdays were at Allan Glen's School, then housed in a brand new building in Cathedral Street near the centre of the city. It was founded in 1853 as a Secondary school for boys with nominal fees for tuition: in this latter respect, it was similar to my own school, Greenock Academy. The original building had been further west in Cathedral Street on the corner of North Hanover Street, but the school had moved to the new building as recently as 1964 (both it and the old building have now been demolished). It had acquired a reputation for excellence in science and engineering, but the curriculum included all subjects. The architect Charles Rennie Macintosh was a pupil, as was the actor Duncan Macrae.

The head of music there was Alec McDougall. I got on well with Alec: he had a dry sense of humour that I appreciated. But I didn't get to know many of the other members of staff as I was only there for two days a week: indeed, apart from Iain Turpie, I didn't really get to know many of the Glenwood staff either. In my years with the SSC, I met boys from several of the well-known Glasgow and Edinburgh schools although I couldn't recall any from Allan Glen's. But I was pleased to see that the Club did have a branch here, albeit a small one.

The short summer term was a useful way of easing myself into the job, and towards the end of it there was a Summer Ball at the RSAM to which I went with Juliet. But I was thankful to have another long break during the summer holiday which began as usual at the end of June: the English schools went on for another month. One interesting concert in July was a Scottish National Orchestra 'Prom' at Glasgow's Kelvin Hall at which the conductors were Alexander Gibson (with the SNO) and the jazz musician Johnny Dankworth, who conducted his own orchestra. This was a more adventurous programme, and it included compositions by Dankworth himself – the *Zodiac Variations*, *Lysistrata,* in which the vocal soloist was his wife Cleo Laine, and *Improvisations for Jazz Band and Orchestra*, partly by Dankworth and partly by Matyas Seiber (1905-1960).

I was still having harmony and counterpoint lessons with Tom Messenger, and I was beginning to think that if I stayed in teaching it would have to be with post-school work – perhaps teaching harmony and counterpoint at the RSAM or a similar institution; for that I would need some more academic qualifications. And so I decided to try to acquire an external B Mus from Durham University, and went down to Durham in September to sit the first part of the exam, staying with my old SSC friend Ian Matthew in Newcastle. The Professor of Music at Durham was the legendary and somewhat eccentric Arthur James Bramwell Hutchings (he wrote a hymn tune to which he gave the name 'Fudgie' after his pet dog). The exam was held in the music school on Palace Green beside Durham's wonderful Cathedral. The invigilator was one of the lecturers, Dr James Murray Brown, but Arthur looked in at the beginning to say a few words. For no obvious reason he informed us that he had recently been in France – "and you know what French toilets are like!" That was apparently typical of his style, and it may have been deliberate to try to elicit a smile and put us at our ease. Afterwards, I visited the Cathedral. I passed the first part of the exam, and I continued for some time to have lessons with Tom Messenger.

Back from Durham, I went to another SNO concert in Greenock at which the American pianist Ann Schein played

Rachmaninov's *Rhapsody on a theme of Paganini*. This was followed by Sibelius' third symphony – two somewhat more 'modern' works than usual. I was then in Edinburgh during the International Festival, and saw Britten's comic opera *Albert Herring* given by the English Opera Group at the King's Theatre. I also went to a concert at the Usher Hall. This was similar to the Kelvin Hall 'Prom', but this time it was with the BBC Scottish Orchestra conducted by James Loughran, the similarity being that the Johnny Dankworth orchestra was again playing, and the programme included some of the *Zodiac Variations* and the Seiber/Dankworth *Improvisations*.

Shortly after this, Sandy Oliver and I said goodbye to Mrs Duncan, to the elusive Fergie, to Luther the cat and the half-cooked eggs, and moved from Westminster Terrace to new digs in Cardonald in the south-west of the city. We had contemplated a move for some time, but we were galvanized into action by an advertisement in a local paper that rather took our fancy. It was from a young couple, Con and John Moore, who were looking for two lodgers, and it was worded in a way that made the digs sound a fun place to be. And so on Monday October 4, 1965 we moved to 35 Berwick Drive. Con and John were delightful but also somewhat eccentric. Con's own surname was Boyle, the family name of the Earls of Glasgow although I don't know if there was any connection. She wrote poetry. John, who was from Bristol, was a history lecturer who was completing a PhD thesis. He was tall and heavily bearded, and this made his unfamiliar accent even harder to understand. They had several young children – all girls. The house was large, and it had apparently been a manse. There were other students there too, and so it was all quite hectic. Sandy and I had a double bed-sit on the ground floor next to a communal sitting room.

Living in Cardonald meant that it was slightly easier to get to Glenwood if not to Allan Glen's. But I was soon to acquire my first car which was very useful, particularly as I still had various connections in Greenock. There was, for instance, yet another SSC *All Weather Revels* show just after our move to Cardonald, and I was now the accompanist for the Greenock Male Voice Choir, conducted by a versatile local musician, George Parkhill. They gave two concerts in November 1965 with, as a guest artist, the soprano Patricia Hay who had been a fellow student with me at the RSAM. I could now also drive to Edinburgh at week-ends to see Juliet (the family usually had a somewhat formal Sunday lunch – again, something I had not been used to at home). The car was a 1950s four-door Morris Minor with a split windscreen and semaphore indicators between the front and rear doors. It cost £50, which seemed a fortune to me then, but my parents helped me with this.

There was a Christmas concert at Glenwood on December 15 at which Jimmy Geddes and I accompanied some of the numbers. I also arranged four carols for the orchestra to accompany unison singing. These were *Hark! the herald angels sing*, *O little town of Bethlehem*, *In the field with their flocks abiding* and *The first Nowell*. I also made a second arrangement for the brass quintet of four different carols: *Once in royal David's city*, *A virgin most pure*, the *Coventry Carol* and *O come, all ye faithful*.

In January 1966, Juliet celebrated her 21st birthday. She had always wanted to get engaged on this particular day, and despite my misgivings about it, as I was still very insecure in myself and didn't feel ready to 'settle down', I agreed. The birthday/engagement party was held in her parents' house in Edinburgh; my parents were there as were many of our RSAM friends. It was essentially a cocktail party, and it was certainly a convivial affair. But I still felt a bit out my depth. It also didn't help that I had been told that the engagement would be announced in 'the Telegraph'. My parents never bought or read the broadsheets – my father preferred the *Daily Mail* (he once won first prize in its crossword competition) – but we did get the local paper, the *Greenock Telegraph*, and as that was the only 'Telegraph' I was used to I assumed that that was where the announcement would be. Of course, I couldn't find it; it was embarrassing to find out that it was in *The Daily Telegraph*. Once again, the feelings of insecurity and inadequacy surfaced although, ironically, *The Daily Telegraph* later became my favourite newspaper. Suffice to say that the engagement was eventually broken off. This caused a lot of upset all round – to Juliet, to me and to both sets of parents – but I think it was the best solution at the time. Juliet eventually married another RSAM student, Alec Young, whose brother David, I later discovered, had been in the D'Oyly Carte Opera Company some years before me.

In February, I produced another short original piece for Glenwood called *Marche Grotesque*, this time for a wind sextet: Iain was certainly very persuasive in 'keeping me at it'. Shortly after this, I arrived back at Berwick Drive after another visit to Edinburgh to find that a carton of Gibbs' 'Clinic' shampoo that was in my suitcase had leaked, staining various items of clothing. This was the second time it had happened, and while I hadn't done anything about it before, possibly thinking that I hadn't screwed the stopper on tightly enough, I did now write to Gibbs Proprietaries Limited saying that I thought the product's stopper was faulty. They replied saying that they had had one or two complaints about this particular item and were 'working on it'. They also sent three bottles of shampoo by way of recompense, and they asked me to send any damaged items of clothing to see if these could be cleaned. By then, I had managed to clean most of the clothing myself, and so I simply wrote again to thank them for their offer, which I now didn't need to take up, and also for the three bottles of shampoo. At the end of March, the Arts Centre gave an Easter concert which was mainly choral, but with some solos and a contribution from the orchestra. I didn't do any arrangements for this concert, but the following month I made an arrangement of *The Snowy-breasted Pearl* for TTBB. In April, I was in Edinburgh again, this time to see a production of *The Marriage of Figaro* by Opera da Camera at the Gateway Theatre. Figaro was played by my old Greenock friend Peter Morrison.

Like me, Sandy Oliver had come up to the RSAM in 1961, but he had started with what they called a 'prelim year'. He then went on to do the standard three-year course, but at the end of it he did a further year – five in total – and as he was now about to finish in 1966 I wondered what would happen at Berwick Drive. We both ended our time there and went off in different directions, but our departure was preceded by an incident that might have changed our lives for good.

One evening, a number of us – Con, Sandy, me and some of the other students – were in the sitting room, and at one point someone said "Is something burning?" As most of us were smoking, we began to look around – perhaps one of us had dropped ash behind a cushion – but we couldn't find anything. Then the door opened, and John's head appeared: "I don't want to worry you" he said – quite calmly, I seem to remember – "but the house is on fire". And it really was. It had started upstairs (where these young children were all in bed), and it had already taken quite a hold. There was a lot of smoke. The other students' rooms were also upstairs, and so they couldn't do anything, but as our room was on the ground floor we were able to throw our possessions out of the window and into the front garden. John, to his credit, put a wet towel round his head and went upstairs to bring all of the girls down safely. The fire brigade had been summoned, and they arrived shortly afterwards and were able to put out the fire. But one of the firemen told John that they had caught it in time as the floorboards had already been seriously damaged and would not have lasted much longer. I can't remember if we were told how the fire had started, but John was working on his thesis upstairs, and as a heavy smoker himself he may well have been careless with a cigarette. He certainly lost the research he was working on. Apart from that, we were all very lucky, but it was something I wouldn't like to go through again.

In August, I had an unusual holiday with Juliet and an old family friend of the Robertsons, Leszek Pawlowski, a Pole, who said that he would take us to his home in Huntly in Aberdeenshire for a few days. But we went via the Western Highlands, in his Triumph 2000, visiting several places on the way. One was Applecross, on the coast near Skye: at that time there was only one road to it. From there, we made our way to Inverness and eventually to Huntly where we spent a few days. It was good to see parts of the country that I had not yet visited. When we got back to Edinburgh, Leszek treated us to a meal in the village of Dirleton (east of Edinburgh and home to another fascinating castle that I eventually visited) where I first tasted whitebait. I then began another year's teaching.

2 – 1966-1967

From Cardonald, I now returned to the north side of the city, sharing digs with Norman Adam at 34 Victoria Crescent Road near Byres Road and Glasgow University. Our landlady, Mrs Morrison, occupied the ground floor and basement of what was quite a large end-of-terrace house. There were three rooms and a bathroom on the first floor, and a small self-contained flat and another couple of rooms on the top floor. Norman and I had the largest room, a double bed-sit on the first floor overlooking Victoria Crescent Road, and I had now obtained an old upright piano. Various tenants, not all of them students, came and went. Some we rarely saw. One of them, a cheerful individual, was fond of saying "Isn't nature wonderful", but we got on best with two English girls, Virginia (Ginny) Wood and Jill Hickson, who shared the flat above us: they would often prepare a good Sunday lunch for the four of us. Next to the house was a short road that had been blocked off, and this was an ideal parking place for my car.

I found that I was now very close to Iain Turpie, who lived in an even grander house in Kingsborough Gardens just a few streets further on. Iain either couldn't drive, or, for whatever reason, simply didn't have a car at the time, and so inevitably I found myself giving him a lift to Glenwood every alternate day. We had to leave at 08.00 in order to get through the city with all its early morning traffic, and this took a good hour. I am something of a 'night owl', and I have never been good at getting up in the morning, and so I found that it was easier to shave at night, particularly as I was often sitting up later than usual doing arrangements for Iain – and trying not to disturb Norman. Tuesdays and Thursdays were less of a problem as I was at Allan Glen's which was much nearer than Glenwood, and so I didn't have to get up quite so early.

It was a slow crawl through the city to get to Castlemilk, and Iain, a heavier smoker than I was, got through a good number of cigarettes on the journey. As an ordinary member of the staff at Glenwood, I was given a register class, and I had to be there at 09.00 to check who had turned up and who was absent. But when I called at Iain's house to pick him up at 08.00 it was often to find that he wasn't ready, and on a number of occasions we were late in getting to the school. As a principal teacher, Iain didn't have a register class, and so it didn't matter if he wasn't there at 09.00, but after a while I was asked to see the headmaster, Hamish Gardner, and I was gently chastised on my late arrivals. I told him that I was well aware of the situation, but I was in an awkward position: as Iain's assistant I couldn't very well just drive off and leave him if he wasn't ready. Hamish sympathised and said that he would speak to Iain, and the problem was finally resolved.

As I got to know Iain and Kay better, I often found myself at Kingsborough Gardens, baby-sitting for their younger children, Max and Alison. The eldest child, Karen, was a gifted violinist and was already at the specialist music school run by Yehudi Menuhin at Stoke d'Abernon in Surrey: she was soon to be followed by Max, a gifted cellist. I also got to know a protégé of Kay's, an attractive model whose name was Vicky. We went out a few times although it never blossomed into a romance, but in 1969 Vicky acquired her moment of glory as one of the 'Lager Lovelies' whose photographs, on a series of cans of lager, were part of a successful advertising campaign by the brewing firm of Tennent. I kept one of Vicky's cans for many years, but, sadly, with various moves around the country, it eventually disappeared. However, a book written many years later about famous Scottish products featured reproductions of the 'Lager Lovelies' cans, and so I still have a picture of her. (Empty lager and beer cans also formed a large pyramid that Norman and I constructed on the mantelpiece of our bed-sit.)

Despite my continuing unease with teaching, I was settling into a routine that did have plenty of variety: I was still singing in the Bach Choir at the RSAM, and the Friday evenings at the Arts Centre were a welcome relief at the end of a week's teaching. I was also building up quite a folio of arrangements, not only for Iain Turpie but also for Alec McDougall at Allan Glen's, where they had an orchestra of almost fifty, and occasionally for other people.

I was still the accompanist for the Greenock Male Voice Choir, and on November 12 they gave a joint concert with the Greenock Ladies' Choir whose accompanist was Jinty McLean. (Jinty's mother, Mrs Mair, had been a member of the Frank Buckeridge orchestra that my father had played in.) At this concert, George Parkhill and I played a four-movement piece for two pianos – *Interplay (An American Concertette)* – by the American composer Morton Gould. As a finale to the concert, the entire group gave three *Sea Songs* arranged by Gordon Jacob, but with a two-piano accompaniment for Jinty and myself that George Parkhill had fashioned from the orchestral score.

Back in Glasgow, in the old Boys' High School in Holland Street (near the King's Theatre), the Arts Centre gave its annual Christmas concert on December 17 for which I did arrangements of yet more Christmas carols for the choirs and orchestra – *We three kings of Orient are, I saw three ships* and

Wassail, Wassail, all over the town! I ran the three arrangements together and called the piece *Fantasia on Christmas Carols*, having in mind Vaughan Williams' somewhat more original effort of the same name which I had much enjoyed singing in at one of the RSAM concerts. The following day, I drove to Dunfermline to attend a concert, conducted by Harry Stevenson, which included the Vaughan Williams *Fantasia*. Although I didn't realise it at the time, there was someone in the alto section whom I would later get to know well. Next, on December 21, Allan Glen's gave its Christmas concert to which I contributed another piece, an arrangement for bassoon and orchestra of the Scottish country dance tune *Hamilton House* in which I managed to introduce part of the Grand March from Verdi's *Aida*. Combining seemingly disparate tunes sounds 'clever', but it is easy if the underlying harmonic structure is the same. These arrangements were fun to do, but they were beginning to take up more and more of my spare time.

I now had another car. The Morris Minor's big end had packed up, but there had also been other problems. The heater wasn't working properly (I remember one journey to Edinburgh during which I was almost frozen), and one of the semaphore indicators had been broken and was patched up with sticky tape. My second car was a 1957 Austin A 50 (Cambridge), an early model that still had the originally designed rear end that turned in slightly on itself (later models had the rear end extended further back and had a wider rear window). It also had leather seats, a sunshine roof and a column gear change that I liked and actually preferred to the traditional floor-mounted gear change. The car seemed well sprung, and I decided to call it Bouncer (but not after Miss MacKechnie from Greenock Academy's Primary 4!) It lasted a good bit longer than the Morris Minor.

Nineteen sixty-seven was a very busy year. In January, I orchestrated three hymns for the Arts Centre choirs and orchestra. Along with members of the Clydebank Male Voice

Choir and their conductor, Kenneth Hay, they were to take part in one of the BBC Television *Songs of Praise* programmes under Iain Turpie's direction (Sandy Leiper orchestrated the other hymns). The congregation consisted of members, parents and friends of the Arts Centre. The tele-recording was made in the Couper Institute in Clarkston Road, Glasgow on Friday, March 10, and it was broadcast on Sunday, May 7; the announcer was my old friend Murdoch McPherson. Like many people, I had grown up with the well-known hymn and carol arrangements of Reginald Jacques and David Willcocks in the first *Carols for Choirs* book, and when an opportunity such as this presented itself you tried every trick in the book to make each arrangement, particularly that of the final verse, different from anything that had gone before. The three that I arranged were *All hail, the power of Jesus' Name!* (sung to the tune Diadem), *A safe stronghold our God is still* (Ein' feste Burg) and *Ye gates, lift up your heads on high* (actually a Psalm, to the tune St George's, Edinburgh). As usual, I let my harmonic imagination run riot!

There was another Greenock Male Voice Choir concert in March, the soloist this time being Elaine Blighton, but she was accompanied by George Parkhill. I played for the choral items.

Sadler's Wells Opera were in Glasgow again at the Alhambra in April, and I took the opportunity to see a less-often performed work, Britten's *Gloriana*. This was followed by a Scottish Opera season at the King's in May and June, and among several productions I saw Puccini's *La Bohème*.

At the end of June, I was one of the staff looking after a party of boys from Allan Glen's on a week's holiday in Switzerland. I was in the staff room one day when the man who was to be the leader of the group, Archie Orrock (who taught history although he was also an ordained minister), asked if anyone would be interested in joining him. Up to that time, my only trip abroad had been to Tossa de Mar in Spain in 1962, and this seemed a good opportunity to see another part of the world. The party consisted of forty boys from the second year with four teachers in charge – Archie Orrock, myself and two female members of the staff, Betty Bell and Ann Inglis. Our destination was the town of Champéry, just south of the eastern end of Lake Geneva (or Lac Leman) and very close to the French border. (Not to be confused with the French town of Chambéry [sic].)

As with our trip to Tossa de Mar, we went by train, starting with a journey to London on June 28: we arrived there at 11 pm. There was a coach tour of the city the following morning followed by another train journey to Folkestone, a channel crossing to Boulogne and yet another train journey overnight, this one south-east through France. By the third day we were all somewhat weary of travelling, but early in the morning of June 30, as we neared the Swiss border, we went into a long tunnel and came out into bright sunshine and a wonderful view that lifted our spirits considerably. We then arrived at Basel where we had a continental breakfast of croissants (which were new to me) and coffee that was by far the best I had ever tasted. Next, it was another train journey, this time to Lausanne where yet a further train journey took us to Aigle at which point we boarded a coach that took us to our destination. In Champéry we stayed at the *Hotel du Parc* where I experienced something new – a duvet on my bed. It was, however, very hot with the duvet.

The week was full of excursions. On one of these, we got inside a glacier via a long tunnel (when you are inside a glacier the ice seems a particularly brilliant blue). But all too soon the holiday was over, and we had to endure another three days travelling home. During the first night of the return journey, the train stopped as there was a terrific thunderstorm, but I was fast asleep and was quite unaware of it, only finding out the following morning. This time, we had a bad Channel crossing. Few of the boys, who had been so sprightly during the holiday, turned up for breakfast: those that did looked positively green. I was used to being on the Clyde steamers, and the rough crossing didn't stop me having a hearty breakfast – but with few of the others for company. We arrived back in Glasgow on July 8. There was a reunion in the school hall in October, and I hoped that if I was still teaching next year there might be a repeat of this holiday.

At the end of the month, I was off again. An annual highlight of the Arts Centre years was a choral camp held during the summer holidays in a school in Campbeltown at the foot of the Kintyre peninsula: these courses were memorable for a variety of reasons. A large quantity of mattresses, blankets and other material, courtesy of Glasgow Corporation, was required for the camp, and this all had to be taken down to Campbeltown by road in a ten-ton lorry that the Arts Centre had hired from Herz. I was asked if I would be the driver, and, with some misgivings, I agreed. We picked up the bedding from the Corporation's store at Clive House in India Street (also near the King's Theatre) and set off. The road by Loch Lomond as far as Tarbet was not as good as it is now, and it was, to say the least, a hair-raising journey, although with the cabin being so high you had a good view of the road ahead. The journey, there and back, was luckily without any mishap, and I duly wrote a poem about the experience entitled *My Herz in the Highlands*. Unfortunately, like Vicky's 'Lager Lovelies' can, the poem too has disappeared. I only drove the lorry once. Shortly afterwards, the law was changed, and you had to have an HGV licence to drive a ten-ton lorry. I was quite happy to say that I wouldn't be able to oblige again.

The tutors and helpers had somewhat better accommodation than the children, and Sandy Leiper and I stayed with the headmaster of the school. My bed had the luxury of an electric blanket – yet another new experience. The camps were very enjoyable, and we had a lot of fun; this included playing a joke on any staff member who arrived after the course had started. He or she was told that the penalty for not being there at the beginning was to do the washing-up after the evening meal on the day of their arrival.

The washing-up was done in a very large sink. The new arrival would stand there, washing the crockery and cutlery and putting all the items down on one side, but although these were ostensibly being dried they were quietly being put back in the sink on the other side. After a while, the unsuspecting victim would say "We've used an awful lot of things tonight" at which point other items such as corkscrews, cheese graters, scissors – anything that the others could find (none of which had been used earlier) – began to surface. Eventually, he or she would say "We didn't use that, did we?" at which point the penny dropped. One of the helpers, Aine Carey, was on the receiving end of this prank one evening when she found herself lifting a large fish out of the water. At that point she screamed! Aine was a good folk singer, and with her twin brother, her sister and her sister's fiancé, they formed a group called the Gleanna Four. They made at least one commercial recording. After the Swiss holiday, and the hair-raising journey to Campbeltown for the Arts Centre, I entered my third year of teaching.

3 – 1967-1968

The SSC celebrated its Golden Jubilee in 1962, but the Greenock branch, founded in 1917, could only now celebrate its own Golden Jubilee for which it produced a substantial booklet with a foreword by Stanley Nairne, who again drew attention to the sizeable contribution that Greenock had made to the Club. There was yet another show in October – *All Weather Revels*, Volume 8.

December 1967 was even busier than usual, with an Arts Centre concert in Paisley Abbey on the 17th, Allan Glen's Christmas concert on the 21st and the Arts Centre Christmas concert on the 22nd. This was specifically a Carol Concert for which I did yet another *Fantasia on Christmas Carols* for choirs and orchestra. It was a more elaborate affair than the previous one. The introduction was based on *Christmas Eve* from Carl Reinecke's *The Nutcracker and the Mouse King*, and the four carols were *Of the Father's love begotten*, *A virgin most pure*, the lovely *O Holy Night* by Adolphe Adam (which I had only recently heard for the first time, and which I set for baritone solo and the senior choir) and *Good King Wenceslas*. I really went to town on the last one with different harmonies and orchestral effects. This occupied me from October until November, and the concert again took place in the Boys' High School in Holland Street. It was in memory of Arts Centre member Alex Black who had been drowned during the summer at Machrihanish, west of Campbeltown, when going to the aid of a boy who had been in difficulties. Before the concert, Iain Turpie spent some time in Denmark as he had plans to present concerts there and perhaps to have reciprocal visits from Danish performers.

If I thought that 1967 was a busy year, I found myself even busier in 1968. As the Arts Centre expanded, there were more and more concerts including one in Airdrie on February 1. Later that month, there was a visit to the Danish Institute in Edinburgh as part of Iain's plan to have a regular cultural exchange with Denmark, and in March the Centre's rehearsal venue changed to Allan Glen's which, of course, was familiar territory. There were another two short arrangements for Glen's, and the annual Easter concert for the Arts Centre, after which came the Easter holiday. I was still not happy in the job, and no further forward in deciding what I was going to do, but I hardly had time to think about it as I was involved in yet another 'arrangement' – a very different one – that took up even more of my time.

Iain Turpie was writing an operetta in three acts (to his own libretto) which he called *Highwayman's Inn*. It was to be performed by the pupils of Glenwood School, both cast and orchestra, and Iain asked me if I would orchestrate it. I don't recall ever seeing a complete libretto although the cast were eventually given typed copies of one. Neither was there a complete vocal score, but as a solo, duet, trio or quartet was required, I would be presented, every so often, with these individual pieces in manuscript (they had the vocal lines and a piano accompaniment) which I then had to orchestrate. One result of there being no libretto or vocal score was that I only ever heard Iain referring to the piece, and I was under the impression that it was called *Highwaymen's Inn*. I wrote this title on all the numbers as I orchestrated them, and when I eventually came to have the score bound I had it printed on the cover. It was something of a shock to find that when the operetta was produced it was called *Highwayman's Inn* in the programme – presumably what Iain had intended – although, confusingly, it did say *Highwaymen's Inn* on the tickets! But in any mention of the piece it always sounded like 'men' to me – another sign of my poor hearing which was only going to get worse.

Once the individual numbers had been orchestrated, I then had to add what is usually called 'additional material' to complete the operetta: this included an overture, introductions to the second and third acts, and the finale to the third act, all based on Iain's ideas. This occupied me from January to June, and there were two performances in the Couper Institute in Glasgow on June 18 and 19, 1968. It had been a labour of love, and it involved many late nights burning the midnight oil in our double bed-sit. Again, I hope this didn't deprive Norman Adam of too much sleep.

The Swiss trip the previous year, with the boys from Allan Glen's, had been voted a success, and the following week, on June 26, another group of second year boys left Glasgow for a return visit. I was happy to be having another 'working' holiday. This time, however, there was a change of venue to Einsiedeln in the north-east of the country, roughly equidistant from both Lucerne and Zurich. Einsiedeln is famous for its wonderful baroque monastery (Benedictine) which contains a Black Madonna, one of a number found throughout Europe. We had a similar three-day journey to get there, but this time we travelled to London by coach: in those days, long journeys were all part of the course. The staff remained the same, but with the addition of another young teacher, Norman Wilson, who brought his bagpipes with him. Norman and I also brought our kilts.

The hotel in Einsiedeln was the *Rot Hut*, and the week was filled with numerous excursions including a day in Lucerne where, at the pier, I saw one of the famous Swiss paddle steamers, the *Schiller*, which was very different from the steamers that I had known on the Clyde. We also visited the Grimsel Pass, the Rhône glacier in the Furka Pass, a gloomy gorge (the Aareschlucht) which you could access by way of a somewhat rickety walkway attached to one side, and a climbable mountain (more of a hill walk) called the Hochstuckli. From the latter there was a spectacular view of an equally *un*-climbable set of peaks called the Mythens.

As Norman Wilson had brought his pipes, I wrote a tune for him that I called *Norman Wilson's Farewell to Einsiedeln*. Not being a piper myself, I didn't know how to add the usual embellishments for pipe tunes, but Norman added them to a separate copy that I gave him. One of the highlights of the week was when we decided to walk down the main street at midnight wearing our kilts, with Norman playing the pipes and me accompanying him on a 'drum': this was an empty catering-size jam tin that I had acquired from the hotel kitchen, and I 'played' it with a couple of wooden spoons (I was really just banging out a basic rhythm). The local constabulary turned up to see what the noise was all about, and we might well have been arrested, but thankfully they decided that we were just a couple of harmless tourists. All too soon the holiday was over, and we set off on our homeward journey, arriving back in Glasgow on July 6.

A week later, I was in Campbeltown again. Iain had gone down earlier, and I drove down with Kay and their dog, Jingles, as my travelling companions. The weather was warm and sunny, and I had the sunshine roof open. With far less

Einsiedeln, 1968.

traffic in the 1960s, we virtually had the road to ourselves. We were bowling along, enjoying the lovely scenery in that part of the world, when we came, rather unexpectedly, to a hump-backed bridge. I was really going too fast, and I couldn't slow down in time, and so we actually took off momentarily, coming down with something of a bump. It was just as well that the sunshine roof was open as Kay and I had a brief encounter with the fresh country air. Jingles was in the front seat with Kay, and he too went 'through the roof'.

We did many concerts, often in care homes and hospitals, and one that year (for Biafran Relief) was held in the village hall at Carradale, about twelve miles away. The hall seemed to be in (or to border on) an open field, and as it had been very hot that day a door at the back of the stage had been left open for ventilation. The choir was in front of this door, and they had their backs to it so that they couldn't see it, but I could see it as I was the accompanist, and many of the audience could see it too. During the performance, a cow suddenly appeared at the door and looked in. Unaware of this, the choir carried on singing, but they were wondering why many in the audience were laughing.

The last night of the course was an occasion to let our collective hair down, and another of the tutors, Iain Campbell (a B Mus graduate of Glasgow University), and I did a 'vent' act with Iain as the ventriloquist and me as the dummy, 'Davey', sitting on his knee. We didn't try to emulate any of the famous ventriloquists such as Arthur Worsley, Peter Brough (the voice of 'Archie Andrews', a famous child character on a radio show called *Educating Archie*) or the wonderful Sandy Powell with his spoof vent act (a classic piece of comedy from the years of Variety). Our dialogue was corny in the extreme (mirroring my "Weelie and Jeem" act with Malcolm Cook), e.g. Davey: "My uncle has just bought a matterugly"/Iain: "What's a matterugly?"/Davey: "Nothing, fish face!" There was also a mock strip-tease and the appearance of suitably attired 'ghosts'. It was all good fun.

4 – 1968-1969

As well as the teaching, the Arts Centre and the orchestration of *Highwayman's Inn*, I was still having harmony and counterpoint lessons with Tom Messenger, and at the beginning of September I went down to Durham again to sit the final part of the B Mus exam. But this time I didn't pass. I seemed to be getting involved in too many other things such as doing arrangements. Norman Adam now had a choir, the Falkirk Junior Singers, and for them I made a three-part arrangement (SSA) of *Stille Nacht*. I had also begun to take a regular evening class in general music appreciation in Airdrie, and I enjoyed this more than the daytime teaching. I now began to wonder if it might be possible to become a full-time student again in the hope that I could eventually complete a

B Mus as I would need a university degree if I was going to apply for a teaching job at college or university level. Being a student again would also solve the problem of getting out of school teaching, but I realised that if I did give up my job I would have no income.

The Arts Centre concerts continued. At the Christmas concert, held this time in the City Hall in the Candleriggs (once used as a fruit market), there was another performance of the second *Fantasia on Christmas Carols*. I hadn't been able to write anything new for the Arts Centre as I had decided to write a *Fantasia on Swiss Melodies* for Allan Glen's choirs and orchestra following our second Swiss holiday in June/July. In Einsiedeln, I had bought a book called *Unser Singbuch* (actually published there) which had the words (I presumed in German but perhaps with some Schweizerdeutsch) and music of almost three hundred songs from various sources, and I finally selected three – *Keis Burebuebli...?*, *Spinnliedchen* and *Mein Vater war ein Wandersmann* – which I arranged and orchestrated between October and November. The piece was performed at Allan Glen's on December 19 and 20.

The next big arrangement was a *Fantasia on Scottish Songs* for the Arts Centre. It included *The Yellow-haired Laddie*, *The Deil's awa' wi' the Exciseman*, *The Gallant Weaver*, *I'll Aye ca' in by Yon Toun* and *Mairi's Wedding*, along with snatches of numerous other songs and instrumental tunes that had similar harmonic structures and could therefore be used as counterpoints to the main themes. There were other arrangements too, but these were much less elaborate.

An interesting departure, thanks to Iain Turpie, was to produce two pieces for BBC's *The Epilogue* that used to come at the end of the evening's programmes. The first was another original piece to words by Iain – *Hail King, Hail King, blessed is He!* – and the second was *The First Miracle of Christ* which was in a simple ABA form with the A section by Iain and the B section by me. This *Epilogue* was during Christmas week 1968. It had certainly been the busiest year so far. And so into

1969 which would finally see a big change to my life, including the end of my teaching years.

I had now decided that I should try to obtain a place at Glasgow University to study full time for a B Mus, and at the end of February I had an interview with Frederick (Fred) Rimmer who was the Gardiner Professor of Music. He was quite happy to accept me, but there was a problem – not that I would be a 'mature student' but because I had not managed to obtain even a Lower certificate in a foreign language at school, and that was a requirement laid down by the University: my sin of omission had finally caught up with me. I hadn't required a language to gain entrance to the RSAM, and that was probably why I didn't try hard enough in my last year at school; now I did require one. But all was not lost. Fred told me that if I wanted to pursue the degree course I should try to obtain a language certificate. I could sit the University entrance exam in French, and as I was determined to get into the University I now had an incentive to brush up on the French that I had only half learned at school and pass this vital exam. As ever unsure of my ability to accomplish this on my own, I enlisted the aid of one of the modern language teachers from Greenock Academy, Peter Crumlish, who agreed to give me a crash course. I still considered my parents' home in Greenock as my main home, and I was often there at week-ends when I would go out on a Sunday morning to photograph older parts of the town that would soon be demolished. This time, I would be there during the summer holiday when I could really concentrate on the French. I hadn't had Peter Crumlish as a teacher, having been in 'Biscuit' McFarlane's class, but he had been the producer of the school's *Iolanthe* in 1961 in which I had played the Lord Chancellor, and so he wasn't a complete stranger. I also knew his son Brian, a little younger than me, who had been a member of the tea committee that was part of the school's stamp club run by Harold 'Pot' McNeill.

Two interesting concerts now took place at the City Hall in the Candleriggs. First of all, on Sunday April 27, there was a

recital by Benjamin Britten and Peter Pears. The first half
consisted of Haydn and Schumann, but the second half was all
Britten – the cycle *Winter Words* and four of his folk song
arrangements. Candour compels me to admit that Britten is
not my favourite composer, and Pears is not my favourite
singer, but this was still a rare event, and an occasion not to be
missed.

The second concert was given by pupils from the Menuhin
School on May 25: an equally rare event as Menuhin preferred
his pupils to be practising. But as Karen and Max Turpie were
both at the school, Iain had persuaded the great teacher and
performer (he had recorded the Elgar violin concerto under
the composer's direction in 1932) to allow the pupils to do
this: proceeds from the concert were to go to the school. Karen
and Max were both involved, as was an angelic-looking boy
of about twelve: this was Nigel Kennedy before he adopted a
rather different outward appearance. The full ensemble also
played the *Larghetto* from Elgar's *Serenade for Strings,* a
lovely performance from these young and very gifted players.
It was an outstanding concert, and a rare chance to enjoy it
without being involved. As well as programme notes and brief
biographies of the children, the programme contained a short
history of the Arts Centre, written by Iain, which now had
between 600 and 700 members.

At the beginning of June, I enrolled for the French exam,
and the following week I had my first session with Peter
Crumlish: these would continue until I sat the exam. If I didn't
pass, I would not be accepted for the B Mus course, and so
there was every incentive to concentrate: being older and a bit
more mature certainly helped. But there were still other
pleasures, and on June 25 we set off again for Switzerland
with yet another party of second-year boys from Allan Glen's.
This year, we returned to Einsiedeln; once again, it took three
days to get there although to get to London we reverted to a
train journey, this time overnight, which was notable for an

encounter with someone who was then one of the up-and-coming stars of the entertainment world.

Having got the group more or less settled, we (the staff) were sitting in a separate compartment (it was a corridor train) when one of the boys appeared at the door. I refrained from saying "Yes, what is it, this boy?", but Archie Orrock asked him what he wanted. "Please sir, Jimmy Savile is on the train. Can we ask him for his autograph?" At that time, Savile's famous *Jim'll Fix It* programme had not started, but he was already a big name on *Top of the Pops*: it was only after his death, years later, that the truth about his activities became known. Archie's first reaction was to say "No, you mustn't bother him", but after much pleading he gave in and allowed them to do this. I went up with the boys, and apologised for the intrusion, but he was very affable, and signed as many bits of paper as were offered. I even got his signature myself although it too has disappeared. In the light of what we now know about Savile's life, any surviving autographs might be worth something. Perhaps some of the boys retained theirs.

And so my teaching career effectively ended – but not quite yet. I spent the summer cramming for the French exam, but as the schools started before the University I had agreed to do another month's teaching from the end of August: an extra month's salary (after deductions) of £70.7s.2d was going to be useful. This time, I was sent to a school in Easterhouse, the largest of Glasgow's post-war estates, but I remember little of it. I sat the French exam on September 12, and shortly afterwards I began my first year at Glasgow University.

Chapter 5: Glasgow University – 1969–1972

Year 1 – 1969-1970

The music department at Glasgow University was in University Gardens, a road that runs off University Avenue near the University's main entrance. No. 14 was at the end of a long row of Victorian houses, most of which had been acquired gradually by the University. I duly arrived there at the beginning of term with a certain amount of trepidation. The results of the University entrance exams had not yet been announced: if I didn't pass I would have to leave the course after perhaps the shortest time ever as a full-time student – a possible contender for an entry in *The Guinness Book of Records*. I was also worried that as a mature student (now twenty-five, going on twenty-six) I might not fit in with all these young people just out of school. But I needn't have worried: despite the fact that the music department was much smaller than the RSAM, I still found that I was one of several older students, and not even the oldest: that distinction was held by Dave Milne, a jazz pianist who wanted to improve his general musical knowledge. Dave was thought to be in his late thirties (he was very cagey about giving away his exact age), took his studies very seriously, and would seldom join the rest of us for a drink or any other relaxation, invariably saying "So much to do; so little time!" Two others were William (Bill) Mann and Gerry Goldberg, one being slightly older than me, and the other, slightly younger. Another mature student was Ian Robertson, a very good pianist, who had also been at the

RSAM but had come straight up to the University after that and was now in his final year. Like Ian, I was able to start in the second year of the course by virtue of having a Dip Mus Ed, RSAM. With all of these older students I had no need to feel too old myself.

I can't remember how long I had to wait for the results of the University entrance exams to be published, but it wasn't too long into the first term. They were posted on the University notice board, and when I heard that they were there I was so nervous that I had to get someone to look for me. But, to my great relief, I passed. I also seem to remember that there were just two of us who passed the French exam although I couldn't remember how many actually sat it. But I could now relax and enjoy my second stint as a full-time student.

I had given up a job, but I still had a car, and I was still smoking. These were both eating into my meagre finances, and I had to make some savings. I wanted to hang on to the car, and so the obvious thing was to cut down on smoking or perhaps cut it out altogether. Even then, I had quite a bad cough, and so cutting down on cigarettes seemed a sensible thing to do. There used to be an idea that if you gave up smoking overnight you would have withdrawal symptoms, and so I began to cut down slowly from perhaps twenty a day (one packet: many people got through several packets in a day) to just a few. Once I had got used to this, it was quite easy to give up cigarettes altogether, although for many years I still enjoyed a cigar after a meal, particularly if eating out. Now you can't do that in a public place, and so I have become a complete non-smoker. Cutting out the 'fags' certainly helped to keep the car running, but it was also beneficial to my health.

I found most of the B Mus course, which was much more academic than that of the Dip Mus Ed, very much to my taste, particularly in harmony and counterpoint, orchestration, orchestral score-reading and history, but there were other aspects which were a bit beyond me (and, indeed, beyond many of us) such as acoustics and composition. We had to attend lectures on acoustics in the science department, and they were complicated and hard to follow: we were arts students, and many, like me, would have given up science in their fourth year in Secondary.

As for composition, completing a harmony exercise in the style of Bach, Mozart or whoever was one thing, but there was always general grumbling about original composition, either word-setting or an instrumental piece. I tried setting words from various poets, among them Burns' *Epitaph on a Wag in Mauchline*, Gerard Manley Hopkins' *Inversnaid*, and two short poems by the twelfth century Chinese poet Yang Wan-Li, but, like most of us, I was happier with straightforward pastiche. One instrumental effort was a short piece for oboe and piano that I hoped was in the style of Richard Strauss (I had recently discovered *Der Rosenkavalier*), and another one was a short piano piece in a vaguely early twentieth century style. I didn't give either of these a name, but the piano piece might well have been called *Scherzino*. Beyond these efforts, my musical writing has been primarily arrangements, but I have written a number of Scottish country dance tunes as I have played for many Scottish country dance classes, some of them run by my old friend Stewart McMillan, since my schooldays. For the Golden Jubilee of the SSC in 1962, Stewart devised a dance called *The Jubilee Jig* and I wrote the music.

The first lecturer in composition that we had was Hugh Wood. An established composer himself, he was often quite dismissive about our efforts (usually pastiche) which elicited the general response that we were not composers, and few of us had any original thoughts in that direction. A subsequent lecturer, Martin Dalby (another established composer, who also held the post of Head of Music, BBC Scotland), was much more sympathetic.

Other members of the teaching staff were Edward (Teddy) Garden, Michael Tilmouth, John Currie and Kenneth Elliott, while among the younger members were Peter Dennison,

Warwick Edwards and, later, Stephen Arnold. Kenneth Elliott was a clever and respected academic, and an acknowledged expert on early Scottish music, but he could be prickly. One of our subjects was transcribing lute tablature into modern notation, another part of the course that most of us found very abstruse. Few of us really got to grips with it, but Kenneth, to whom it was probably second nature, couldn't understand this: after one particularly gruelling session he walked out of the room in a huff at our collective incompetence. But in other ways he could also be encouraging. He took a class in orchestral score reading, and one day he asked us to bring along a prepared piece. I brought the score of Bizet's youthful *Symphony in C*, and his eyes positively lit up with delight – at the piece itself rather than at my performance of it, I should add. But it showed another side to his character.

I soon got to know the other students, among whom were John Fisher (who later moved into the world of opera), Jim McCulloch (Jim and I would eventually share a flat) and Iain MacFadyen, known as 'Fudge', who was quite a character. Among the ladies were Elaine Geddes (whose father, Jimmy, had been one of Iain Turpie's assistants at Glenwood), Ann Young (originally from South Africa) and Sheila Hennessey.

Having given up my teaching job, I now had almost no money. Luckily, my fees were paid by the Carnegie Trust as I was deemed to be 'furthering my education', an admirable concept for which I heartily thanked Andrew Carnegie (born in Dunfermline) who had made his fortune in the United States and had become such a memorable benefactor to his native Scotland in so many different ways. (I also discovered that we shared a birthday.) Having already given extra-mural lectures in Airdrie, I was allowed to continue doing this thanks to the composer Thomas Wilson of the University's extra-mural department; this gave me something of an income. These classes were held in Airdrie Public Library on Wednesday evenings. Most of the attendees seemed to want only a bare minimum of information about the music itself, and I was once reprimanded by a lady for talking too much – "We just want to hear the music!"

The music department was also the home of the Glasgow University Music Club whose president was Iain 'Fudge' MacFadyen. Membership was open to anyone, and most of the music students were members. Club meetings took the form of informal concerts given by the members every second Friday evening in the ground floor of the department where there was a grand piano. It was the responsibility of one member of the committee to organise each concert, and a good number of the music students usually took part in them. Inevitably, I became involved with these concerts, and in January 1970 I accompanied a singer, Elizabeth Johnston, in some Handel arias. I don't recall Elizabeth being a member of the music department, but she may have been taking music as a subject for the MA degree. She sang with the University Chamber Singers.

On February 6, at a concert organised by 'Fudge', I accompanied another singer, Josephine Donnelly, who also sang with the University Chamber Singers. Josephine, too, was not a member of the music department, but I had known her from the Glasgow Arts Centre. She sang Thea Musgrave's *Bairnsangs*. One of the music students performing at this concert was Anne Goodwin, who was also from Greenock. Her father, Bobby, was another well-known local musician, a good pianist who had played the famous *Scherzo* by Henry Litolff (part of his *Concerto Symphonique No. 4*) at a concert many years previously when my father played in the orchestra. The following evening, in an entirely different situation, I played at a Burns Supper for a singing teacher I had recently met, Margaret (Maggie) Cotter – another of life's characters. It was a Saturday evening, and this gave an entirely new slant to Burns's famous poem *The Cotter's Saturday Night*.

The term finished (ominously) with an exam on Friday March 13, after which came the Easter break. The following day, I was in Greenock to hear Verdi's *Requiem* given by one of the many excellent amateur choirs in the town, the Greenock Philharmonic Society, which that night fielded all of ninety-nine choristers – forty-one sopranos, twenty-three altos, fourteen tenors and twenty-one basses. Still in existence as I write, their numbers, as with so many other groups, are now just over half of that: some groups, such as the Greenock Male Voice Choir, no longer exist.

I had now decided to try to obtain an ARCM accompanist's diploma in the hope that further letters after my name would be useful in applying for jobs when I had finished my degree. One of the set pieces for the exam was Brahms' non-too-easy *Sonata in A major* op. 100 for violin and piano, and my partner for this was another former colleague from the RSAM, Christine Leiper, yet another musician who had joined the Arts Centre along with her pianist sister Carol, also ex-RSAM. I discovered that I had known Christine's husband, David, when I was still at school as he had been a member of the Glasgow branch of the SSC. It's a small world. I had previously passed the paper work for the ARCM, but the practical was held in London at the RCM on April 22. Thankfully, I passed.

Back in Glasgow, my pianistic ability was tested to the full at another Music Club concert on April 24 when I had to accompany a performance of Schubert's *Erlkönig (The Erl-King)*. This is a notoriously difficult piano accompaniment because of the constant repetition of octaves in the right hand: without a supple wrist, the hand can simply seize up. I actually worked out a way of playing it, using the left hand at certain times when it isn't otherwise occupied. According to the programme, several of the students, including Ian Robertson and Sheila Hennessey (Sheila had organised the concert), took part in this epic, and so it must have been acted out in some way although I don't remember much about it, presumably because I was concentrating on just getting through the accompaniment. The first item on the programme was a performance of Gabriel Fauré's *Dolly Suite*, played as a piano duet by Ann Young and myself. The *Berceuse* from the *Dolly*

Suite was well-known to people of my generation as it was used as the signature tune for the old radio programme *Listen with Mother* with its polite and iconic "Are you sitting comfortably? Then I'll begin".

Although I was a full-time student again, I hadn't given up all of my various outside interests, including the SSC in Greenock: there had been yet another *All Weather Revels* show over two nights in the Arts Guild Theatre in October 1969. I had stopped playing for the Glasgow Arts Centre, but I hadn't given up my association with it. On May 23, 1970 they gave a concert in the City Hall in the Candleriggs with Karen Turpie as soloist in works by Tartini and Novacek. Knowing Menuhin's reluctance to let his pupils perform, I think she had probably left his specialist music school by this time. But I was involved in the concert too as Iain had asked me to do some more arrangements; this time I did three for the choirs and orchestra – *Blowing in the Wind, Tomorrow shall be my Dancing Day* and *All creatures of our God and King.* This was all good practise for the orchestration exercises that we had to do at the University.

Shortly after this, at the beginning of June, we had the end of term exams: two mornings of 9.00 am-12 noon and three afternoons of 2.00 pm-5.00 pm. I was a bit nervous about these although my work had seemed perfectly all right during the year, and there should have been no need to worry: I think I was just feeling that I had to justify my time there. Afterwards, we had to see Fred Rimmer individually when he went through all of our papers. Most of mine were all right apart from acoustics which occasioned a "H'm... yes... well..." from him. But I think that applied to most of us.

And so my first year at the University ended, and I found myself once again with a summer job. I can't remember how I came to apply for this, but I became a caretaker in a twenty-storey block of flats, part of the Sighthill Estate at Springburn, just north of the city centre: built towards the end of the 1960s, these blocks were demolished early in the present century. My duties included cleaning and sweeping out the lifts, mopping out the foyer and dealing with the bins. The lifts could be problematic: sometimes they were filthy, and they would occasionally break down from misuse, forcing the tenants, who were often older people or young women with prams, to use the stairs. As I was the caretaker, I didn't want to risk being caught in a lift if it broke down, and so I used the stairs to trudge up to the top of the building most days to check that all was well in the block. I was standing on the ground floor one day, along with two ladies, when the lift doors opened. I obviously wasn't going in, and this prompted the following exchange:

First lady: "Hive ye changed yer mind?" Me: "Beg pardon?" First lady: "Hive ye changed yer mind? Are no' gaun on the lift?" Second lady: "Weesht, he's the caretaker!" First lady: "Oh my, ah thocht he looked awfy brainy!"

Comments such as these were always worth recording. One day, when I was sweeping up, I heard a lady say to her friend "There the boay still at it." When I looked up, she said to me "If ye keep the place that clean, son, theys'll oaffer ye the joab permanent!"

The bins in these high-rise blocks were very large, and they sat underneath the ground floor openings of the refuse chutes that ran through the building. Each floor had access to the chutes, and there were notices beside the entry points. It was clearly stated on these that the chutes were only to be used between 8.00 am and 8.00 pm, that all refuse was to be wrapped, and that no bulky materials such as cardboard cartons were to be put into the chutes. But these rules were generally ignored. Some tenants would often use considerable force to try to put the most ridiculous things into the chutes: one day, I found a broken drawer, and on another occasion there was a roll of old carpet. These objects invariably caused blockages, and if someone on one of the lower floors was responsible this meant that waste material from above could accumulate as it couldn't reach the bin, and we might end up with a solid column of rubbish, even up to twenty storeys high, inside the building. I had to check the bins regularly, move them when they were full, and put another empty one underneath the chute exit. If I found that a bin wasn't filling up I knew that there was yet another blockage, and I had to report it. A firm (I believe it was Rentokil) would then come to try to clear the chute, and I would be told to "stand well back!"

The stairwell ran up through the centre of the building, and on each landing there were windows – not just ordinary panes of glass, but long horizontal strips with wire through them. There were several of these in each window frame, but they were angled rather like a Venetian blind. On the ground floor of the block, directly under these windows, was the caretaker's office. The office door was on the outside of the building, and one sunny day I was standing in the doorway looking out when one of the panes of glass from several storeys above came crashing down in front of me: it may have become dislodged due to vandalism. It was just as well that I was actually standing inside the office or this might have proved fatal. It certainly gave me quite a shock. On another occasion, a resident, Mr Hood, smashed the office window with his arm as he needed access to the telephone because his wife required medical aid: not surprisingly, Mr Hood also required medical aid after this! The job had something in common with my earlier stint as a pan washer at Butlin's; it was certainly a useful insight into how people lived in these high-rise blocks.

After this, I had a holiday in Spain with Sheila Hennessey and another music student, Stephen Clemes. By now, Sheila and I were beginning to feel a mutual attraction, which must have been difficult for Stephen, and by the time we got back we were definitely, in modern parlance, 'an item'. This relationship lasted until the end of my time at the University, but it too finally ended although we did keep in touch over the years. During the writing of this book, I was looking through a box of old programmes, and I found the one for Harry

Stevenson's concert in Dunfermline, in 1966, which had included Vaughan Williams' *Fantasia on Christmas Carols*. I now discovered that it was Sheila who had sung alto in the choir at this concert. Of course I didn't know her at the time, but I wasn't even aware of the connection when we were together at the University. Sadly, I wasn't able to tell her of this as she had recently died. At her funeral, I met one of her University friends, Anne Spence, whom I remembered, but I also saw one of my RSAM friends, Bob Harvey, whom I hadn't seen for a long time. Bob had come to know Sheila later through a family connection. Small world indeed.

As I was growing up, I became aware that every year my father wrote to a lady, Mrs Player, in Glasgow. Her late husband, Harry, had been a working colleague and friend of my father, and the letters were timed to arrive (hopefully) on his birthday. I believe I met Harry a few times when I was young, but I have only a hazy memory of him: he died around 1950. He was older than my father, and he had been working in Germany on the outbreak of the First World War. Not being able to get home, he was interned, with many others, in a civilian detention camp at Ruhleben near Berlin (it had formerly been a racecourse), and perhaps as a result of this he suffered from bouts of illness throughout his life. These would often occur at work, and my father would look after him.

Harry was involved in the camp's various activities that included sport and productions of the G&S operas. He had a number of fascinating photographs of his time in Ruhleben, several of which were of the G&S productions (*The Pirates of Penzance, The Mikado, The Yeomen of the Guard* and *The Gondoliers* – the female parts played by men, of course), and having taken part in the operas myself at school I found these ones particularly fascinating. Some of them show the musical director, J. Peebles Conn, who eventually conducted the Greenock Orchestral Society in which my father had played (when it disbanded he played in Frank Buckeridge's little orchestra). My father later acquired these photographs,

The Gondoliers – Ruhleben, Germany, 1917.

presumably after Harry's death. I now realised that Mrs Player lived very near me in Observatory Road, just off Byres Road and near my own digs in Victoria Crescent Road, and I duly visited her occasionally. My father continued to write to her until she died.

Year 2 – 1970-1971

The Martinmas term started in October. My second year was really the last year of the ordinary degree course, but I was hoping that I might get an honours degree, and this would entail an extra year. The course continued in much the same way, with an ever-increasing number of harmony exercises in the styles of various composers (this was 'style study'). These exercises included complete fugues, which I enjoyed doing, and writing in up to five parts in the purer styles of the 16th century composers Palestrina, Victoria and di Lasso: this was much harder and less enjoyable. Not only did you have to avoid all the usual pitfalls such as writing parallel fifths, but these exercises had to be written in open score (a separate stave for each part) using not just the treble and bass clefs familiar to all pianists but also the alto and tenor clefs (much less familiar) for the appropriate voices. It was often very frustrating, but it was, as W.S. Gilbert says in *The Mikado*, "a useful discipline". Our exercises were scrutinised by Fred, and they would be returned with corrections and invariably also with his trade-mark 'See me' which implied that you had committed some musical solecism.

This was also a time of discovery. One evening in the department, when most of the students had gone home, Dave Milne came into the library where I was working and asked me if I had ever heard any music by Erik Satie (1866-1925). I knew more about Satie's eccentricities (somewhat akin to those of the composer Lord Berners (1883-1950), who was sometimes labelled 'the English Satie') than his music. Some of his pieces have strange titles (such as *3 Pear-shaped Pieces*: there was actually a performance of this at a Music Club concert on November 13), and the music is often peppered with equally strange instructions for the performers. Dave Milne had just acquired a recording of some of Satie's piano pieces. We went into the lecture room, put on this record, and I heard the *Gymnopédie no. 1* for the first time. That was definitely an eye- (or should that be ear-) opener. We both agreed that the music was haunting, and that it seemed to come from somewhere very far away. Hardly known at the time in this country, the piece has now become justly famous.

I was still in touch with Iain Turpie and the Arts Centre, among whose members were identical twins Tina and Mairi Boyd who were both brass players – Tina, a trumpeter and Mairi, a trombonist. They had been students at the RSAM, and they became good friends. I now became involved in a BBC *Songs of Praise* programme with the Arts Centre choirs, orchestra, drama group and folk singers. I think it had been put together by Iain and Kay Turpie. It was a very dramatic presentation called *The Suffering of the Innocents,* and it was for Palm Sunday, 1971 although it was recorded on November 25, 1970. For this programme, I had to orchestrate the *Procession of Palms* by the Australian composer Malcolm (later Sir Malcolm) Williamson, a future Master of the Queen's Music, but I also had to produce some original work including various fanfares and a setting of words written by Iain Turpie under the title *The Herod Sequence*. This ran as follows:

'By the shadows cast by flickering lampions ....to his soldiers said: "Go forth and rid me of this King. Every boy child – new-born babe – child in arms – those who take their first tottering steps. All shall be slain. All those but recently learned to walk, slay them. Pluck them from behind their mothers' skirts. All shall be slain. Ignore their trusting eyes, ignore their fright, beware their blessed innocence. Slay them, kill them all"'.

Strong stuff indeed. Some of the material was considered quite provocative, and this was stated at the beginning of the programme. The introduction ended with the words "We hope that the next thirty minutes or so will stimulate, interest and entertain as we present our thoughts for Palm Sunday". Despite having little aptitude for original composition, I managed to produce a setting of Iain's text for baritone solo and choir; this was finished on October 28. I then set about orchestrating the *Procession of Palms* and writing the brass fanfares, the latter being completed by November 20 – just in time for the recording on the 25th.

As at the RSAM, the various singing groups at the University, such as the University Chamber Singers and the University Chapel Choir, gave concerts. Among these, very close together, were a Chamber Singers concert, with the University Chamber Orchestra conducted by Peter Dennison, on February 4, 1971, and a Chapel Choir concert on February 6, the choir conducted by 'Teddy' Garden with Fred Rimmer at the organ. I wasn't involved in either of these, but, as at the RSAM, we were expected to attend.

Most of the music at the Chapel Choir concert was by sixteenth and seventeenth century composers such as Byrd, Gibbons and Weelkes, but Fred played a modern piece, *Shima B'koli*, by Vincent Persichetti (1915-1987). Fred also gave organ recitals, and his programmes invariably included contemporary music; sometimes, his own compositions. At one of these recitals he included a piece that required him, at one point, to play as many notes as possible. The only way that he could do this was to more or less sprawl across the manuals with his arms outstretched, producing a really excruciating sound. He was in full view of the audience while he was doing this, and a lady who was watching him thought he had fallen over and was heard to say "Oh, he's fainted!" So much for the *avant-garde*.

Fred definitely had a predilection for modern music, and our choral concerts reflected this. One piece that we did was Thea Musgrave's *The Five Ages of Man*. This was given on Sunday March 14, 1971, along with Verdi's *Four Sacred Pieces*, in the University's Bute Hall. Another work that we performed under Fred's direction was Stravinsky's *Symphony of Psalms*. Fred was also a Director of 'Music Nova', a series of concerts devoted to contemporary music.

I was still taking classes in Airdrie on Wednesday evenings, and, as many of us were, I was singing in the University Choral Society – but not only singing: Fred had asked me if I would take on the job of secretary, and I felt that I couldn't refuse. Membership of the Society cost 10/- (ten shillings, or fifty new pence in today's money) while students had to pay 5/-.

I had to organise one of the Music Club concerts for May 14, 1971, and I based it on settings of Shakespeare, the earliest of these by Henry Purcell (1659-1695), the most recent by Gerald Finzi (1901-1956). The programme also included four settings by Thomas Arne (1710-1778), the delightful *Lo! – here the gentle lark* (from Shakespeare's poem *Venus and Adonis*) by Sir Henry Bishop (1786-1855), set for soprano, flute and piano, and three songs by Sir Arthur Sullivan

(1842-1900). Once again, I was dealing with Sullivan's music although I didn't realise at the time that very soon it would loom very large in my life. Maggie Cotter sang Mrs Ford's aria from the opera *The Merry Wives of Windsor* by Otto Nicolai (1810-1849). To break up this succession of Shakespearean songs, I also persuaded Ian Robertson to play something, and he obliged with the first movement of the *Sonata in D minor*, op. 31, no. 2 by Beethoven and the *Nocturne* op. 15, no. 3 by Chopin. I accompanied all of the settings apart from those by Purcell: they were accompanied by an ensemble that included another student, John Kitchen (harpsichord). John went on to study at Cambridge, and later became a university lecturer in Edinburgh and the city organist there.

There were exams again at the beginning of June. Following these, Norman Adam and I and our respective partners went to the wedding of Ginny Wood, one of the tenants at 34 Victoria Crescent Road: Ginny was marrying a Scot, Ross Jenkins. Next, I started a short but interesting job in the Scottish Music Archive at 7 Lilybank Gardens (this cul-de-sac was near the music department but was approached from Great George Street, off Byres Road). Founded in 1968, with Fred as its Director, the Archive's purpose was to collect and document music by Scottish composers, concentrating at first on music written from 1920 onwards. The advisory committee included representatives of the original four Scottish Universities (St Andrews, Glasgow, Aberdeen and Edinburgh), Kenneth Elliott being the Glasgow representative. The RSAM was also represented, not by Henry Havergal, who had retired by this time (although he was also on the committee), but by Kenneth Barritt, who was now the Academy's Principal. The Archive's Secretary/Librarian was James (Jim) McAdam, who had been Ian Barrie's assistant in the Glasgow Corporation office when I started teaching. Being a relatively new foundation, much cataloguing of material was still required, and Fred had asked me if I would help Jim McAdam with this.

When I finished my stint at the Archive, I had yet another job as a caretaker. It started in August. This time, again a temporary employee of Glasgow Corporation, I was in different blocks of flats: one block, a mere eight storeys high, was at Hillpark in the south of the city while another, higher, block was in Garngad (an area now known as Roystonhill), north-east of the city centre. The duties in these blocks were similar, but I have few memories of that summer – no falling window panes and no blocked refuse chutes: the residents must have been very well behaved!

I enjoyed the various holiday jobs that I had during my time at the University, and there were two that I remember clearly enough although I seem to have no written record of either of them. In one, I was a postman over one Christmas break. The job itself was fine, but I had to be up very early each morning; as this is not my favourite time of day, I found that very difficult – particularly in winter.

The other job might have been during an Easter break. Along with a number of other students (but not my fellow music students) I was working for the Scottish Legal Life Assurance Society whose offices were in the Scottish Legal Life Assurance Building at 95 Bothwell Street. This imposing edifice, near Glasgow Central Station, has a frontage that fills the entire space between West Campbell Street and Blythswood Street, and it extends back to Bothwell Lane, one of a number of narrow lanes between the main streets in the central grid-like part of the city, halfway between Bothwell Street and Waterloo Street.

The Society's information about its clients, some with very odd names that greatly amused us, was contained in a then standard filing system that consisted of thousands of handwritten cards. This information was now being transferred to a newly acquired computer, and they were having a trial run. It was our job to check that the details that came to us on sheets of green computer paper tallied with the information on the old cards: the information, often on two sides of one card, could sometimes be contained on just one line in the computer. We worked in a small room in the heart of the building, and spent all day checking everything, the routine broken by innumerable cups of tea. One day, a member of the staff asked us if we would like to see the computer, and we all said "Oh, yes please." Few of us had any idea what to expect. We then went upstairs to another room where we saw this enormous piece of equipment – so large that we could walk round it. Computers have certainly changed since those days.

Shortly before my last year started, Jim McCulloch and I moved in to a ground-floor flat in Holyrood Quadrant, just off Great Western Road and directly behind St Mary's Cathedral where I had sung numerous times when I was at the RSAM. I can't remember why I left Victoria Crescent Road, but despite the fact that the new flat had plenty of space – with a lounge, kitchen, bathroom and two bedrooms – it was also very damp (our landlady was somewhat reluctant to do anything about this), and so it wasn't exactly a great improvement. We took possession of it on Saturday September 11, 1971, our rent being due weekly each successive Saturday. Sheila and I then had a holiday, and a month later, on Thursday, October 7, I started my last year at the University.

Year 3 – 1971-1972

As a mature student, I had applied myself to the B Mus course perhaps more than I had done at the RSAM. There were only a few students in each year of the course, but this had been whittled down to just two of us, myself and James (Jimmy) Laird who was also from Greenock, in the honours year. I believe Jimmy went on to Jordanhill and became a school-teacher: I had come to the University to get away from that. In this final year, we had to choose one period of study in which to specialise – the earliest times up to 1680, a middle period (1680 to 1890), or the modern period from 1890 to the present day – and we had to produce a dissertation of about 11,000 words on a topic from that period. I chose the middle period, and my topic was *Settings of Lyrics from Shakespeare's Plays*. I had already performed a number of these at a Music Club concert in May; another one was "Come unto these yellow sands" from Sullivan's incidental music to *The Tempest*: incidental music for the theatre was an area of Sullivan's considerable output that was much less well-known.

Soon after the start of term, Sheila and I went to Ledlanet House in Kinross, home to the 'Ledlanet Nights' arts festival founded by the publisher John Calder. We saw a production of Purcell's *Dido and Aeneas* in which the role of Dido was taken by Lorna Brindley, who had been a student with me at the RSAM.

The Music Club concerts continued every second Friday, and if I wasn't performing in them I was usually in the audience. But there were other concerts too. Ian Robertson, who had now left the University, was conducting the Helensburgh Dorian Choir, and as part of a programme given at Bridgend Church, Dumbarton on October 27 Ian and I played a number of piano duets: there were items by Handel, Haydn, Moszkowski, Johnson and Walton. I always enjoyed playing duets, partly from the fuller sound you can get from a keyboard but also because I felt less nervous with two of us playing. As regards this 'safety in numbers' aspect of duet playing, I once took part in a performance of the famous arrangement of the overture to Rossini's opera *Semiramide* by Rossini's contemporary, the pianist and pedagogue Carl Czerny (1791-1857). The arrangement is for sixteen pianists playing as eight sets of duettists, and the performance took place in the piano showroom of Wylie & Lochhead at the lower end of Buchanan Street in Glasgow. (With the adjacent McDonald's these stores became, first of all, 'House of Fraser' and then 'Frasers' [sic].) There are now numerous performances of this curiosity available online, but a little bit of our performance in the 1960s was broadcast as part of a radio news item, and there may well be a copy of it somewhere. The sound of sixteen people playing on eight grand pianos is, as they say, 'something else'.

Although Fred Rimmer was a champion of modern music, the Choral Society did give concerts of more traditional music, one such being on Sunday, December 12 when we presented the *Messa Concertata* by Cavalli (1602-1676), the harpsichord concerto in D minor by J.S. Bach and the *Magnificat* by one of his many sons, C.P.E. Bach (1714-1788). That was the start of a very busy week.

The period that I had chosen to specialise in (1680-1890) included the life and work of Richard Wagner (1813-1883), and one of the year's highlights in Glasgow was Scottish Opera's ground-breaking presentation of Wagner's '*Ring*' cycle (*Der Ring des Nibelungen*), seldom seen in its entirety outside Bayreuth. We had interesting sessions on this mighty conception with a lecturer, Robert (Bob) Meikle, who had recently joined the department.

Scottish Opera had previously staged each of the four operas separately, and they decided to capitalise on this and present the complete cycle. This takes at least four days, but with suitable gaps 'for rest and refreshment', particularly for the hard-worked orchestra, it usually takes almost a full week. The cycle was given during the second week of December 1971: *Das Rheingold* (Monday 13), *Die Walküre* (Tuesday 14), *Siegfried* (Thursday 16) and *Götterdämmerung* (Saturday 18). People came from all over Europe, and possibly from further afield, for the event, and enterprising hotels offered packages for the week. Just to have sat through it all was an achievement, but as impecunious students we were in the cheapest seats in the gods. With the best will in the world, it was hard not to nod off occasionally. But it was still a privilege to have seen it; we were even allowed to go to a rehearsal of *Götterdämmerung* the previous week.

And so into 1972 and my last months at Glasgow University. The old piano from Victoria Crescent Road was now at Holyrood Quadrant, and I spent a lot of time at it, playing over my various harmony exercises. Jim McCulloch also played the oboe, and as well as playing piano duets we would sometimes play pieces for oboe and piano. Jim was now at Jordanhill; I think he disliked it almost as much as I did. During his time there he met Mairi Boyd (whom I knew from the Arts Centre) who was in training for instrumental teaching. Sometime later, he happened to meet Tina Boyd, and was initially somewhat confused, thinking that she was Mairi and that he had already met her. He hadn't known that Mairi had an identical twin sister, and he wasn't the first person who found it difficult to tell them apart. Jim and Tina eventually taught at the same school in Glasgow.

Another of our University colleagues, John Fisher, came to live in the flat, but he didn't stay very long, possibly because of the dampness. One evening, Jim's brother, David, paid us a visit, and we all went out for a drink; while we were out, we were burgled. I don't remember losing anything, but Jim lost a radio which had been a Christmas present from his parents, and our intruder helped himself to the contents of the electricity meter. But we had some good times in the flat. There were occasional parties, and there were visits from other friends, one of whom was Liz Sinclair, who had been at the RSAM with me and who was now teaching.

I too had a radio, and one Friday morning I was in the kitchen listening to Radio 3's *Composer of the Week*. At the end of the programme, the announcer said that Brahms would be next week's composer, and the first programme on Monday would begin with a very rare recording, namely Brahms himself playing one of his *Hungarian Dances* – and actually speaking. Brahms died in 1897, and although I knew that there were a number of late nineteenth century recordings I didn't know that there was one of Brahms. I also had an old tape recorder, and so I decided to try to record this rarity. On the following Monday, I duly set up the recorder and waited in breathless anticipation. Barely audible through a haze of crackle, you could just about hear the composer saying "ich bin Johannes Brahms", and this was followed by the music. But there was so much surface noise that it was almost impossible to hear anything clearly. Nevertheless, I managed to record this little fragment of history – and I may still have it somewhere although it is doubtless now available commercially with the crackle removed thanks to modern technology.

Boys of my generation were seldom encouraged by their mothers to spend much time in the kitchen, and they were rarely taught cooking at school, so that if they found themselves in a self-catering situation when they were first away from home they were often at a loss as to how to prepare even a simple meal. But by this time I had become a fairly tolerable cook, and I was able to pass on some of this expertise to Jim as he too had left school with little or no idea about cooking, so much of which is dependent on timing. One meal I introduced him to was pasta with bacon.

The Music Club concerts continued, and on April 21 I again played the piano part in Bishop's *Lo! – here the gentle lark*, this time with Josephine Donnelly as the soloist and Ben Pateman as the flautist. The Choral Society gave two performances in March (that may have been the Stravinsky *Symphony of Psalms*); I also played for my old school friend Peter Morrison, who was now living in Glasgow and making a name for himself as a singer. But time marches on, and soon our finals loomed. Before this, the very last 'style study' exercise that Jimmy Laird and I had to complete was the rondo *Les Adieux* by Dussek (1760-1812). We were given the first nine bars of the original; my completed exercise was eventually 164 bars long, taking up a full eight pages of manuscript. The significance of the title was not lost on us.

I had now been a full-time student for six years (or six and a half if I include the two terms at Jordanhill Training College), and during this final year of the B Mus course I had to consider what would happen next. Even if I hadn't enjoyed it, I had left a secure and pensionable school-teaching job to try to obtain some more qualifications that might help me find a more congenial post, possibly in a college of further education such as the RSAM, or perhaps even in a university. But I was well aware that such jobs are few and far between, and I couldn't assume that I would automatically find one: I might have to go back to school-teaching. However, it now transpired that I could put off worrying about this as a further three years of study awaited me.

As well as thinking about how to resume my working life at the end of the B Mus course, the possibility of continuing my studies by doing research had been considered before the final exams. It looked as if I was in danger of becoming the eternal student, but the idea was appealing, and if I was offered the chance it would be silly not to take it. But to do research I would have to get a good degree, and even before that I would have to have some idea of the area I wanted to work in. I was writing a dissertation entitled *Settings of Lyrics in Shakespeare's Plays*, and I had taken part in two of the Music Club concerts as the accompanist in several Shakespeare settings, and so I wondered if I might be able to take this idea further as I felt I had only scratched the surface of it. During the early part of 1972, I began to look around to see where I might possibly become a research student with 'Settings of Shakespeare' as a possible subject.

After some initial probing (which wasn't very successful), I received a much more positive letter, dated May 19, from Dr Nigel Fortune of Birmingham University. He said that they would be interested in considering me for a place as a post-graduate student although I would have to get at least a good second-class degree. For the moment, even before the exam results, I would have to complete the enclosed application form; this I did immediately. I then received an acknowledgement, dated May 24, from the Assistant Registrar. Nigel Fortune's letter also touched on the subject matter I had suggested, saying that he had spoken to the staff member likely to be my supervisor if I was accepted. He felt that the subject I proposed was rather narrow (in scope if not in time), and would I be interested in a broader investigation into English Song in the nineteenth century? They were also considering an application from another candidate who wished to work on English Song in the twentieth century, and these two fields seemed to be complimentary. I was more than happy to accept the suggestion: all I needed now was a good enough degree.

Next, I received a letter, dated June 5, from Birmingham's music department secretary Margaret (Maggie) Costello, who said that they were pleased that I could come for an interview on June 15, and would I ring them when I knew the result of my finals. This must have come shortly afterwards as I did get the required degree (a 2(1) – 'good upper second'), and I hoped that the interview would be successful. This was my first visit to Birmingham. I went down by train on June 15, and somehow found my way to the University which is in the Edgbaston district, south-west of the city centre. I got a bus that went down the Bristol Road and dropped me off at the edge of the campus near a pub called *The Gun Barrels*, much frequented by the students. I too would soon get to know it. The interview was successful, and shortly after I got back to Glasgow I received another letter from Nigel Fortune (dated the day of the interview) to say that they were happy to accept me to do an MA by thesis on the subject of Nineteenth Century English Song, convertible to PhD if appropriate. The only proviso was that I was able to obtain the necessary money to continue my studies, but I had already applied to the Scottish Education Department for an award under the Scottish Studentship Scheme, and this was successful. On receipt of Birmingham's acceptance, I wrote to thank them, and I began to look forward to another three years as a student. But before that there was the B Mus graduation followed by one more summer job.

The graduation took place on Friday July 7 at a ceremony in the University's Bute Hall. Unlike the Dip Mus Ed graduation in 1964, academic dress was now required, and I had to hire a gown and the appropriate hood for the B Mus degree. My parents came to the ceremony, and afterwards we had a meal in a local restaurant, something of a novelty for them as they seldom ate out in Greenock.

As a graduate, I could now become a member of the Glasgow University Graduates [sic] Association: it published a journal called *The College Courant*. Some years later, with the end of the D'Oyly Carte Opera Company in sight, I was asked to contribute an article to vol. 66 of the *Courant* (March 1981) on the thorny topic of 'tradition' in the Company. I duly complied, calling my piece *G&S and D'Oyly Carte: The Lively Tradition*. It was in connection with this article that I contacted Muriel ('Poppy') Dickson who had been on the staff at the RSAM. Although I had never spoken to her during my time there, she was very helpful, giving freely of her own time and recalling her years in D'Oyly Carte.

For my last summer job, I was a house porter at the Manor Park Hotel. This was a large nineteenth century building, a former mansion, some miles south of Greenock in an isolated position overlooking the Firth of Clyde between Wemyss Bay and Largs: it was believed that Winston Churchill had stayed there during a war-time conference, held in Largs, on some aspect of the planning of the D-Day landings. There was no accommodation for most of the staff at the hotel, but I had moved out of the flat in Holyrood Quadrant and was living at my parents' home in Greenock. I still had my old car, Bouncer, and I drove to and from the hotel every day.

Being a conversion from a private house, albeit a large one, the hotel only had ten bedrooms, but it had several public rooms, was situated in very attractive grounds, and was popular for wedding receptions. If there *was* a wedding reception, or any other function, the hotel would usually be fully booked, and one of my duties was to go round the following morning to pick up any trays that had been left outside the bedrooms (sometimes, shoes would also be left there to be cleaned) and take them down to the kitchen. Another duty was to clear the tables after receptions, and this included collecting empty wine bottles that had to be disposed of. But some bottles often had wine left in them (perhaps just half a glassful, but sometimes a good deal more), and so before getting rid of them I used to take these (sometimes quite expensive) left-overs back to Greenock and enjoy a glass of Château something-or-other with a meal before returning the empties to Manor Park. That was the best perk of the job.

There was a small storage area in the hotel's outbuildings where, amongst other things, I kept all the empty bottles until they were collected for disposal. As I was the only member of the staff who used this area I decided to brighten it up a bit, and I decorated it with various items including a number of the popular and iconic Chianti bottles with their raffia coverings.

The country had recently adopted the decimal system, and the hotel's restaurant had an *a la carte* menu with the prices listed in new pence. They seem laughable today – caviar £0.55, fresh salmon £1.40, and a T-bone steak £1.75. If your budget could stand the expense you might then have cream [sic] caramel for a whopping £0.20.

The hotel's owner was a Mr Clifford Sabire: I think he came from the Channel Islands. He had become the manager in 1959, buying the hotel in 1967. He was a hard taskmaster. The back stairs down to the kitchen were narrow and steep, and once, when carrying some trays, I misjudged my footing near the bottom: the trays and contents went flying, and I literally bumped my way down the last few steps onto the kitchen floor. I lay there, winded, for a few minutes before Mr Sabire came to see what had happened. He did ask me if I was all right, but I think he was more concerned with the breakages. When I said I thought I hadn't injured myself he said "Well, get up and get back to work now". Other than experiencing back pain for some time afterwards I don't recall any lasting problems from the fall. On another occasion (I forget the circumstances) Sabire complained about something I was doing that didn't please him. I then said "Mr Sabire, this is not a permanent position. I am a student doing this as a summer job. If you don't like what I'm doing I'll be happy to leave at any time, and you will have to find someone else". That seemed to mollify him, and I stayed on at Manor Park until the end of the summer, almost certainly continuing to do whatever it was that had displeased him.

The only other member of the staff that I remember was the barman, Eric, who came from Largs. We would often exchange thoughts about our difficult employer, and Eric certainly helped to make the summer pass more pleasantly. Now it was time for yet another phase of my life; this time, there was also a complete change of scenery with a move away from Scotland.

Chapter 6: Birmingham University – 1972–1975

Year 1 – 1972-1973

I spent three happy years in 'Brum', following in the footsteps of an earlier and better-known fellow-Greenockian, James Watt. I had been told that there was a chronic shortage of digs in Birmingham, and I was advised to contact the University's Lodgings Warden. Accordingly, I went down again in September for a couple of days to look at various possibilities. I wasn't allowed to have even temporary accommodation at one of the Halls of Residence, but I had been given a list of B&Bs in the area, and I stayed at one of the cheaper ones – £2.50 per night! Having looked at several possibilities, I eventually settled for a small flat on the top floor of a house at 5 Frederick Road in Selly Oak, about half a mile from the University. The cooking facilities there consisted of a two-ring electric contrivance (it hardly merited the appellation 'cooker') which took about half an hour to heat up sufficiently to boil an egg. But it was a start. Perhaps I would be able to move to a better place, possibly with other students when I got to know them. I had started at the RSAM not knowing anyone else, although I was still living at home and had my own Greenock friends, but I soon found new friends in Glasgow, and I hoped that I would eventually do so here too.

The first term began on October 2, 1972. I had my car, Bouncer, with me, and it would prove very useful, not just for getting around the city but also for journeys further afield. I had heard of the infamous 'spaghetti junction' at Birmingham, and when I drove down for the start of the term I was a little apprehensive about negotiating it as it was known far and wide for the complexities that had given rise to its apposite nickname. Its official name was Gravelly Hill Interchange, but to most people it was just 'spaghetti junction'. Luckily, I managed to cope with it, and I didn't get lost; in due course I became quite familiar with it.

The music department at the University was in two separate buildings, the main teaching rooms being in the Arts Block that also contained the Elgar Concert Room, Sir Edward Elgar having agreed, somewhat reluctantly, to be the University's first Professor of Music during the years 1905-1908. The Elgar Room had an excellent grand piano. The department's office, under Maggie Costello, and the music library, run by Ken Wilkins (who, strangely, later moved to the RSAM in Glasgow), were in a splendid building, the Barber Institute of Fine Arts, that was almost a mini National Gallery. Its wonderful collection of paintings included works by Turner, Gainsborough, Monet, Van Gogh and Picasso (among many others). There was also, given due prominence, a portrait, by Sir J.J. Shannon, R.A., of Dame Martha Constance Hattie Barber who had set up the institution in the 1930s (following the wishes of her late husband Sir Henry Barber who had died in 1927) as a centre 'for the study and encouragement of Art and Music' at the University. The building also contained a concert hall, and, in the basement, a number of booths where, with headphones, one could listen to recordings.

The supervisor for my research was Dr John Drummond (his recently completed doctoral thesis was on post-Wagnerian opera), who later became Professor of Music at Otago University in New Zealand: he was actually a year younger than me! I saw him from time to time in his room in the Arts Block, but I spent most of my time in the music library. It had a 'stack' [sic] room in the basement where I found long runs of nineteenth century publications such as *Musical News*,

Musical World and *The Musical Times* that I could consult at my leisure – very useful in the days before the internet.

There was much else in the basement including musical scores that had belonged to Sir Barry Jackson, founder of the Birmingham Repertory Company and later director of the Shakespeare Festival at Stratford-upon-Avon: these were bound, with 'B.V. Jackson' stamped in gold on the covers. Some years later, on revisiting Birmingham, I found some of them for sale in a second-hand shop as much had been removed from the stack room to make way for new material. Among these scores was Sullivan's last completed opera *The Rose of Persia* (1899) which I duly acquired.

The Professor of Music was Ivor Keys, a fine pianist (at one concert he took part in a performance of Brahms's *Piano Quartet in A*) who, not surprisingly, was known as 'Ivory' (do parents always think about the names they give their children?) As well as Nigel Fortune, the music staff included the distinguished composer John Joubert (referred to as 'Jumbo' by the students and perhaps best known for his carol *Torches*), Peter Dickinson, Colin Timms and John Whenham, now Emeritus Professor of Music History.

Following Nigel Fortune's letter, I had received one from John Drummond that went deeper into what would be the precise nature of my research: would it be confined to solo song? – would it include several Celtic revivals? – would I have to deal with the influence of German lieder? – and so on. He also asked if Shakespeare still figured in my scheme, and would I kindly let him have a copy of my B Mus dissertation? I did let him read the dissertation, but I said that I wasn't adamant that my research had to concentrate on settings of Shakespeare although there might well be some of these, possibly including the ones I had looked at in Glasgow. I didn't have any clear idea exactly what I wanted to do: all I knew was that they had accepted me to research some aspect of Nineteenth Century English Song, and I trusted that my supervisor would steer me in the right direction.

John Drummond didn't have any specific idea himself about what I might do, but he said that I should begin by making a list of relevant composers to see if anything suggested itself. This initial list consisted of as many well-known composers as I could find who had lived and worked in some part of the nineteenth century and who had written at least a few solo songs, but I was quite surprised to find just how many names it contained – somewhere around 500. I then thought that I should compile another list, this time of both known and now forgotten composers who qualified under these criteria. I compiled this second list from numerous sources, old and new, and I was astonished to find that I ended up with something in excess of 2,500 names. This all took weeks, if not months, and it was becoming unworkable. It clearly wasn't getting us anywhere, and so John Drummond said "Right, we must find one composer who is well-known and who has written a reasonable number of songs that, to our knowledge, have not yet been studied in depth". And so I narrowed this list down to a handful of names, and the one that stood out was Sir Arthur Sullivan.

Three-quarters of the way through the twentieth century, Sullivan's name was still known mainly through his operas written in collaboration with W.S. Gilbert (1836-1911): these came to be known as the Savoy Operas from the author's and composer's association with the Savoy Theatre (built by Richard D'Oyly Carte (1844-1901) and opened in 1881) where most of them were first produced. The best known of them are HMS *Pinafore*, *The Pirates of Penzance* and *The Mikado*. But the Savoy Operas were only a part of Sullivan's extensive output which included a symphony, a cello concerto, the grand opera *Ivanhoe,* other light operas, concert overtures (including the *Overtura di ballo* that was still occasionally played), incidental music for the theatre, oratorios, cantatas, church music including anthems and numerous hymn tunes (the best-known being *St Gertrude*, sung to Sabine Baring-Gould's words "Onward, Christian soldiers"), and also a large number of solo songs of which perhaps only two – *The Lost Chord* and *Orpheus with his lute* – were still sung regularly.

Little of this music was known to the general public (including me) other than to a small band of enthusiasts. The cello concerto was deemed 'lost' as it had not been published (it had been available for hire), and the original manuscript was destroyed in a fire at the music publishers Chappell & Co in 1964. (Some years later, I was able to make a reconstruction from a surviving solo part that had not been at Chappell's, and this, following collaboration with Sir Charles Mackerras who had actually conducted a performance of the work in 1953, was eventually published by Josef Weinberger Ltd.) But the eighty or so original solo songs with piano accompaniment – a large but not excessive number to deal with – seemed fertile ground for research, and Arthur Sullivan (1842-1900) fitted very neatly into the period having lived and died entirely within the reign of Queen Victoria (born 1819) which was from 1837 to 1901. And so finally we had a peg on which to hang something, and it was decided that I should concentrate on some aspect of the songs of Arthur Sullivan. But I was told to stick to these solo songs and not to include other songs, particularly ones from the operas.

Here at last was a subject I could get my teeth into, but we still had to find some way of dealing with it that complied with the academic discipline of research. As so few of these songs had remained in the repertoire, I first had to assemble the material. I had in fact already acquired some of them, including a collection published by the firm of Paxton: this volume contained not only *Orpheus with his lute* but most of the other Shakespeare settings – *O Mistress Mine*, *Sigh no more, ladies* and *The Willow Song*. The one missing from this list was *Rosalind*, and I had to acquire a copy of that along with all the other songs. But I needed to find the earliest published copies, and also, if possible, the actual manuscripts, to find out exactly what Sullivan wrote, including the original key of each song: any popular song would be made available by its publishers in anything up to four different keys to suit high, medium or low voices. Most of these songs were long out of print, and while I was able to find a number of original copies in second-hand shops, I had to obtain most of them from the British Library and other sources. But, after something of a false start, I now had a goal. As there had been, so far, little interest in Sullivan aside from the Savoy Operas this was perfect for me: however it turned out, my research would throw some light on another aspect of his career. As it happened, it was one of the first attempts to look seriously at his other work in a process that continues to this day, ironically as the Savoy Operas themselves are now perhaps less well-known to the general public than they were when I was taking part in productions at Greenock Academy.

As I didn't have to attend any of the B Mus classes, I took a little longer to get to know the younger students, but several of the research students, like me, spent much of their time in the library, and they were among the first that I got to know. Someone who *wasn't* there was the one I had been told might be a companion researcher into Twentieth Century English Song. I never found out why he or she didn't take up this possible course of study.

Among the research students was Hilary Bracefield from New Zealand. Hilary seemed to be about my age and to be another eternal student. She had not completed her B Mus degree as she still had to produce a composition, and she was always saying "I must get this done some day". I don't know if she ever did. I think her research area was Music and Literature in the Eighteenth and Nineteenth Centuries, but she was also very much into the latest developments in music, an area that didn't interest me as so much of it, particularly at that time, seemed very *avant-garde*. When I arrived at Birmingham in the autumn of 1972, Hilary was the associate editor of a contemporary music magazine called *Contact* (the editor was a former student, Keith Potter), and she spent much of her time going to concerts of new music and writing reviews for the magazine. I made half-hearted efforts to support some of these concerts, but I never acquired a liking for any of the music. Later, on Sunday December 17, along with some other students, I did take part in a performance of John Cage's *Musicircus* [sic] at London's Roundhouse during which we did our own thing regardless of what else was going on around us: it might be better described as 'a happening'. Despite our differing spheres of interest, Hilary and I became good friends, and we remained so until her death. She was really *Mrs* Hilary Bracefield, but all we ever gleaned about Mr Bracefield was that he had exited stage left some time previously. Hilary was definitely a 'one-off'.

Another of the research students I became friendly with was Jonathan (Jo) Burton (brother of the television presenter and producer Sir Humphrey Burton), a Cambridge graduate whose research area was 'The Musical Language of the Late Works of Richard Strauss'. Jo introduced me to the world of the clerihew, a distinctive four-line verse invented by Edmund Clerihew Bentley, the author (as E.C. Bentley) of the famous detective story *Trent's Last Case*. The subject matter of Bentley's clerihews is essentially biographical. I don't regard myself as a poet, but I enjoy writing clerihews, and I have produced many examples over the years, often for friends or just for fun, including a number that I entered for a clerihew competition in *The Sunday Times*. One of these ran as follows: 'Richard D'Oyly Carte/Fostered Gilbert and Sullivan's Art/But it was really just a ploy/To help him build the Savoy'. I thought it was quite good, but it didn't win a prize. Another research student was Tony Carver: Tony and Hilary both ended up in the 'groves of academe' in Northern Ireland.

As I began collecting the source material for my research into Sullivan's songs, I also began to fit in with the department's activities such as joining the University Choral Society (as at Glasgow) and attending lunchtime and evening concerts in the Barber Institute's concert hall. Most of these concerts were given by visiting artists (one was Jane Manning, who was known as an interpreter of contemporary music), but one of the lunchtime ones, on November 17, 1972, was given by a student string ensemble from the University directed by one of the B Mus students, James Young, a violinist who came from Edinburgh. With our Scottish backgrounds, James and I soon became friends. Among the other students were James's future wife Vivienne Fuller, Martin Delgado, Peter Wall, Eric Cross, Eric's girlfriend (and later wife) Lindsay Young, Helen Ireland, Nigel Argust and Frank Bowler, these last three being then on the University Musical Society's committee. Frank's girlfriend was another music student, Ruth Cuckson. One day, when I was driving south-west down the Bristol Road (the A38), I saw a destination sign to 'Frankley and Rubery'. These, I discovered, were two areas near the famous Longbridge plant (formerly the home of the Austin car and the famous Mini, and at one time Europe's largest car factory). The similarity to 'Frank and Ruth' amused me, and ever afterwards I always thought of them as 'Frankley and Rubery'. Two other students were identical twins Martin and Paul Hindmarsh who, strangely (like Tina and Mairi Boyd in Glasgow), also played trumpet and trombone. Later, they both graduated with first class honours.

On Wednesday December 6 the University Choral Society and Orchestra, conducted by Ivor Keys, gave a performance of Elgar's *The Dream of Gerontius* with no less a mezzo soloist than Janet Baker. Already a CBE, although not yet Dame Janet, she was still a very big name, but at one of the early choir rehearsals Ivor told us that she had agreed to sing. The other soloists were Richard Lewis (tenor) and Robert Lloyd (bass). As a tenor, I found that not only were we few in number (as in most choirs) but we were further exposed as the *Gerontius* chorus sub-divides at several places, and I found myself singing in the semi-chorus. In one short passage, only the semi-chorus tenors sing with the Angel (the mezzo). The few singing with me appeared to have taken stage fright at this point as, for a mercifully brief moment, I seemed to be the only chorister singing with the distinguished soloist – a truly unnerving experience! Following this, I heard Peter Pears again, this time singing in Britten's *Saint Nicolas* with the Birmingham Bach Society in Birmingham Cathedral.

I then attended a Music Research Students' Conference that was held in Nottingham University, the Professor of Music there being Denis Arnold. There were almost one hundred people present (some of them still undergraduates), with over a dozen of us from Birmingham. Our contingent included lecturers John Whenham and Nigel Fortune, the latter leading a discussion group for, mainly, third-year students who were contemplating research once they had graduated. The range of subjects covered by the research students was remarkably wide, from 'Latin liturgical polyphony in post-Reformation Tudor England' to 'Computer analysis of music', with just about every conceivable subject in between. My research area was listed as 'Nineteenth Century English Song'.

I enjoyed my time in Birmingham, but it was quite a shock to find that much of its architecture was so different, particularly its domestic architecture which was often in a mock-Tudor style. And there were no familiar tenements, just seemingly endless rows of little terraced houses, and all built of red-brick: in Scotland, most of the older buildings are stone-built. Although I had already been in England, this aspect of so many of its buildings had not struck me before. When I was young, most films were in black and white (as was television), and if you saw footage of places in England you were not aware that most of the building material was red-brick and not honey coloured stone (or 'grey granite' as in Aberdeen). My various digs were all in red-brick terraced houses. Later, living in London, I found that much of the brick there is darker (sometimes almost yellow) and, to me, much less glaring: I always felt that Midlands red-brick was particularly unattractive. It wasn't the best introduction to the various building materials to be found elsewhere in England – Cotswold stone, Norfolk flint, or half-timbered work as seen at Lavenham, perhaps the country's best-preserved mediaeval village. Apart from the architecture, I also missed the sea breezes on the Clyde.

As I got to know the other students, both under- and post-graduate, I became aware of any changes in their accommodation, and by the end of 1972 I heard that there would a place available at 49 Harbury Road in the Cannon Hill district, close to the Warwicksire County Cricket Ground at Edgbaston. This was a little further away from the University, but not too far away, and I would now have the company of James Young and Jo Burton. The vacancy was due to Tony Carver leaving to take up a lecturing post at Queen's University, Belfast. Tony had founded and conducted a group called the St Paul's Orchestra, named after St Paul's Church in Birmingham's Ludgate Hill where they gave concerts (James Watt held the freehold of pew 100 there). The first St Paul's concert that I attended was on Saturday November 18. The orchestra's new conductor would be James Young.

One other tenant at Harbury Road, Malcolm Haynes, was not a musician, but he and Hilary Bracefield were 'an item' and so we also saw Hilary regularly too. My first tenancy, at 5 Frederick Road, ended with payment of my last rent – £8.00 – on Christmas Day, and on Sunday January 7, 1973 I moved into Harbury Road. I was there for over a year. Apart altogether from the red-brick, it was a rather dingy house that suffered from an infestation of mice: we set traps at the front door and caught several. Draped over the bannisters were a number of towels that each of us thought belonged to someone else in the house. Eventually, it transpired that not one of us laid claim to them, and so we had to assume that they had belonged to a previous tenant. They were then removed. As Scots, James and I hosted Burns Suppers at Harbury Road in 1973 and 1974.

Having taken extra-mural classes in Glasgow, I wondered if I might be able to earn some extra money (and also get more useful experience for the sort of job I was hoping to get eventually) by taking some classes here, and so I contacted Dr John Waterhouse of the extra-mural department. He was another eccentric individual, prone to cycling around the University with a briefcase on his handlebars. Students who knew him would take delight in waving at him in the hope that he might feel obliged to wave back, with the hoped-for result of him dropping the briefcase and losing at least partial control of the bicycle. But he did give me seven weeks' work between February and April.

Shortly after I moved into Harbury Road, John Drummond asked me if I would take over a role in an eighteenth century opera that he was producing. This was at short notice as someone had dropped out. Although I don't consider myself a singer (certainly not a soloist) I agreed so that the opera could go ahead. I have little memory of the piece although I think the plot involved two brothers. It also contained dialogue, and in that sense it was similar to the G&S operas that I had taken part in. It was staged in the Elgar Concert Room between January 27 and February 3.

As I was now researching the music of a Victorian composer, and with my interest in architecture, I joined the Victorian Society. Based in London, it also had regional groups, and on February 14 (St Valentine's Day) the Birmingham group organised a Victorian Music Hall Entertainment. It was held in a private house in Edgbaston, and tickets were limited, but thanks to Nigel Fortune I was able to get one at a cost of £1.50 which included a fork supper with wine. At the end of February, I went to a performance of *The Yeomen of the Guard* given by the Queen Elizabeth Hospital Operatic Society in the Arthur Thomson Hall in the University's Medical School. The producer was Bill Slinn of the Birmingham branch of the Gilbert and Sullivan Society, and the orchestra, conducted by Roger Flinn (who, I believe, was a doctor), was called the 'Asklepios [sic] Orchestra (Orchestra of the United Birmingham Hospitals)' after Asclepius, the god of medicine and doctors in ancient Greek mythology. Shortly after that, there was another St Paul's concert at which one of the soloists was the clarinettist Colin Lawson, also a research student and later Director of the Royal College of Music.

Next, I was again standing in for someone, but this time as a pianist. Jo Burton played the bassoon in a group called the Icknield Ensemble, founded by another of his brothers, Tony, a Radio 3 announcer and producer, and he was shortly to be taking part in a performance of the *Quintet for piano and wind* (flute, clarinet, horn and bassoon) by Louis Spohr (1784-1859). Shortly before this was due to take place, the pianist had to drop out, and Jo asked me if I would step in. The piano part was difficult, but I somehow managed to get through the performance (at Little Gaddesden) on Saturday, March 3, 1973. Jo's then girlfriend, Mary King (also a student but not in the music department), sat with me for moral support. Mary has since had a high-profile career as a vocal coach.

After all this excitement, things quietened down somewhat, and I was able to get on with my research, trying to narrow it down to a specific aspect. The beauty of research was that I could plan my own day without having to appear at lectures, apart from tutorials with John Drummond, and while I was at the University I volunteered to be a guinea pig at Birmingham's dental hospital – a good way of having your teeth looked after by experts. I would go there from time to time, and, under supervision, the students would start to deal with a filling or whatever. But if they weren't going through the proper procedure, the expert would step in and do it for them. My teeth certainly benefitted from this for many years afterwards – and at no cost whatever.

As I had a car, I was able to visit places like Stratford-upon-Avon, Warwick and Kenilworth; later in the year, after the undergraduates' exams, some of us would have picnics in the countryside. In those days you could get three gallons of petrol for £1 – and even get a few pence change. I got to know other students too. Not all of them were in the music department, but they usually had some interest in music, and often had a musical skill: among them were Alison Nuttall, an oboist, Joy Puritz, a singer herself and granddaughter of the famous German singer Elisabeth Schumann (Joy later translated her father's biography of Elisabeth into English), and Clare Shirtcliff. Clare was reading English and history, but was also a singer, and while still at school had already met some of the Birmingham students that I was now getting to know myself.

Occasionally I would drive down to Hay-on-Wye on the Welsh border, the town of second-hand bookshops. I thought that I might pick up some of Sullivan's songs there, and on my first visit I found a copy of his only song cycle *The Window* of 1871. In its early days, there were plenty of bargains at Hay. As its fame was spreading, large quantities of material would arrive, and often there were crates of books and music lying around, none of the contents processed or priced. You could sift through all of this yourself, and if you found something interesting, the bookseller would quickly think of a price that was often less than you might pay elsewhere. As well as material relating to Sullivan, I found piano music by Moszkowski, Godard, Chaminade and others. On later visits, I found that most of the stock had been processed – higher prices and fewer bargains!

Another of the music students was Geoff Abbott, who had an interest in the music of Kurt Weill (1900-1950). Geoff wanted to put on a performance of one of Weill's shorter pieces, *Das kleine Mahagonny* or *Mahagonny-Songspiel*, portraying Berlin in the 1920s, and I found myself involved in this too. There were numerous rehearsals for it after the undergraduate exams, and the performance took place at one of the Barber Institute lunchtime concerts on July 3. But that wasn't the end of my association with Kurt Weill. After this, on July 6, the St Paul's Orchestra gave a concert in which I played percussion along with Hilary Bracefield. The final number was the famous *Champagne Galop* by the Danish composer Lumbye (1810-1874) in which I had to produce the sound of champagne corks popping at appropriate moments.

The concert was repeated the following evening in Brighton, but it was eventually decided that while it was good to do as many concerts as possible they should be within the Birmingham area.

I then went back to Greenock to see my cousin Muriel, who was here again from Australia. This time, her husband Jimmy was with her. We took them on the *Waverley* whose future at that time was still far from secure. We had a pleasant day, but later there was a long delay because of a damaged paddle float. She eventually limped into Largs, and we had to get coaches back to Greenock. Shortly after this, I was in Birmingham again to begin my second year of research.

Year 2 – 1973-1974

It had taken a good part of the first year to narrow down my subject from the rather too general 'Nineteenth Century English Song' to some aspect of Arthur Sullivan's songs. That was a start, but still more focus was required. The first task was to make a list of all the published songs (a number in excess of one hundred), sorting out the original solo songs with piano accompaniment from others that had come from a variety of sources, the piano parts of these usually being reductions of orchestral scores. Some of the latter group were songs from incidental music to plays; others were melodies from the Savoy Operas with new words (such as *In the Twilight of our Love*, originally Lady Jane's song "Silvered is the raven hair" from Act II of *Patience* (1881)). Another song was *Little Maid of Arcadee*, the only published number from Gilbert and Sullivan's first collaboration *Thespis* (1871). (Although the original score is, like that of the cello concerto, deemed to be 'lost' it is known that Sullivan used at least some of the music in later works.)

So few of the eighty or so original solo songs with piano accompaniment were currently known that we felt that something had to be said about each one, and just sorting out all of this became the main drift of the research. Eventually (it's difficult to say precisely when we fixed on the title) my research subject became 'The Songs of Arthur Sullivan – a Catalogue and Commentary'. Despite being at Birmingham for three years – fully enough time to set anyone on the road to a PhD – I had now used up one year of this before really starting. As a preliminary towards possibly completing a PhD, my first task was to present my research as an MA thesis, something that might have been accomplished in a year if I had known from the beginning exactly what I was going to do.

When I got back from Greenock, I received a letter from John Drummond asking me if I would be prepared to do some teaching in the department the following year. It would be unpaid, but he said that it would be useful experience, and it was something that would look good on a CV. I did eventually do some work that included taking second year keyboard classes and playing for dance classes in the drama department – and I *was* paid for at least some of this.

As I could plan my own time, I paid a visit to Glyndebourne in the middle of August. My old friend Sandy Oliver was singing in Monteverdi's *Il ritorno d'Ulisse in patria*, and family and friends of artists could visit them with rather more freedom than I suspect is the case today. Among the performers were Janet Baker, Laureen Livingstone (another former RSAM student) and John Fryatt whom I didn't know at the time but later got to know well as he had been a former D'Oyly Carte principal.

With my research interest now centred on Sullivan, I found myself involved with the Birmingham branch of the G&S Society. Despite having to avoid dealing with the Savoy Operas, except where necessary (as with *In the Twilight of our Love* and *Little Maid of Arcadee*), I still had a great fondness for these masterpieces, and I eventually became a Vice-President of the Birmingham branch. Later, I also became the

Hon. President of the Glasgow branch of the G&S Society, and it is an interesting reflection on the changes in the country at large, and in attitudes to Sullivan in particular, that, as I write, both of these societies – in the two largest cities outside London – no longer exist. Two members of the Birmingham Society were Bill Slinn (who had produced the Queen Elizabeth Hospital *Yeomen*), Chairman when I joined, and Moreen Moss, Hon. Secretary, who would later become Chairman. Bill died young some years later, but I kept in touch with Moreen for many years.

Sullivan's songs were originally issued by publishers such as Boosey & Co and Chappell & Co, and I wrote to as many of these as still existed to see if they had retained the manuscripts that they had worked from. Any such manuscripts would have perished in Chappell's fire in 1964, but, during July and August 1973, six of them turned up in the archives of Boosey and Hawkes: these related to the original Boosey & Co. Two others were in the archives of Novello & Co. Any such finds are a godsend to researchers, particularly if one is hoping to include hitherto unknown material when presenting a thesis for examination. I was grateful to Novello and to Boosey and Hawkes for supplying me with photocopies of these manuscripts.

Sullivan was unmarried and left no issue although his brother Frederic did have a large family. I have since made contact with one of Frederic's descendants, but without the internet in the 1970s I was unaware of these family connections. One personal contact I did make during this time was with Barry Sterndale-Bennett, a direct descendant of the composer Sir William Sterndale Bennett (1816-1875) who had taught Sullivan at the Royal Academy of Music – a tentative connection, perhaps, but an interesting one.

Along with my research, the year continued with tutorials, concerts in the Barber Institute, visits to the dental hospital and to Hay-on-Wye. There were also occasional visits to the Birmingham Film Society (in association with the University's extra-mural department) where there were talks or screenings of interesting films such as Rossellini's masterpiece *Rome Open City* of 1945.

In November, Geoff Abbott sent out a letter saying that as a sequel to the *Mahagonny-Songspiel* he planned to present another short piece by Kurt Weill, *Der Jasager*, which would be given at the Barber Institute in April 1974. He also intended reviving the *Mahagonny-Songspiel* and presenting both pieces during the 1974 Edinburgh Festival as one of the Fringe events. This definitely sounded interesting, and I agreed to play for *Der Jasager* and to perform at the famous Fringe.

December, as usual, was a busier month than most. On the 5th, the Choral Society gave a performance of Walton's *Belshazzar's Feast*, and on the 11th the University Musical Society's Carol Concert took place in the Debating Hall of the Union; this was followed by an evening in Staff House on the 12th when some of the carols were repeated. Among all my varied activities, I had now taken over the conductorship of the University's Wind Band. Open to anyone in the University, many of the players, not all music students, were flautists and clarinettists, and at rehearsals we often had a glut of these instruments, the music lacking a solid harmonic basis. It was often only at final rehearsals that I would get anything resembling the sound envisaged by the composer (or arranger) when other players, sometimes from the Birmingham School of Music, joined us. But we took part in the two carol concerts, and I orchestrated three of David Willcocks's arrangements – *Of the Father's love begotten*, *The First Nowell* and *O come, all ye faithful* – for the band.

As if all of this wasn't enough, there was now another research conference, this time in Sheffield University, from December 14-17. Overall, the numbers attending were slightly down on the previous year, and there were considerably fewer from Birmingham. But there was one student from Nottingham, Robert Manning, who would soon come to Birmingham to study for a PhD.

And so into 1974. I was now on the committee of the Musical Society as the Wind Band manager, but I was concentrating on finishing off my thesis and getting it typed, bound and ready for presentation. In March, I had another change of address, and I moved to no. 13 Windsor Road in Stirchley, further south of the University. I don't remember why I had to leave Harbury Road, but another of the music students, Rosalind Adams, told me that there was a vacant room in her digs, and I was there for just a month while I completed my thesis. Ros's boyfriend (and later husband), John Bagshaw, lived nearby, and he was at Windsor Road regularly. The house also had a piano.

Around this time, the Scott Joplin piano rags were enjoying great popularity, having been rescued from virtual obscurity by the American pianist Joshua Rifkin. I acquired a volume of these, and I played them regularly as a relaxation to finishing my thesis, often into the 'wee small hours'. John and Ros still remind me of that brief period at Windsor Road.

I had written out my thesis by hand, leaving spaces for the musical examples that I would have to put in, again by hand, once it had been typed and bound. The University required two copies, but the lady who typed it up (Ellen Arnold of 'Cartland Duplicating') told me that she could do a third copy, on thin paper, if I wanted one for myself, and I was happy to let her do this – all for the very precise sum of £34.24. The copies were ready by the end of April, and I then had to have them bound – for a further £8.40. The two required copies were then submitted to the University, and after this I had a *viva voce* examination at the end of the month. For the moment, there was plenty to keep me occupied. The Choral Society had given a performance of Bach's *Mass in B minor* on March 20 (I had sung in it when I was at the RSAM), and, amazingly, there was yet another opportunity to see Wagner's complete *Ring* cycle, now being presented by English National Opera (formerly Sadler's Wells Opera) at the Hippodrome Theatre in Birmingham. This took place during the week of

Monday 6-Saturday 11 May. I still nodded off occasionally. As well as opera, there were regular orchestral concerts in the historic Town Hall given by the City of Birmingham Symphony Orchestra (CBSO), principal conductor Louis Frémaux. I once had an opportunity to play the organ in the Town Hall, and I was told that it had been played by Mendelssohn and had not been altered since. I'm sure that is no longer the case.

By now, I had moved yet again, this time to 149 Mary Vale Road (part of yet another red-brick terrace) in the Bournville area near Cadbury's factory. I was familiar with Bournville chocolate, but I didn't realise until I came to Birmingham that the brand name was taken from the area. Coming back in the evening, you could smell the chocolate well before you got to the house. It was a slightly bigger house than the previous ones I had lived in. The move came about through yet another student connection, this time with Simon Street, the boyfriend, and later husband, of oboist Alison Nuttall. Among the other tenants, not music students, were Rupert Best and Charles Shotton. I was there for just over a year, but we finally had to move because of 'multiple occupancy': apparently this was frowned upon by Birmingham City Council.

My *viva voce* took place on Friday, May 31 at 11.00, and my external examiner was Dr Percy Young, author of numerous books on various aspects of music. Among these was a biography of Arthur Sullivan that had been published just three years earlier in 1971: it was considered the most comprehensive account of the composer's life to date. I was naturally apprehensive about the interview – who would not be? – but there was an added worry. In the course of my research I had discovered that a piece of music thought to have been by Sullivan (an exercise in fugue 'after Mozart'), and which had been accepted by Percy Young as such, was in fact a student exercise by Thomas Attwood (1765-1838) when he had been a pupil of Mozart. Attwood was in turn the teacher of Sir John Goss (1800-1880), who taught Sullivan at the Royal Academy of Music. On Attwood's death, Goss had acquired some of his manuscripts, and Sullivan had obviously seen this particular exercise and had simply copied it out. But he had signed it – A.S. Sullivan – thus blurring its true provenance. I had stumbled on the truth of the matter, and I mentioned it in the introduction to my thesis. While such little nuggets are the stuff of research (good for the individual and always welcome in academic journals), I was now going to be examined by the man who 'got it wrong' and who could pass or fail my thesis. Of course he couldn't fail me on that account. New evidence is always coming to light that changes current views of just about everything: it's an accepted part of research. But as this was an examination, I was wishing that my external examiner was anyone but Percy Young. However, I needn't have worried. I had met the requirements, and my thesis was accepted: perhaps that little piece of research impressed him as, I hoped, the unearthing of all those hitherto unknown manuscripts would have done. Later, I became a good friend of Percy and his wife Renée. Thanks to the wonder of technology my thesis can now be accessed via the following link: http://etheses.bham.ac.uk//id/eprint/15030/.

There were three graduation ceremonies, on 11, 12 and 13 July; mine was on the 13th in the Great Hall of the University at 3 pm. Before it started, there was a recital by George Thalben-Ball, the University organist. The higher degrees were awarded first – two PhDs followed by seven of us graduating MA. I was the last of these, and I had been issued with a printed card reading 'Graduand – seat no. 9. Graduands to be in their seats by 2.30 p.m.' Among the students graduating B Mus were Helen Ireland, Geoff Abbott, Nigel Argust, Ros Adams and Eric Cross. Alone of some sixteen of them, Eric graduated with first class honours, and he also collected the Arnold Goldsborough Memorial Prize. Once again, I had to hire academic dress, this time from the famous London firm of Ede & Ravenscroft in Chancery Lane.

After this, I went down to see my cousins in Liss, and then headed back to Scotland for a well-earned holiday. As a child, my father had spent holidays in Kirriemuir, north of Dundee, and as I had the car we went there for a week to let him visit old haunts. We even managed to see one of his old school friends who now lived at the head of Glen Clova, some miles north of Kirriemuir, a journey that would have been difficult for my parents without transport. After this, I spent another week at the SSC camp at Bruar, and then caught up with the Crawfords. Now it was time for the Kurt Weill pieces – both with libretti by Bertolt Brecht (1898-1956) – at the Edinburgh Festival Fringe.

The performances, presented by Birmingham University Music Society, and conducted by Geoff Abbott, took place in the hall of Old St Paul's Church in Jeffrey Street (just off the Royal Mile and very near the Fringe Club) from Thursday August 22 until Friday August 30. We gathered in the city on August 16, and had several days of intensive rehearsals before we opened. *Der Jasager* (sung in English) was given at 1.00 pm, and the *Mahagonny-Songspiel* at 10.45 pm, one exception being on Sunday August 25 when there was a double bill at 3.00 pm. Tickets cost 35p, and programmes, 10p. The gap between the week-day performances gave us plenty of time to take in the delights of the Festival and all the other Fringe activities: Edinburgh was busy, but not quite as busy as it later became with the development of the Fringe. The operas were scored for a small chamber orchestra which included a piano in *Mahagonny* (which I played), with two in *Der Jasager* (myself and Helen Ireland). There were some half dozen principals in each opera, among whom was Geoff's girlfriend Jane Wynn Owen who, like many other singers and instrumentalists, was often in the music department although not part of it. There was a small chorus in *Der Jasager*, and with cast, orchestra and backstage staff there were about forty-five of us in all. The group had rented several flats, and I stayed in one of these at no. 11 Lauriston Park, not far from The Meadows. We catered for ourselves and supplied our own bed linen – in my case, a trusty old sleeping bag.

It was a marvellous experience, and great fun, marred only by the fact that during the rehearsal week I managed to get a parking ticket. Although I don't recall the details of how this happened, I tried to get out of it by writing to the appropriate authority, but it is seldom that there is a way out of these situations, and while still at Lauriston Park I received a letter to that effect which returned the fixed penalty ticket. I was told that in the particular circumstances "the wardens were acting correctly", and you can't argue with that. But it was a small price to pay for such a good time.

While still in Scotland, I took the opportunity to catch up with my old school friend Allan McEwan and his wife and family who were now living in North Berwick, but soon after that I was back in Birmingham again for my last year of study.

Year 3 – 1974-1975

I could now add MA to my qualifications, and I had registered to convert to a PhD, but I would only be at the University for one more year, and there was no possibility of completing a PhD in that time. But I was still hoping that I might obtain an academic teaching post somewhere at the end of the year, and that I would be able, concurrently, to continue my studies at Birmingham. However, despite having now found a subject – Sullivan's songs – I still had to find some aspect of them, beyond just a 'Catalogue and Commentary', to take my research to the next level. But I knew that I wouldn't complete a degree in a year, and so there wasn't any particular pressure, and I was also getting involved in many other activities, both choral and instrumental.

Having already made a great many arrangements, I felt that I now had a decent, legible 'hand', and I wondered if I might be able to utilise this by doing some professional music copying as this was still being done by hand at that time. John Joubert, who was on the music staff, had written a concerto for bassoon and chamber orchestra, and he had produced a reduction for bassoon and piano that had to be copied. He suggested that I contact his publishers, Novello & Co, who then asked me to send them some specimen pages of this work. They were happy with what I had done, and so I copied out the reduction for them. That occupied me throughout the first term, with a deadline of January 17, 1975. The work itself was first performed in March 1975 although it wasn't published until 1977. In November 1978 I received a copy from the composer with the following inscription – "David, Please accept this example of our joint handiwork! John Joubert. With greetings". I did some more work for Novello, but technology was taking over, and copying by hand was coming to the end of its days. And so that source of income soon dried up.

The extra-mural work started up again with a class in Leamington Spa, but it wasn't well-supported, and had to close after just two weeks. Many years later, as a free-lance musician, I became used to work ceasing fairly soon after a promising beginning.

On the night of November 21, 1974, bombs exploded in two Birmingham public houses, killing twenty-one people and injuring one hundred and eighty-two others. This, the worst act of terrorism in England since the Second World War, was supposedly the work of the Provisional IRA and part of what was known as 'the Troubles'. I had planned to see a ballet production the following evening, and I wondered if it would now go ahead – and even if I would be able to get into the city centre. But I did get in as planned, and I was surprised to see that the theatre was open, probably as an act of defiance. However, many people had clearly stayed away, and it was a half-empty house – a rare occurrence in the world of ballet. The programme that night consisted of Tchaikovsky's *Swan Lake*, *Études* (the music based on Czerny's piano exercises) and *Prodigal Son* (the music being the piano rags of Scott Joplin that I had played during the time I was preparing my thesis).

The next major event at the University was a production of Carl Orff's famous *Carmina Burana* of 1937, the second half of a concert that also included Bach's motet *O Praise the Lord, All ye Nations* and the *Te Deum* from Verdi's *Four Sacred Pieces* (1898). Yes, *Carmina Burana* was a production and not just a performance: it was the first danced performance by an English company, and as the songs are student songs it was appropriate that it was given in a university. The producer was my supervisor John Drummond, the orchestra was the CBSO, conducted by Ivor Keys, and the action was provided by the drama department (under Jocelyn Powell) and the Birmingham University Studio Dance Company. The soloists were Sandra Dugdale, whom I had previously met at Glyndebourne, Robert Bateman and Bonaventura Bottone. I would later work with all three although at the time I had no idea that this would happen. There were two performances, on November 29 and 30, in the Great Hall of the University where a huge wheel – the 'wheel of fortune' – had been erected behind the choir, soloists and orchestra. The work is exciting to take part in simply as a concert performance, but this staging gave it something extra: not merely exciting, these performances were thrilling.

On December 7, I took part in a Victorian Evening at the Midland Institute. Again, I played Bishop's *Lo! – here the gentle lark*, and a similar composition of his with flute obbligato, *The Gypsy and the Bird*. The programme also included vocal duets, piano duets, music for clarinet and piano, and an arrangement for six hands at one piano of *Qui Vive* by Wilhelm Ganz. That was great fun to do.

I was still conducting the Wind Band, and as it was also being used for the 1974 Carol Concert I did some more arrangements including a re-arrangement of *Good King Wenceslas* that I had previously arranged for choir and orchestra. One of the players said that he thought it was like a miniature symphonic poem. Following the end of term, a couple of days later, there was yet another research conference, this one at Southampton University, but this time I didn't attend.

Birmingham University had its roots in several nineteenth century colleges, but while it did not receive its charter until 1900 its starting point was deemed to be the founding of Mason College in 1875. And so, as we entered 1975, I found myself in its centenary year, and I became involved in various activities associated with this. In the first of these, John Drummond asked me if I would be the musical director for Stephen Sondheim's *A Funny Thing Happened on the Way to the Forum* that was being staged by the drama department. John had been asked to do this, but he had declined, and I was delighted to take it on. I had already had some contact with the drama department which resulted, among other things, in yet another relationship, this time with one of the students, Nikki Sturdy. I had seen Nikki in the department's production of Shaw's *Major Barbara* in October 1974. Alas, that was yet another relationship that didn't survive, but I still treasure a book that she gave me at Christmas 1974 – A.A. Milne's *Winnie-the-Pooh*. Having learned that I hadn't read it, she wrote inside "Now we are 31 it's time we met Pooh!", a reference to one of Milne's books of poetry *Now We Are Six* with its iconic illustrations by Ernest H. Shepard.

The theatre in the University had a steep auditorium and two aisles. The design of the stage enabled performers to come off easily, go up one aisle, along the back of the theatre, down the other aisle and back onto the stage. The cast of *Funny Thing* used this to great advantage. The performances took place during January 21-25, 1975. It was also great fun to do. One of the drama lecturers involved in the production was David Hirst, and one of the students was Bob Howie to whom I lent a pair of open sandals for the show as they looked suitably Roman.

At the end of January, the music students put on another eighteenth century opera *The Pirates*, again produced by John Drummond. February saw another G&S production, this time of *Iolanthe*, given by the Queen Elizabeth Hospital Operatic Society with the Asklepios Orchestra, again in the Arthur Thomson Hall. The producer this time was Jill Burrows.

Another drama student that I got to know was Fidelis Morgan, known as 'Fid', and it was thanks to her that I found my fifth and last digs in Birmingham. Fid's parents had bought her one of these red-brick terraced houses – no. 75 Dawlish Road, very near the University – and it so happened that she had a spare room that she wanted to let, just at the time I had to leave 149 Mary Vale Road, and so I moved into Dawlish Road shortly after the production of *Funny Thing*. Fid had a 'thing' about the well-known department store Harrods in London's West End, and she had decided to call her house by this name which she painted on the front door in the style of the store's own distinctive logo (I wonder if Harrods or Mohamed Al Fayed ever found out). The unattractiveness (to me at least) of these endless terraces was compounded here by the fact that the doors and window frames of several houses in

'Harrods' – 75 Dawlish Road, Birmingham, 1975.

this row were all painted in different colours: Harrods was a garish pink, two on one side were yellow, and the one on the other side was a bilious light green – "..and they clash, my Lords, they clash!" (W.S. Gilbert – *Iolanthe*). But the house did have a piano, which was useful.

One of the drama students at Birmingham at that time was Jane Wymark (daughter of the actor Patrick Wymark) who starred in the TV drama *Poldark* and was later well-known as Tom Barnaby's wife Joyce in *Midsomer Murders*. I didn't know her although I had seen her in Congreve's *The Way of the World* presented by the drama department in 1973: Fid was also in that production as was Jane Wynn Owen. But one student, a friend of Fid, whom I did see regularly was a slightly plump girl who had been the stage manager for *The Way of the World* and who used to come to Harrods to play over songs that she had written – no less a person than Victoria Wood. I recognised that they were clever songs, but universities are full of clever people who write clever material, and I never dreamt that she would become such a major figure. Two other friends of Fid that I saw regularly were Celia Imrie, who appeared in many of Victoria Wood's programmes (and also in many films including *Calendar Girls*), and Pam St Clement who was perhaps best-known as Pat Butcher in *EastEnders*. Later, I saw Jane Wymark at the Birmingham Repertory Theatre in Peter Shaffer's *Equus*, the cast also including Patsy Byrne who later became well-known as Nursie in the *Blackadder II* series.

After *Funny Thing*, the next big event as part of the centenary celebrations was a performance of Mahler's Symphony no. 8 (the 'symphony of a thousand') by the combined choirs and orchestras of the University and the Birmingham School of Music, and children's choirs from several schools. The orchestra alone consisted of one hundred and twenty players – including nine horns. The score calls for tubular bells, and a set of these had been designed and made in the University's Department of Industrial Metallurgy. Once again under Ivor Keys' direction, the performance took place in the city's Town Hall on March 17: like Orff's *Carmina Burana*, it was a very exciting experience.

In April, there was another season of opera at the Birmingham Hippodrome presented by English National Opera, and once again I saw Britten's *Gloriana*; also Gilbert and Sullivan's *Patience*, possibly my favourite of all the G&S operas. The eponymous heroine was played by Sandra Dugdale, and the fleshly poet, Reginald Bunthorne, by Derek Hammond Stroud. Later, I would also work with Derek.

My relationship with Nikki now came to an end, but we decided to part amicably, and we had a farewell meal at a rather expensive restaurant, the French-styled Château Impney near Droitwich Spa in Worcestershire. The meal was excellent, if something of a drain on the finances: I remember having escargots (snails) as a starter. With my interest in architecture, I also found the building itself fascinating: formerly the home of the nineteenth century Droitwich MP John Corbett, it seemed out of place in the English countryside.

There were a number of events, again all part of the centenary celebrations, which kept me busy. The first of these took place on May 29 in the Barber Institute – a performance of Handel's *L'Allegro* (to words by John Milton), again conducted by Ivor Keys, in which I was part of a chorus of some two dozen singers. We had been specially chosen for our ability to sight read, thus saving Ivor the trouble of teaching us the parts: in my case, the choice certainly wasn't for any great vocal contribution.

Next came the Wind Band concert that was held in the Great Hall on Friday June 20. As usual, with so few members attending rehearsals regularly, I had to wait until the performance itself to get a full band, and so I had to make sure that we didn't do anything too difficult as so many people would effectively be sight-reading. Essentially, it was a Light Music programme. The first half consisted of the overture *Plymouth Hoe* by John Ansell, movements from Handel's *Water Music* and the easier movements from Percy Grainger's

A *Lincolnshire Posy* (it was still the most difficult work in the programme). We opened the second half with Eric Coates's suite *London Every Day,* and followed this with Strauss's *Emperor Waltz* (I was told afterwards that some members of the audience were dancing at the back of the hall). We ended the programme with a march *Old Comrades* by Teike that I had re-scored from the orchestral version.

This would normally have been the last concert for the Wind Band, but the University wasn't finished with us just yet. The most important part of the centenary celebrations, a visit by Her Majesty the Queen, was coming up the following week on Friday June 27, and, along with the University's Motet Choir, the Wind Band had been asked to provide some music. Her Majesty arrived first at the Barber Institute where the Motet Choir under another staff member, John Harper, gave a short 'vocal fanfare'. The Queen then moved to the Library, and for half an hour before this (from about 11.40 to 12.10) we played in the open air – luckily it was fine. I had been given instructions that as Her Majesty arrived we were to end on a loud chord. I can't remember how (or even if!) we managed that. The Queen then entered the Library where the Motet Choir sang again to the assembled guests. Ivor Keys had been presented to Her Majesty on her arrival in the morning.

As usual on such occasions, there were numerous instructions to be followed; we were given labels to be stuck on instrument cases and to be attached to the windscreens of any cars on the premises. I received an official letter, signed by Ivor Keys, that authorised me as conductor of the Wind Band to enter the Barber Institute and the main Library. Despite all of this, we weren't aware of any obvious security around these buildings, particularly as musicians were arriving with instrument cases that might have had anything inside them (shades of the prohibition days in Chicago), but there must have been a lot of security, particularly after the bombings of the previous November.

That evening, in the Elgar Concert Room, there was the first of three student performances of Handel's *Tamerlane*. The libretto had been adapted and translated by Nigel Fortune and Brian Trowell; the opera was produced by another student, Andy Adamson, and conducted by Eric Cross. The cast included Mary King and Jane Wynn Owen.

Next day, Saturday 28th, was an Open Day, with most of the departments offering exhibitions and demonstrations. Staff were on hand to answer questions. The Faculty of Law mounted a mock criminal trial, with faculty members acting as counsel, witness and judge. Members of the public were invited to take part as jurors. The galleries in the Barber Institute were open all day, with a variety of music provided by the music department from 10 am-4 pm. I took part in this, playing piano duets with fellow-student Nigel Argust from 12-12.30. These were two very interesting days.

The term was now winding down, but my grant extended to the end of the summer, and I would carry on with my research until it was time to leave – hopefully to start some gainful employment. But, as always, there were plenty of other activities including attending other performances. The week of the centenary celebrations at the University coincided with the start of a three-week season of G&S given by the D'Oyly Carte Opera Company, and following our busy week-end I saw *The Pirates of Penzance* on Monday June 30 at the Alexandra Theatre. At the end of the next week, on Thursday July 10, I saw *The Sorcerer*, one of the lesser-known operas. Between these two, I travelled down to London with some of the other students to see something quite different – Benjamin Britten's *Death in Venice* – at the Royal Opera House (as usual we were in the gods, in the cheapest possible seats). Before the opera began, we sensed that there was a definite buzz of excitement in the theatre, and it turned out that Britten himself was in the audience. He was already a sick man, and he died the following year.

Throughout this last year (1974-1975), knowing that my student days were finally coming to an end, I began to look around for any job that I thought might be congenial – not that I expected just to walk into one, but I had to start applying. Unfortunately for me, there was an economic squeeze at this time, and many university and college jobs were frozen, existing staff being asked to do extra teaching each week. This was particularly annoying as I had spent the last six years acquiring more qualifications in the hope of finding a suitable job. Now, few jobs were being advertised, and there would be more and more people applying for any job that did come along, among them, undoubtedly, some PhDs who would be nearer the front of the queue than I would be.

With little prospect of a job in the academic field, I also began to look elsewhere for work. I applied for a post with the Arts Council in Scotland for which I had to attend an interview in Edinburgh on July 1, the day after I had seen *The Pirates of Penzance*. That involved getting a train at 8.10 and not getting back to Birmingham until just after 10 pm. I didn't get the job, but at least I had been interviewed. Among the few academic posts that were advertised was a Lectureship in Music at the University of Newcastle upon Tyne: I applied for that, but I wasn't interviewed. Another position, Music Officer with Southern Arts, resulted in a letter thanking me for my application but regretting that "in an unusually strong field we were unable to invite you for interview". Somewhat surprisingly, during this economic squeeze, the Welsh College of Music and Drama in Cardiff advertised vacancies for no less than three Lectureships in Music, but my application to them resulted in a letter informing me that I had been "unsuccessful", and that "all three posts have now been filled". But these letters only arrived after I had in fact found a job – one that came out of the blue and turned me in a completely different direction, transforming my life.

I had always preferred being an accompanist or playing for rehearsals and shows, and I now had an ARCM (accompanist).

With so few jobs available in the academic world, I began to wonder if it might be possible to get work as a repetiteur although I had had no training as such, there being no tuition for repetiteurs when I was at the RSAM. But now I had nothing to lose, and so I wrote to all the major opera companies – Scottish Opera, Welsh National Opera, English National Opera, The Royal Opera at Covent Garden, Kent Opera (which no longer exists) and the D'Oyly Carte Opera Company. With one exception, they all replied saying more or less the same thing – "Thank you for your letter. We have no vacancies at the moment, but we will put your name on our list should a vacancy arise". The only one that didn't reply was D'Oyly Carte.

In July, I saw yet another production of *The Bartered Bride*, this one given by the City of Birmingham Polytechnic at the city's Crescent Theatre. By the end of the month, my student days were almost over; still no possibility of work. The latest job I had applied for was an extra-mural one based in Louth in Lincolnshire, but so far I had heard nothing. On Friday August 1, I was in the library in the Barber Institute trying to do some work. It was a hot day, and everyone was finding it difficult to concentrate – and, indeed, just to stay awake. I then heard the phone ringing in the librarian's office. He too was almost asleep, but he roused himself and went to answer it. He came back and said to me "It's for you". This was strange as nobody had ever rung me there before, but I went into the office, picked up the phone and said "Hello?" A voice then said "Hello, this is Royston Nash of the D'Oyly Carte Opera Company " (Royston was the Musical Director of the Company, and he had conducted the performances I had seen recently). He then went on "We had a letter from you some time ago, but we didn't reply as we didn't have any vacancies. However, a vacancy has arisen somewhat unexpectedly. Are you still interested?" By now I was fully wide awake, and I said "Yes, certainly". He then said "We are playing in London just now at the Royal Festival Hall. When could you come for an interview?" "More or less any time", I said. "Could you come down next Wednesday? We could see you between the matinee and evening performances". "Yes", I said. "Thank you very much".

The next few days were quite tense, and the waiting seemed interminable, but I duly turned up at the Royal Festival Hall on Wednesday August 6 and was interviewed by Royston Nash, his assistant Glyn Hale and the assistant producer Jimmie Marsland. This was in the conductor's room during the break between the matinee and evening performances of *The Yeomen of the Guard*. They gave me a score of *Iolanthe* and asked me to play part of the opening chorus – "and could you sing in some of the parts?" I knew *Iolanthe* as I had taken the role of the Lord Chancellor when I was at school, but the opening chorus is for ladies only – the fairies! Nevertheless, I managed to get through it.

Afterwards, they were at great pains to tell me that the Company was on the road for forty-eight weeks of the year, doing eight shows a week, and that if I was taken on I would have to find digs in all of these towns and cities. Did I think I could cope with this? I said that I was single, had no ties, and that the touring life didn't hold any terrors for me; in any case I was looking for work – any work – as my research days would soon be over. They also said that the payment would be £50 (£32 actual salary with a touring allowance of £18) to which I said "Is that a week or a month?" It was, of course, a week, but I had been a student for so long that I had got used to living on next to nothing (if they had said 'a month' I think I would have accepted it). They then said that they might be seeing someone else (at which my heart sank), but also suggested that I go back to Birmingham and think about it. Next, I was invited to go to the Royal Festival Hall bar with Jimmie Marsland and Glyn Hale, and I met Glyn's girlfriend Gill Burrows, a chorister in the Company. I was also invited to attend the evening performance, but I said that I had to get back to Birmingham.

During this season at the Royal Festival Hall, D'Oyly Carte was also performing *Utopia Limited*. This opera was not in the Company's normal repertoire: it had not been performed professionally since its initial staging in 1893. But this year, 1975 (as at Birmingham University), was taken to be D'Oyly Carte's centenary year, and a new production of *Utopia Limited* had been part of the centenary celebrations at the Savoy Theatre during March and April. There had been such a demand to see this rarity that extra performances had been scheduled in the present summer season. If my interview had been on a *Utopia*, rather than a *Yeomen*, day I would have wanted to stay and see it although I don't know how I would have got back to Birmingham.

I spent a sleepless night wondering if I had actually got the job. Royston Nash rang the Barber Institute again the following day, Thursday, and asked me if I was still interested. I said "Yes, I am", and he said "Good. Can you start on Monday?" I said that I could, and spent the next few days arranging a somewhat hastier end to my research than I had been planning just days before. This involved contacting the Scottish Education Department to say that I now had a job that would be starting immediately. I also had to find somewhere to stay in London, but I managed to do this too. On Monday August 11 I duly turned up at Sadler's Wells Theatre where the new choristers were being rehearsed prior to the 1975-1976 tour. And so began my working life with the D'Oyly Carte Opera Company, something I had never actually contemplated, but which, on reflection, seemed to be the culmination of so much involvement with the music of Arthur Sullivan. I had taken part in several of the Savoy Operas while still at school, and I had produced a dissertation on settings of Shakespeare, which included some by Sullivan, for my B Mus at Glasgow University. My initial efforts to look at 'Nineteenth Century English Song' had coalesced into *The Songs of Arthur Sullivan – a Catalogue and Commentary*, and now I was in the world-famous D'Oyly Carte Opera Company which performed only Sullivan's operas. It did seem as if fate had determined that this was where I should be.

After its season at the Royal Festival Hall, the Company had its annual four-week vacation while the new choristers were being rehearsed. During the first week I didn't do much playing, but stood by the piano watching another pianist, the London-based Stewart Nash (no relation to Royston) who was not part of the Company but who was familiar with the operas and with D'Oyly Carte's way of performing them. At the end of this four-week period, the Company assembled for a week's rehearsal of the five operas we would take out on tour, and on September 15 the tour began with two weeks in Oxford. We then went up to Glasgow, and I was able to stay at home in Greenock. Glasgow was followed by dates in Billingham, Edinburgh, Newcastle and Liverpool before we were back in London in December. During this tour I received the replies from Southern Arts and the Welsh College of Music and Drama, but fortunately their negative responses were now of no consequence.

As it was D'Oyly Carte's centenary year, there were constant toasts to 'the next hundred years', and I thought I had landed a job for life, but, although I didn't realise it at the time, the writing was on the wall, and D'Oyly Carte's days were already numbered: it closed just short of seven years later. But they were perhaps the best years of my working life, a truly one-off experience. With the constant touring, I had to abandon any further research, at least for the time being, but if any information about Sullivan's songs surfaced I would add it to my own copy of my thesis. But I never managed to complete a PhD. I told the University that it would be difficult to continue with my studies, and at the end of September I received a letter from Ivor Keys to say that if the University PhD committee couldn't agree to my studies being suspended for a year then it would be taken as read that I had actually resigned. When D'Oyly Carte closed in 1982 I might have managed to pick up the threads again, but instead I spent a year reconstructing

Sullivan's cello concerto, and eventually I became a free-lance accompanist, repetiteur and conductor. But in the years 1975 to 1982, after a false start in teaching and further years of being a student, I had at last found what was the perfect area of work for me. I have written about these years in *Nothing Like Work or Right in the D'Oyly Carte*, and about the post-D'Oyly Carte years in *A Bit More Like Work or Life After D'Oyly Carte*.

THE END